KU-317-203

350 LEGAL PROBLEMS SOLVED

350 LEGAL PROBLEMS SOLVED

Keith Richards

WHICH? BOOKS

CONSUMERS' ASSOCIATION

Which? Books are commissioned by
Consumers' Association and published by
Which? Ltd,
2 Marylebone Road, London NW1 4DF

Distributed by The Penguin Group:
Penguin Books Limited, 27 Wrights Lane, London W8 5TZ

Contributors: Jane Bell, Eileen Brennan, Rebecca Evans, Paul Gurowich, Susan Hayward, Phillip Howells, Lara Massey, Sonia Purser
Typographic design by Paul Saunders
Cover design by Ridgeway Associates
Cover photograph by ACE/Mark French

First edition October 1993
Revised edition May 1995

Copyright © 1993, 1995 Which? Ltd

British Library Cataloguing in Publication Data

350 Legal Problems Solved –
A catalogue record for this book is available from the British Library

ISBN 0–85202–536–X

Help at hand
If you have ever been faced with the sorts of problem described in this book, you'll be glad to know that Which? has a service, open to all, whereby you can consult a qualified lawyer by telephone at any time Monday-Friday (9am–6pm). For details of how to subscribe to Which? Personal Service, either write to Consumers' Association, Gascoyne Way, Hertford X, SG14 1LH or telephone 0171–830 6000. Information about *Which?* and its sister magazines can be obtained from the same address.

No part of this publication may be reproduced or transmitted in any form or by any means, electronically or mechanically, including photocopying, recording or any other information storage or retrieval system, without prior permission in writing from the publisher. This publication is not included under licences issued by the Copyright Agency.

Typeset by J&L Composition Ltd, Filey, North Yorkshire

Printed and bound by Firmin-Didot (France)
Groupe Herissey
No d'impression: 30321.

CONTENTS

How to use this book

If you already have a consumer problem to which you want to know the answer, check the **contents** listing first to find out which chapter would cover it. Or, if you want to check a point of law, use the **index**. The questions and answers throughout the book explain how the various laws apply in practice.

For an overview of how consumer legislation works, read the **introduction**, which also includes a *Which?* Guide to Complaining: this takes you through the practical process of making a complaint, whatever the problem, and explains how to deal with the most common excuses made by shops and traders to fob customers off.

For matters which cannot be simply resolved, you should read **Chapter 13**, on taking a case to court, and if you need to check the meaning of any terms used in this book, or in a legal document, try the **glossary**.

The names, **addresses** and telephone numbers of the most important contact organisations are listed at the end of the book, and where these appear in the text they are accompanied by the symbol †.

INTRODUCTION

CONSUMER problems are, unfortunately, a continuing theme of modern life – purchases you wish you'd never made, insurance claim stalemates, holidays that disappoint – and for over three decades *Which?* has been advising its readers on how to deal with them. As a nation, the British are now very much more aware of their rights than was once the case: the Office of Fair Trading has reported that in 1992 alone consumers made nearly 700,000 official complaints about goods and services. Now, for the first time, some of the questions most frequently asked of Consumers' Association's legal experts have been brought together in one volume, allied to concise, easily comprehensible answers that show you, first, exactly what your legal position is, and, if it seems that you've got a case, how to proceed.

350 Legal Problems Solved advises on making the best use of trade associations, ombudsmen, conciliation and arbitration schemes, and on taking a case to court. It will give you the confidence, and the legal grounds, to seek redress or compensation, and should save you time, money and hassle.

The book is designed to explain the law as it applies in everyday consumer situations. There is nothing magical about the law. It is largely based on common sense. But the chapters that follow should do much to dispel its mystique, show you how to use the law to your advantage, and enhance your bargaining power when dealing with shops, businesses, professionals – and even your neighbours.

As well as explaining key legal terms which you are likely to come across in documents, and how to use some of them (such as 'time is of the essence' or 'under protest') to protect your rights, the book describes the best way to complain, and to whom.

While some of the above may suggest that almost everything consumers do is fraught with difficulty, this is of course not the case. Many thousands of goods are bought and sold, services provided and jobs done every day without problem. But if problems should arise, you will want them to be sorted out as speedily as possible and at minimal cost. Legal costs, even for a consumer matter, can be very high – hence the importance of self-help, at least in the first instance. Let *350 Legal Problems Solved* be your guide and ally, whether or not you subsequently decide to consult a solicitor.

The *Which?* Guide to Complaining

The following action points should help you to make an effective complaint in most circumstances. We also list the most common excuses you may come up against when you do complain, and advise you how to deal with them.

- **Act quickly** Don't let your complaint go stale. If you discover a defect in goods, say, go straight back to the shop or, if that is inconvenient, write.
- **Know your rights** Check in this book what you are entitled to so you can let the person to whom you are complaining know the legal basis of your claim.
- **Target your complaint** Write or insist on speaking to someone in authority – the manager of a local branch, for example, or the managing director of a company. Don't vent your anger on the telephonist or the cashier: he or she may not have the authority to make a decision about the problem.
- **Keep a record of your action** Even if you complain in person, or by phone, make sure you keep a record of what was said and when, together with a note of the name and position of the person you dealt with.
- **Follow up in writing** Unless your problem is resolved immediately, follow up your complaint by letter, and keep a copy. By sending your letter to a named individual you

reduce the risk of it being passed around the organisation and perhaps being ignored or lost. Type (or write as neatly as possible), date it, and, if appropriate, give the letter a heading (if it is an insurance or holiday dispute, say, state the name and number of your insurance policy, or your holiday booking reference and so on). Use this heading, and any reference given by the organisation, every time you write.

To avoid committing yourself by mistake when negotiating settlement terms, write '**without prejudice**' at the top of that part of your letter, but don't use it on all your letters as this may cause problems (p. 20).

You may be sent a cheque in '**full and final settlement**' of your claim. If this happens, be very careful: even if you do not consider the amount to be enough, by cashing the cheque you *will* have accepted it, in settlement of your claim, so you will be unable to claim any more (p. 144). If the amount proffered is not sufficient, it is best to send it back.

- **Keep to the point**
  - A brief letter setting out the facts in short paragraphs, rather than an angry or emotional letter making personal remarks, will help your claim. But be firm.
  - Quoting the relevant law, such as the Sale of Goods Act 1979 if you are complaining about faulty goods or the Supply of Goods and Services Act 1982 in respect of inadequate services, shows you are aware of your rights and mean business.
  - State what redress you want: if you want your money back, a repair or a replacement, or if you want financial compensation, spell it out.
  - Give a reasonable deadline for a response: 14 days for a simple matter, but longer if it's a more substantial problem such as building work.
  - Use recorded delivery and keep copies of all documentation.
- **Get evidence** Get and keep any evidence you can to support your claim: receipts, invoices, brochures, contract terms and conditions, advertisements, estimates, bills, statements from witnesses, photographs of damage, etc., and technical expert evidence if appropriate.

- **Be persistent and don't be fobbed off** If you are not happy with the response to your complaint, or you've had no response at all, write another letter. Don't fall prey to attempts to fob you off with less than you're entitled to. Here are some of the most common excuses:
  - **'You're too late. You should have complained within 30 days'** Don't accept time limits of this sort. Whether it is goods or services, or a bad holiday you are complaining about, your rights to claim compensation for breach of contract or negligence last for six years (five years in Scotland), and three years in personal injury claims (pp. 20–1). So, even if you have lost the right to reject faulty goods, say, because the 'reasonable' period of time has elapsed (pp. 29–30), you can still claim compensation. Even if there's a term in a contract (for example, a holiday brochure) and you don't complain within the set time limit, you may be able to challenge this under the Unfair Contract Terms Act 1977 (p. 72).
  - **'We don't give refunds'** If you have bought goods that are faulty, unfit for their purpose, or not as described, you are entitled to a refund if you act quickly enough (pp. 29–30). Notices saying 'No refunds' are against the law, so don't be put off by them, and report any you see to your local Trading Standards Department.
  - **'We don't guarantee our products'** Ignore this. Your rights as a consumer in all circumstances apply whether you have a written guarantee or not (p. 29).
  - **'*You* caused the problem, not us'** Don't be deterred by this. For example, a pair of children's shoes should be designed to withstand the rough and tumble of the playground, so if they fall apart soon after purchase the trader cannot blame the way your child used them. But if it's not as clear-cut as this you may need an independent test on the product or service.
  - **'It's not our problem. Try the manufacturer'** If you have bought something faulty, it is up to the retailer to deal with it, not the manufacturer. But all too often the retailer will try to pass you on to the manufacturer or force you to claim on the manufacturer's guarantee on the grounds that

'we only sell them'. Don't accept this and tell the retailer that it is his legal responsibility to address the problem (p. 29). This also applies to complaints about goods supplied via services – for example, materials used in work done for you by a builder or plumber.

- **'We can't do anything without a receipt'** There is no legal requirement to have a receipt, but you may have to prove when and where you paid for the goods or service. So if the trader asks for proof of payment, a receipt is useful. But a credit card voucher, say, would be legally acceptable.
- **'No refunds on sale items'** If you buy goods in a sale you still have your normal rights. If you buy goods that are seconds you cannot expect them to be perfect, but they must still be of satisfactory quality (i.e. free from hidden defects, p. 28) and as described. But you cannot complain about any defects which were pointed out to you or which you could have spotted before buying (p. 33).

- **Be reasonable** Be prepared to come to a compromise if you receive a fair offer, even if it is not exactly what you wanted. But be warned that once you have accepted an offer of compensation you cannot ask for more later (p. 144).
- **Follow the right complaints procedure** If you cannot come to an agreement it is time to let somebody else decide on the rights and wrongs of your complaint. If the trader is a member of a **trade association** which operates a **code of practice**, you may be able to get help there (p. 237). Most have a free conciliation service to help settle disputes.

Many industries and professions now have their own formal mechanisms for dealing with complaints. You'll find detailed explanations in the relevant chapters of this book. Broadly, the following courses of action may be open to you (see Chapter 13):

Court In almost all cases you'll have the option of going to court. The small claims court (part of the county court) offers a cheap and relatively informal way of dealing with fairly straightforward cases (p. 246). If you have reached the end of your negotiations, the final stage before starting court action is to send a 'letter before action', telling the other party that unless you receive redress within a specified period (usually seven days) you will take the matter to court.

Ombudsmen Many professions and industries operate ombudsman schemes. Usually the trader or company you are complaining about must be a member of the particular scheme and membership is not always compulsory, so check first. The service is free, and you can still pursue your claim in the courts if you are not happy with the final decision (p. 243)

Arbitration If you have a dispute and both you and the other party agree, you can ask for the dispute to be referred to arbitration, which is generally operated by the Chartered Institute of Arbitrators† (Arbiters in Scotland), so that an independent decision on your dispute can be made. This will be binding, so that you cannot subsequently go to court if you are not satisfied with the outcome. And it can also be expensive. But many trade and professional bodies offer their own low-cost schemes, so check first (p. 239).

Q *Where does consumer law come from?*

A There is a huge body of law specifically designed to help the individual consumer, some made by Parliament in the form of **statutes**, some by judges in the form of cases argued out by lawyers in the court room (known as **common law**), and some direct from the European Community.

- **Statute law**, set down in Acts of Parliament (such as the Sale of Goods Act 1979) and in Regulations and Orders under the general authority of Acts of Parliament, sets out the rights and duties of specified people in specified circumstances
- **Common law** is based on the decisions of the courts in actual cases which also set out the rights and duties of people in different circumstances. These are recorded in law reports and form 'precedents' for the future. In this way the courts can adapt the law to new situations without having to wait for Parliament to introduce legislation. And many cases that

come before the courts are interpreting and defining the words in various Acts of Parliament.

Q *Which **statutes** give protection to consumers?*

A The following statutes form the main body of legislation aimed at consumer protection:

- **Sale of Goods Act 1979** (as amended by the Sale and Supply of Goods Act 1994) Perhaps the most important single piece of consumer legislation, this sets out the obligations on businesses that sell goods to consumers (pp. 28 and 29)
- **Supply of Goods and Services Act 1982** This Act defines the standard of the service consumers can legally expect when engaging a trader to provide a service; it also covers the quality of the materials used and other criteria such as price and timescale (pp. 59 and 60)
- **Consumer Arbitration Agreements Act 1988** If a disputed sum of money falls within the limit for the small claims procedure in the county court, currently £1,000 (£750 in Scotland), consumers are not legally bound by clauses in contracts which state that any dispute must be referred to arbitration; they have the choice of court *or* arbitration (p. 240)
- **Consumer Credit Act 1974** This regulates credit agreements and stipulates that advertisements for credit schemes must show true rates of interest without hidden extras; it also confers upon purchasers the right to pay off the debt earlier than the time for payment laid down in the agreement; and it gives purchasers who sign a credit agreement at home a 'cooling-off' period during which they are allowed to change their minds and cancel the agreement (p. 124)
- **Consumer Protection Act 1987** and, in Northern Ireland, the **(N.I.) Order 1987** This states that (1) manufacturers are strictly liable if the products they make are defective and cause personal injury, or damage to property over £275, and (2) all goods must comply with a general safety requirement (pp. 46–9); it also (3) provides guidance to prevent traders quoting misleading prices for goods and services (p. 24)

- **Consumer Protection (Cancellation of Contracts Concluded Away from Business Premises) Regulations 1987** This gives purchasers a seven-day cooling-off period during which they have the right to cancel certain contracts made during an unrequested visit by a salesman to their home even when they are not buying on credit (p. 233)
- **Occupiers' Liability Act 1957** This gives individuals the right to claim compensation if they are injured due to negligence while visiting someone's premises (pp. 227–9)
- **Misrepresentation Act 1967** and, in Northern Ireland, the **Misrepresentation Act (N.I.) 1967** If purchasers enter into an agreement on the basis of a statement purporting to be a fact but which turns out to be untrue, they have the right to cancel the deal and get their money back if they act quickly, or to compensation. The Act does not apply to Scotland. However, Scottish law is broadly similar (p. 50)
- **Unfair Contract Terms Act 1977** The small print in contracts for the sale of goods cannot take away purchasers' rights under the Sale of Goods Act. These and other notices or conditions in contracts which exclude or restrict liability for financial loss or damage to property have to be fair and reasonable. If they are not, they will be invalid under the Act and will not affect a claim (p. 72). This is supplemented by a new EU law set out in the Unfair Terms in Consumer Contracts Regulations 1994
- **Unsolicited Goods and Services Act 1971** This gives recipients of unrequested and unwanted goods the right to get rid of them without paying for them (p. 45).

Certain **criminal laws** also affect consumers. Although they do not entitle consumers to get compensation directly, reporting a criminal offence will provide support for the complaint. The most relevant laws are:

- **Consumer Protection Act 1987** This stipulates that only safe goods should be put on sale and prohibits misleading price indications (pp. 26 and 47)
- **Food Safety Act 1990** This covers food standards and

hygiene wherever food is manufactured, prepared or sold, as well as other aspects of food and drink (p. 195)

- **Trade Descriptions Act 1968** This makes it a criminal offence for traders to make false statements about the goods they sell (p. 57)
- **Weights and Measures Act 1985** and, in Northern Ireland, the **(N.I.) Order 1988** This stipulates that (1) all weighing and measuring equipment should be accurate; (2) many commodities (especially foods) should be marked with the quantity supplied, and that certain commodities should be sold only in certain specified quantities; and (3) all aspects of quantity control in trade should be open to official inspection.

Q *What is the difference between* ***civil law*** and ***criminal law****?*

A **Civil law** This is the branch of the legal system which is of most use to the individual seeking compensation and redress. The civil law is concerned with rights and duties that relate to individuals in their dealings with other individuals (including companies and other groups of people). If you suffer loss because someone else breaches these laws then you have a right to redress and are entitled to take that person to court. The main areas of civil law are **tort** (which includes negligence) and **contract**. The courts which deal with civil claims are the **county court** (in which the **small claims procedure** may be used) and the **High Court**.

Criminal law This is the branch of law which is concerned with offences against the public, such as the Trade Descriptions Act 1968. Criminal law is generally enforced by the police, but the specific criminal law affecting consumers is enforced by public authorities like Trading Standards Departments and Environmental Health Officers (both based at your local council offices). You cannot get compensation directly by reporting a criminal offence such as a false trade description, but evidence of such wrongdoing will lend added weight to your complaint. The courts which deal with criminal matters are the **magistrates' courts** and the **crown courts**.

Q *What is a **tort**, and how does it affect me as a consumer?*

A A tort (in Scotland a 'delict') is a wrongdoing in civil law, entirely distinct from breach of contract. Anyone who suffers a wrong can claim in tort against the wrongdoer. There does not need to be a contract nor does a criminal offence need to have been committed. The commonest 'consumer' tort is lack of duty of care or negligence – for example, you could tear your clothes or injure yourself in a shop by slipping on a wet floor (pp. 228–9). What is important is the relationship between the wrongdoer and the person who suffered the damage. For example, all road-users owe a legal duty to other road-users and, of course, pedestrians. If they break that duty by being careless, they will be responsible for the consequences.

Q *What does **caveat emptor** ('let the buyer beware') mean?*

A This legal principle means that the risk of buying something that is faulty in any way rests with the buyer, so it would be up to the buyer to check the quality of the item before purchase. Any defect that the inspection failed to identify would be the buyer's responsibility. Fortunately, when a consumer buys 'goods' this principle does not apply. The Sale of Goods Act 1979 makes the trader who sells the goods 'strictly liable' for the quality of those goods. So there is no legal requirement to inspect goods thoroughly before buying: if you buy goods from a trader and they turn out to be defective, the seller is responsible.

But this principle still applies to the sale of property, so the burden is on the buyer of property to check the quality before going ahead with the purchase. If no checks are made by the buyer and the property turns out to be defective, the seller is not generally responsible (p. 109).

Q *Am I better off dealing only with shops and traders who are members of trade associations?*

A Don't assume that you'll be better protected just because a trader belongs to a trade association. Contact the relevant trade association to check that the company is a member and to see what protection is offered. Some will offer you the choice of paying an additional premium which covers you in the event of insolvency, and occasionally in the event of bad workmanship even if your trader is still in business (p. 65).

Q *How can I find out whether a trader is financially sound?*

A There is no sure way of knowing, and well-known names are no guarantee. Strong signs of trouble are dead phones, being constantly fobbed off with lame excuses, near-empty shelves, endless sales, or hefty deposit demands before the trader will deal with you. If any of these criteria apply to a firm you are thinking of dealing with, it may be best to avoid it, or to take extra precautions, like paying for goods or services by credit card (p. 132), or taking out an insurance-backed guarantee for work (p. 65). Also, contact the Trading Standards Department local to the trader, to see whether it has any further information to help you decide.

Q *Does a contract* have *to be in writing?*

A No. This is probably the greatest misunderstanding of the law of contract. Every day we make contracts without putting them in writing, or even speaking a single word: we buy food in shops, pay taxi or bus fares, etc. All these have the same standing as written contracts and are governed by the same laws as other contracts. Whether written or verbal, a contract is an agreement that can be enforced by the law and gives rise to rights and responsibilities for those involved.

Some rights are always implied into certain transactions: for example, when you buy goods (pp. 28–30), or when you employ a trader to do work for you (pp. 59–60), the rights embodied in the relevant legislation automatically come into play and can *never* be taken away (pp. 18–19).

Spoken agreements can cause problems if it later becomes necessary to prove the precise terms agreed, such as the price or a delivery date. It is always worth keeping receipts for goods in case you need to prove later where they were bought and how much you paid. If you do not have a proper written contract keep any evidence you do have.

The only contracts which *must* be in writing are:

- contracts for the sale or leasing of land
- hire-purchase agreements and similar credit and hire transactions (see p. 123).

Q *I've just signed a contract which had lots of terms and conditions on the back. I didn't have time to read everything before signing it and I'm now worried that my rights may be restricted by the* ***small print****. Am I bound by these terms, whatever they say?*

A If you sign a document you will normally be bound by it whether you have read it or not, and the terms of a written agreement will almost always override anything that you have agreed orally. Even if the terms are contained in a separate document, if you are referred to that document (for example, by the words 'full terms and conditions available on request') you will probably be bound by them, even if you didn't see them and didn't ask to see a copy. You can challenge some of the small print (p. 72), but to avoid such situations:

- *always* ask for a copy of the final agreement bearing both your signature and that of the other person
- *never* sign a document until you have read it. *If in doubt, don't sign.* Ask to take the document away to think about it
- if you are not happy with some of the terms in an agreement cross them out and ask for it to be re-typed, or make sure your amendments are signed by the company representative
- if the small print in contracts for goods or services attempts to take away or limit your rights to claim under the Sale of Goods Act 1979 (pp. 28–9), it is illegal: your statutory rights cannot be taken away
- other notices or conditions in contracts have to be fair and reasonable. If they are not, they will be invalid under the Unfair Contract Terms Act 1977 and can be ignored

- if defective goods or workmanship cause death or personal injury, your right to claim compensation can *never* be taken away by a notice or contract term.

Q *Can I* ***cancel*** *the contract I've just signed?*

A Most contracts become legally binding as soon as they are made, and you cannot get out of them simply because you have **changed your mind**. Moreover, most contracts do not have to be in writing and signed, but it prevents disputes about the precise terms agreed if they are written down. Only specific types of contract can be cancelled after signature. They are:

- **credit agreements** The Consumer Credit Act 1974 provides for a five-day cancellation period for credit contracts that are signed anywhere other than at the creditor's or trader's business premises. So if you have just signed a credit contract at your or a friend's home, say, you have five days to cancel if you change your mind (pp. 124–5)
- **timeshare contracts** The Timeshare Act 1992 provides for a 14-day cooling-off period in timeshare contracts signed in the UK. When you sign you should be given a notice of your cancellation rights and a blank form for you to complete and return. If you cancel during the cooling-off period, you are entitled to recover any money you have paid in connection with the contract (pp. 182–3)
- **contracts made at home** The Consumer Protection (Cancellation of Contracts Concluded Away from Business Premises) Regulations 1987 give you a seven-day cooling-off period during which you have the right to cancel a contract which is made during an 'unsolicited visit' by a salesman to your home. An 'unsolicited visit' is one in which you have not expressly requested the salesman to make: it includes appointments made as a result of unrequested telephone calls or after delivery of a card proposing a visit. If you initiated the visit, you are not protected by the Regulations.

Q *What does* ***'without prejudice'*** *on a letter mean?*

A Either you or the other party in a dispute may make a 'without prejudice' offer in an effort to reach a settlement. This is useful to avoid making a commitment by mistake when negotiating figures. Any letter which is 'without prejudice' may not be used against you and may not be revealed if you finally have to go to court to fight the claim. For example, a trader may be asking for £100 from you, but you may feel you owe only £50. If you make an offer of £50 'without prejudice' and this is not accepted by the trader, in the event of the dispute going to court you can still refuse to pay and the judge will never learn that you were prepared to pay anything.

It can therefore be useful to put the words 'without prejudice' at the top of a letter, since that letter cannot be used against you. But do not use the words on any letter you might later need to prove your case. If you want to make an offer, or if you are responding to an offer from the trader, you could send two letters, one 'without prejudice' which mentions the offer, the other open, ignoring the offer completely and pursuing the main basis of your claim.

Q *Have I the right to have my complaint decided in a courtroom, even if the other side doesn't want to, or wants to go to arbitration?*

A Yes. If you have a valid case, it is your choice whether to go to court or choose any alternative means of sorting it out (Chapter 13). If the amount in dispute is £1,000 or less, a company cannot take away your right to go to court. The Consumer Arbitration Agreements Act 1988 prevents this. Court action is your right, which would be forfeited only if both sides were to agree to arbitration.

Q *How long do I have to start a claim in the courts?*

A This depends on the type of claim, but the Statute of Limitations does put a time limit on starting a formal claim.

Once a claim falls foul of the time limit it is said to become **statute barred**. If you do not issue a court summons against a trader within a certain time, you lose your right to do so. The most common periods are:

- six years for claims for breach of **contract** from the date of the breach: this covers *any* dispute arising from a claim under a contract (for example, those arising under the Sale of Goods Act 1979 or the Supply of Goods and Services Act 1982)
- six years for claims of **negligence** from the date of the negligent act: this covers any claim for damage, say, to your property where there is no contract between you and the person who caused the damage. Such claims would include, for example, damage caused to your car by another driver
- three years in the event of **personal injury**, whether the claim is for breach of contract or negligence. This would include claims for personal injury under the Consumer Protection Act 1987 (p. 47)
- defective design or building work may not become apparent until long after the design or work was done. In some cases the Latent Damage Act 1986 can extend the time period for a claim up to a maximum of 15 years from the date of the work. If your claim is complex, a solicitor may be the best source of advice on this point.

Q *Is the law the same in Scotland, Northern Ireland, England and Wales?*

A No, although most of the rules which apply to the purchase of goods and services are broadly the same throughout the UK. For example, the Sale of Goods Act 1979 applies to the UK as a whole (pp. 28–9), whereas the Supply of Goods and Services Act 1982 does not apply in Scotland; however, if you receive substandard service in Scotland (faulty building work, damage by a dry-cleaner, photoprocessor, and so on) your rights will be covered by **common law** rather than the **statute**.

There are some differences:

- manufacturers' guarantees ensuring repair of any faulty parts are legally enforceable in Scotland, whereas elsewhere they might not be (pp. 35–6). This is because certain promises, such as guarantees, are treated by Scots law as contracts
- in Scotland the equivalent of the **county court** is the **sheriff court**
- the **small claims procedure** in the county court in England, Wales and Northern Ireland will deal with almost all consumer cases up to a value of £1,000. In Scotland the **small claims** limit is £750
- free booklets are available from all county and sheriff courts which will tell you how to begin your action, and how much it will cost (pp. 245–7).

Q *How can I get further help with my consumer dispute?*

A If you cannot resolve your dispute with help of this book, try:

- the sister publication to this book, entitled *120 Letters that Get Results* (also published by Consumers' Association)
- your local Citizens Advice Bureau (CAB) or Consumer Advice Centre or Law Centre, which all provide free advice
- a solicitor who can give you advice under the 'fixed fee interview scheme' – you should be able to get about half an hour's advice for £5. Ring the solicitors in your area to check whether this scheme is part of the services they offer.

CHAPTER 1

BUYING GOODS

MOST of us buy goods every day – groceries, newspapers etc. – and often clothes, records and so on. Occasionally we buy more substantial and more expensive items, such as furniture and cars. And the way we make our purchases can vary enormously. We may buy from a shop, order over the phone or from a mail-order catalogue, or from a door-to-door trader. And we may pay the full price, use a cheque or credit card, haggle for a reduction, rummage in the sales for bargains or in the small ads for something second-hand.

Traders may go bust, or may sell you a defective product which causes you injury. Fortunately, whatever we buy, wherever we buy, and whatever we pay, the law provides protection when things go wrong. This chapter spells out your rights when buying goods.

Q *What are 'goods'?*

A For the purposes of the law, the term 'goods' applies to all personal possessions that are bought and sold, excluding money and property. The Sale of Goods Act 1979 and the Supply of Goods and Services Act 1982 cover a huge variety of products, from cars, electrical goods, toys, clothes and kitchen and bathroom equipment to food. No matter what type of goods you buy, if they aren't up to scratch, your legal rights as set out in those Acts apply (pp. 28–9 and 59–60). However, the Acts do not cover property, so if you buy a house, for example, your rights are very limited and you will have no legal protection from the law on 'goods' (p. 109).

Q *I saw a jumper I wanted in a shop window, but when I went to buy it the assistant told me it was wrongly priced. Could I have insisted on paying the price marked?*

A This is a popular belief, but unfortunately it is wrong. Under the civil law a price displayed on the shelf, on the goods themselves, in an advertisement or on a price list, or in the window of a shop is called an **invitation to treat**, i.e. an invitation for the public to go to the till and make an offer to buy the goods at that price. But if the shop realises it has mis-priced the goods displayed, you cannot insist on buying them at the price marked:

- in fact, a trader can refuse to sell anything to you for no reason at all
- you can try offering the marked price, and the trader *may* agree to sell the item to you at this price
- you can always bargain by offering any price for goods, and if the shop accepts your offer then a contract is made
- if the shop does sell something at the wrong price by mistake, it can't insist you pay the extra later (pp. 27–8).

Under the criminal law the trader offering the goods at the 'wrong' price (if the price is higher) could be liable to prosecution. The Trade Descriptions Act 1968 makes it an offence to give an indication that goods exposed for sale are being offered at a lower price than that at which they are in fact being offered. Also, the Consumer Protection Act 1987 makes it an offence to give a 'misleading price indication'. You should report cases such as this to the Trading Standards Department at your local council offices. But if the price displayed was a genuine mistake then the shop would not be prosecuted.

Q *When I ordered a sofa, the store asked me for a £100* ***deposit****, which I paid. I was then made redundant and cancelled the order. The store refuses to return my deposit. Can it do that?*

A By placing the order you have made a legally binding contract to purchase the sofa. By cancelling the order you have broken the contract, because you agreed to take delivery of the goods and to pay the balance of the price. In most cases a deposit is taken as security, to make the buyer think twice before attempting to cancel the contract, so the store is entitled to keep the deposit. In addition, it may be entitled to claim from you any loss of profit over and above the amount of the deposit: for example, if the sofa had been specially made for you to a precise size and could be difficult to sell to anyone else. Fortunately, if the goods are of a standard design and size stores should not have problems selling them on to recover their loss, so you may lose only the deposit.

Q *I paid a deposit for a new sofa, but I've just heard that the store has gone bust. Can I get my sofa, or at least my money back?*

A When a business collapses and cannot pay all its debts, a strict order of priority operates concerning creditors. As an ordinary customer, you are what is known as an 'unsecured creditor', and unfortunately you come last in the queue: other creditors, such as the Inland Revenue and the company's employees, are ahead of you. You may miss any chance of getting your deposit back if you do not act quickly. So make a claim to the liquidator or receiver straight away (p. 142). There may well not be enough money to go around, so you could end up getting back less than you paid, or nothing at all. However, all may not be lost in the following circumstances:

- you can get your money back if you paid the deposit by credit card, provided the goods cost more than £100 (the actual deposit paid can be less than this – it is the cost of the *goods* that counts) (pp. 54 and 132)
- if the goods had been clearly labelled as yours and put to one side when you paid the deposit, they belong to you, not the trader, so you should go to the shop or warehouse and try to collect them. If you have problems, get in touch with the liquidator or receiver immediately (p. 142).

Q *I was told that the goods I bought in a sale had previously been £50 but were now £35. I have discovered that they were on sale at £20 just before the sale began. Can the shop do this?*

A The shop may be committing a criminal offence by misleading customers into thinking that they are getting a better deal than they really are. The Consumer Protection Act 1987 sets out guidelines on misleading prices. If a shop is making a comparison with its previous prices:

- the previous price should be the last price at which the goods were available in the previous six months
- the goods should have been available at the higher price for at least 28 consecutive days during the last six months
- the goods should have been on sale at that previous, higher price for that period at the *same* shop.

The law aims to prevent customers being misled. However, retailers can give notice that these conditions do not apply, as long as they spell it out clearly – for example, that the earlier price was only available for one week previously, or that that price had been available only in selected branches. If they don't give you this information and you suspect that you have been misled, report the matter to the Trading Standards Department for the area where the shop is.

Q *I paid £40 each for some theatre tickets from a ticket agent, but have since discovered that the box-office price for the tickets is £19 each. I wasn't told this by the agent. Can I claim the extra back?*

A No You must expect to pay more when buying tickets from agents – they will add on their commission and there is no limit on the amount of commission agents can charge. And you agreed to pay the £40 price. But the agent has ignored a government code of practice designed to protect consumers from misleading prices, so he could be breaking the law. The code, which comes from the Consumer Protection Act 1987, states that if prices are higher than those charged at the box office, then the **face value** of the ticket should be made clear.

This applies to prices given over the phone as well as those quoted in advertisements and so on. Although the code is not mandatory, failure to comply could go against an agency if it is taken to court on a charge of quoting misleading prices.

If you use a ticket agency:

- check prices with the theatre first
- ask the agency what the face value of the tickets is and where the seats are – if it can't, or won't, say, don't buy
- always ring around a few agencies. Prices vary enormously, depending (especially) on the night you want
- if you think you have been misled over price, contact the Trading Standards Department (at the council offices local to the agency).

Q *Is there a difference between an* ***estimate*** *and a* ***quotation****?*

A The words have no legal definition. Nevertheless, there's an increasing tendency for an **estimate** to be a provisional guide to the price for the completed work and a **quotation** to be a firm price. So, if you find you're in dispute over a bill, the real issue is whether the price given was intended to be a rough guide or a fixed amount.

If a trader gives you a document with precise details of the work required plus detailed costs, you should not be charged more once that work is done. Some industries, like the motor trade, have codes of practice which follow this general tendency (p. 238). So if a dispute arises over the meaning of the words in an agreement the relevant code of practice will provide a useful guideline.

Before you engage someone to do work for you, be sure to get an **exact and firm quotation** in writing, specifying precisely what is to be done (p. 62).

Q *I ordered a new car last month and, after some discussion, agreed a price of £11,600. The garage rang to tell me the car is ready for collection but say I must pay an extra £500 as they made a* ***mistake*** *in their original calculations. Should I pay this?*

A No. Because you agreed a fixed price with the garage and knew nothing of their mistake, a contract was made and you can insist on buying the car for that sum.

If the garage refuses to let you have the car at the agreed price, you should write giving them a time limit of seven days (say) in which to deliver it. If they don't you may buy the same model somewhere else as cheaply as possible, and, if the price is higher, claim the additional sum from the garage.

Q *What happens if, when I buy a car, the manufacturer's recommended price rises between the time I place the order and the time I take delivery?*

A It's important to remember that when you sign a contract you will be bound by the terms of that contract. So you must look at your sales agreement. If this doesn't allow the seller to pass on to the buyer any rise in the seller's costs then you can insist on paying only the original contract price. So check any contract before signing. If there is a term which lets the seller increase the price to take into account increases in the manufacturer's prices, strike it out before you sign and ask the seller to agree the amendments you've made (p. 18).

Q *I bought a coat to take on my holiday, but after I had worn it only twice the colour started to fade and became rather patchy. I did wear it in the rain, but that's why I bought it. Is the shop responsible?*

A Yes. There's clearly something wrong with a coat that fades and becomes patchy so early in its life, so the shop is responsible. The **Sale of Goods Act 1979** (as amended and strengthened by the Sale and Supply of Goods Act 1994) is perhaps the most important consumer protection legislation ever passed by Parliament. This says that when you buy goods from a trader (whether they're new, secondhand, or in a sale) those goods must:

- belong to the person selling them – if the seller doesn't have **title** to the goods (i.e. own them) then you won't normally become the owner, even after paying your money (p. 52)

- fit any **description** given of them – whether this was on the label, packaging, in an advertisement, or otherwise. So if you were told the coat was suitable for all kinds of weather it must fit that description
- be of **satisfactory quality** – hence, in good condition and free of minor and major faults, safe and able to do the job expected (taking into account the price, age and so on) and last a reasonable length of time. So your coat should have been able to withstand ordinary wear and tear
- be reasonably **fit for their purpose** – if you told the seller you needed the coat for a specific purpose (for example, to withstand rain/be waterproof) then it should be fit for that purpose as well as general use
- correspond with any **sample** you have been shown. If you ordered, say, a sofa on the basis of a fabric sample, the goods supplied should accord with the sample.

If the goods don't meet any of these requirements it is the retailer (rather than the manufacturer) who is under a legal obligation to sort out your problem.

Q *Eight months ago I bought a new freezer but the temperature control no longer works properly: last week all the food in it went off. The shop refuses to acknowledge that I have a valid complaint. Can I* ***reject*** *the goods and get my money back?*

A No, although some shops will offer a refund or replacement as a matter of goodwill, and you should check in case you are entitled to a refund under the terms of the guarantee. The problem in this case is that the freezer has not proved **durable** enough, so the seller is in breach of the contractual conditions implied by the Sale of Goods Act 1979 (p. 28) and is obliged to compensate you. This problem illustrates a particularly difficult area in consumer law, where defects are not discoverable initially but show up only during the life of the goods. If goods are not up to scratch the law allows you either to **reject** them and claim your money back, plus compensation for any extra loss suffered; or claim **compensation**, usually the cost of repair, plus any extra loss suffered. Note that:

- your right to **reject** the goods and get your **money back** can be lost with the passage of time, regardless of whether you could have known about the defect before it came to light. You lose the right to reject faulty goods once you have '**accepted**' them. The Sale of Goods Act says that you have 'accepted' the goods if you keep them for a '**reasonable**' time before rejecting them. There is no precise legal definition of 'reasonable' – it depends on the circumstances of each case and can be as little as a few weeks. This means that you probably lost the right to get your money back on your freezer a week or so after purchase, even though you didn't know of the problem at that time. In one well-known case it was too late to reject a new car after only three weeks and 142 miles, even though the defect – which caused the engine to seize up – could not have been discovered earlier. However, in this case, the buyer was fully reimbursed for the **cost of repair** and was also paid compensation for the hassle caused on the day the car broke down. An amendment to the old Act gives consumers stronger rights, so a buyer in a similar situation today would probably be treated better
- even though it may be too late for you to reject your freezer, you still have the right to **compensation**. So the shop ought to pay the full cost of repair of the temperature control plus the cost of the wasted food.

Q *I took a newly purchased computer back to the shop because it didn't work properly. The shop argued that they were not to blame as they didn't realise it was defective, and it worked when they sold it to me. Surely this argument is irrelevant?*

A Yes, you can ignore the shop's plea of ignorance. The Sale of Goods Act 1979 imposes **strict liability** on retailers. This means that the goods they sell must satisfy each of the various implied terms, including the satisfactory quality condition (pp. 28–9). If they don't they will be liable for **breach of contract**. It is no defence for the seller to claim that he did not know about and could not reasonably be expected to have discovered the fault. So although the fault may have been caused by the wiring or a defective microchip which the retailer could not possibly have noticed, the shop is still fully responsible because of his contract with the customer. And if the shop tells you to claim on your manufacturer's guarantee, don't be put off by this – you don't have to (see p. 10).

Q *When my wife bit into a shop-bought apple pie she started choking. She had swallowed a piece of wire which was inside it. The injury was slight, but what are her rights?*

A If you buy food that is contaminated you should take it to your local Environmental Health Officer (EHO – at your local council), who will investigate the matter and may recommend a prosecution. But whatever the EHO does, you are still entitled to claim compensation for any injury or for the stress caused. This gives rise to two possible claims:

- under the Sale of Goods Act 1979 against the retailer. The pie was obviously not of satisfactory quality and so the retailer was in breach of contract (p. 28). Claims such as this, even if there is no physical injury, can sometimes lead to substantial compensation for the stress or trauma incurred
- under the Consumer Protection Act 1987 against the manufacturer. The pie was clearly not as safe as you are entitled to expect and there is no need to prove that the manufacturer was at fault in any way (pp. 46–9)
- you should complain in writing straight away, and make sure you get the necessary evidence to show that the food was contaminated. If you are injured you may need a report from your doctor to back up your claim.

Q *I gave a radio as a* ***gift*** *to my aunt some months ago. It has stopped working and the shop has refused to repair it for her free of charge, as she doesn't have the* ***receipt****. What can she do?*

A An amendment to the Sale of Goods Act 1979 stipulates that goods bought from a retailer must be of satisfactory quality (p. 28). But the law protects only the purchaser and the right to claim a refund or the cost of the repair arises from the contract between the retailer and the purchaser. Your aunt cannot enforce those rights. Good stores won't argue, but if the matter went to court you would have to pursue the claim on behalf of your aunt. And as long as you can prove that you bought the radio, there is no legal requirement to produce the receipt – a credit card slip showing that you bought the item from that shop would do just as well (p. 11).

Q *The carpet we bought has become marked with dark patches. I complained to the shop but they say it is* ***shading*** *and the carpet is not faulty. Is this right?*

A 'Shading' occurs when some of the carpet pile lies in a different direction from the rest, producing light and dark patches which will not go away. Some retailers (supported by carpet manufacturers) refuse to offer compensation for shading, claiming that it is a normal feature of certain types of carpet and has to be accepted. And it often happens that by the time the shading has become apparent, it is too late to reject a carpet and get your money back, because a period longer than a 'reasonable' time has elapsed (p. 30). So your options could be restricted to a claim for compensation. But don't be deterred:

- it may be possible to prove that the problem with your carpet *does* mean that it is of unsatisfactory quality and is unfit for its purpose (p. 28). You may need to get an expert opinion on this point, so contact a local carpet dealer or the British Carpet Technical Centre.† The BCTC also offers an arbitration scheme to handle complaints about appearance, quality or performance, but if you decide to go to arbitration, you cannot later choose to go to court if you disagree with the decision (p. 240)
- if the shop did not warn you about shading before you bought the carpet, you have a claim against the retailer for breach of

contract. You will be entitled to claim the difference between the price paid for the carpet and what it is really worth, taking into account the shading characteristics. So, if the carpet is so bad that it is effectively worth very little, compensation may be substantial enough to allow you to buy a replacement.

Q *I often buy goods in* ***sales*** *or marked* ***bargain, shop-soiled*** *or* ***seconds****. How does this affect my rights if they are faulty?*

A You have the same rights as you do when buying goods for the full price (pp. 28–9). You are free to shop for bargains, rummage in sales, or even haggle to reduce the price, without fear of reducing those rights. Even if described as 'seconds' or 'imperfect' goods must always be of 'satisfactory quality' so the seller can't fob you off with rubbish (unless of course the goods are actually described as 'rubbish'!).

Signs like 'shop-soiled' or 'imperfect' imply that the standard or quality may be below what you might otherwise reasonably expect. Usually the imperfection or area of soiling will be pointed out to you or will certainly be apparent, so you buy knowing the defect is there. For example, the pattern in the weave of a sweater may be imperfect so you can't complain about that specific problem later. But if the sweater unravels when you wear it, or a sleeve becomes detached when you wash it, you have a valid complaint under the Sale of Goods Act 1979.

Q *I bought a television to get the free flights that were offered with it. It seemed such a good deal, but I've got to buy accommodation from a list provided and it's all very expensive. It's not such a good offer after all. What is the law on* ***free offers****?*

A If you buy a product with a 'free' offer attached, you are legally entitled to benefit from that offer, but many free offers will have binding terms and conditions. If you comply with all the conditions to the letter but don't get the goods or services offered, you may have a claim for breach of contract against the company running the promotion. So if you apply for an offer, always read these conditions very carefully *before* you make your purchase – you might have to pay for accommodation at a specified hotel (not likely to be a cheap one), you might have to take all your meals in an expensive restaurant in the same hotel, or you may have only a couple of dates to choose from, or your dates of travel may be imposed upon you.

With some offers the choice of dates is **subject to availability**, so you may be unable to rely on travelling on the date you want. If you are attracted by an offer attached to a product, only make the purchase if you want the product and after reading the conditions.

The British Code of Sales Promotion Practice (BCSP) specifies how these offers are promoted and what information the promotor must give you. If you feel the offer is misleading, report the matter to your local Trading Standards Department, or to the Advertising Standards Authority.† The main points of the Code are:

- the terms and conditions of a promotion should be clear, complete, and easily seen by consumers *before* purchase
- even if an offer is 'subject to availability' the promoter must take all reasonable steps to avoid disappointing the consumer
- the promoter should have adequate resources to administer the promotion to prevent justifiable complaints
- if the promotion provokes an unexpectedly high level of demand and the promoter is subsequently unable to supply the promised goods, then alternatives must be offered of equal or greater value.

Q *The tiles on our kitchen floor are wearing badly after less than two years. We paid a lot expecting the floor to last for many years. The showroom rejected our claim for compensation on the grounds that the tiles were not faulty when delivered to us and said, 'You can't expect floor tiles to last forever.' Have we any legal rights against the store?*

A Yes. The Sale of Goods Act 1979 (as amended by the Sale and Supply of Goods Act 1994) specifically refers to **durability** as a component of satisfactory quality and fitness for purpose (pp. 28–9). This obligation is a continuing warranty:

- it is not enough for the supplier to deliver goods that are OK at the time of purchase – they must continue to be fit for their normal purpose for a reasonable time. No particular time limits are laid down as these will vary from one type of goods to another and will also depend on the price and the related quality of the goods
- although your tiles may have seemed to be of the right quality when they were delivered, the fact that they have worn out so quickly would indicate that there must have been a defect in them initially, although the problems didn't reveal themselves until later
- the showroom might suggest that you have misused the floor tiles in some way (p. 10), although that is more usually argued in the case of cars and other mechanical goods where careless servicing and maintenance may be to blame. But floor tiles are designed to be walked on and to get wet, etc., so you can pursue your rights with confidence
- always be careful not to fall foul of the limitation period laid down by law, which prevents claims being made after the lapse of a specified time – in this case, six years (pp. 20–1).

Q *If I buy an electrical product, or a car which is covered by a* ***manufacturer's guarantee****, does this mean that I can't complain if the product goes wrong after the guarantee (usually lasting one year) has expired?*

A Many manufacturers promise to resolve problems in their products free of charge. Some offer money back, others offer a free repair or replacement. Always check the wording of a guarantee to see what is included. The important things to remember about free guarantees are as follows:

- rights under the manufacturer's guarantee are **in addition to your rights** against the seller of the goods under the Sale of Goods Act 1979 (pp. 28–9) and are not in any way an alternative to those rights. The manufacturer is legally obliged to explain this and should clarify the fact that the terms of the guarantee do not affect the buyer's statutory rights

- strangely, there is not a single reported court case in England or Wales testing the legal validity of such guarantees, and there is some doubt whether such a manufacturer's guarantee is legally enforceable (Scottish law, on the other hand, treats such guarantees as contracts between the consumer and the manufacturer, which makes the terms of the guarantee legally binding)
- in practice most manufacturers *do* honour their guarantees
- the fact that the guarantee lasts for only one year (or six months, or whatever) may give the impression that this is the full extent of the durability which you are entitled to expect (pp. 29 and 34). In fact the extent of the cover offered by the manufacturer has no effect on your statutory rights against the seller
- as manufacturers are under no legal obligation to give a guarantee they may make it as limited in scope as they wish.

Q *When goods are faulty, can the shop from which they were bought insist that I take* ***exchange goods*** *or a* ***credit note*** *when I would prefer my money back?*

A No. You are entitled to **money compensation** because the seller has broken a condition of the Sale of Goods Act 1979 (pp. 28–9). This compensation should be in the form of either a full refund of the price or the cost of repair, depending on how long you have had the goods (pp. 29–30). If the shop does offer a replacement or credit note you may prefer to accept this, particularly if it's too late to get a refund – the decision is entirely yours – but it can't force you.

The usual way to **reject** goods is to return them to the shop and demand an immediate refund. If the shop refuses or if it's a large product, like a fridge, send a letter making it clear that you are rejecting the goods and seeking all your money back. Keep a copy of the letter. If that has no effect, in the last resort you will have to sue the retailer (pp. 245–8).

Q *Recently I bought a blouse. When I got home I tried it on. I found it didn't fit very well and I've* ***changed my mind*** *about the colour* *anyway. I took it back but the shop refused to refund my money. They did offer me a* ***credit note****. What can I do?*

A Nothing. If the blouse is of the right quality and perfectly wearable, you can't blame the shop because you made a mistake in choosing the wrong size or colour. You should have tried the blouse on first, if possible, and checked it was the colour you wanted. So the offer of a credit note may be more than you're entitled to.

It would be different if the blouse had been wrongly labelled, so that you bought what appeared to be your size and it turned out to be a size smaller – this would be a breach of 'description' under the Sale of Goods Act 1979 (pp. 28–9).

Some shops operate a return and refund policy that applies whatever the reason for the goods being returned. But they do not have to do this. If the shop does not state that this is its policy and you're worried about the colour or the size, get the sales assistant to write on the back of the receipt that you can return the goods and exchange them for something else if they are unsuitable, or be given a credit note, or even get your money back.

Q *I went back to the shop where I bought a handbag to complain that the strap had broken. The shop had closed down, so I went to the nearest branch. I was told that each branch was a separate* ***franchise*** *and I could only claim against the branch where I bought the goods. Is this true?*

A Yes. Your contract was with the person or company who owned the franchise to that branch. If it was a franchise the shop would have been legally obliged to display the name and address of the owner (usually by the till, or on its letterhead if it did business by correspondence). Although all the branches may be using the same logo and name, each one could be a different company. So, if the company that was running that particular branch has ceased trading, even though there are many other shops with the same name still trading, you are unlikely to recover your money (p. 25). If you paid by credit card and the price was over £100, you may have a claim against the credit card company (pp. 132–3).

Q *The television I bought from the local branch of a large electrical store came with a 'free' radio-cassette recorder. The television is fine but the radio has stopped working. The shop manager said 'You get what you pay for. As it was a* ***free gift*** *you can hardly complain that it's rubbish!'*

A The retailer is wrong. The shop has supplied the radio as part of the contract of sale and is responsible for the quality of both the television and the radio. They must both be of satisfactory quality and function properly (pp. 28–9). The retailer will have to pay for the repair: if he refuses, you are entitled to get it repaired elsewhere and send the bill to the shop.

Q *I've often seen references to* ***codes of practice****. How can these help me?*

A The Office of Fair Trading encourages trade associations (pp. 238–9) to prepare codes of practice for its members. Such codes now exist for many types of business including double glazing, travel agents and tour operators, laundries and dry cleaning, mail order, and many areas of retail from electrical goods to cars, footwear, and so on. Check with the relevant trade association at the back of this book.† The aim of the exercise is to raise business standards by recommending standards of practice. The recommendations in the various codes have no legal force, however, and no legal action can be taken in the courts if a member does not adhere to them. So their effectiveness is restricted.

Many codes offer free conciliation by the trade association in the event of a dispute between a member and a customer. Some also offer a system of low-cost arbitration through which the dispute can be resolved instead of going to court (pp. 239–42).

The OFT publishes leaflets on almost all the codes and you

can get copies from the OFT† direct, or from libraries, Citizens Advice Bureaux and Consumer Advice Centres.

Q *I traded my old fridge in* **part exchange** *for a new one and paid the difference in cash. What are my rights if there are faults in the new fridge?*

A Your rights are exactly the same as if you had paid in full for the new fridge. Part-exchange deals are common in the case of cars, cookers, washing machines, cameras and an increasing range of other goods. Whatever the goods, you have the full protection of the Sale of Goods Act 1979 (pp. 28–9).

Q *I ordered and paid for a table from a furniture shop, explaining that I needed it in time for a birthday party four weeks away. What can I do if the table does not arrive in time?*

A There is no legal requirement that goods be delivered within a fixed period, so it's up to you to tell the retailer if you have a deadline. The Sale of Goods Act 1979 says that the seller must deliver the goods to you within a 'reasonable' time. There are no hard and fast rules about what is 'reasonable'. It depends on the circumstances – the type of goods, their availability and so on. Note that:

- if the date of delivery is important you should make **time of the essence** in writing when making the contract. Then, if delivery is delayed by even a day, you are entitled to cancel the contract and receive a full refund of the price paid. And if it costs you more than the price you paid originally to get the same goods elsewhere, you can claim the extra cost from the original supplier
- if no specific date was agreed in this way you can give notice in writing to the shop imposing an ultimate time limit. The period specified in the notice must be reasonable, and if the goods do not arrive by that deadline you may cancel the contract and get your money and any extra costs back. You

would then be within your rights to go to another supplier who has the table in stock and get it immediately. If in doing so you have to pay more, the additional cost can be recovered from the first shop

- sometimes it is clear from the nature of the goods (Christmas cards, or an Easter catalogue, say) that the goods ordered are required by a particular date. So even if you have not specified a date, if such goods do not arrive in time then you are entitled to cancel the contract and get a refund of your money plus any extra costs.

Q *The furniture I bought was delivered to my home. I was asked to sign a* **delivery note** *which stated: 'I acknowledge that the goods have been delivered in good order.' When I unpacked the furniture I found it badly scratched. Should I have signed the note?*

A It is better not to sign a delivery note such as this one because you could lose your right to reject the goods later (pp. 29–30). Your signature is a sign that you 'accept' the goods in the condition they are in even though you haven't inspected them. You should always inspect goods very carefully on delivery.

If you have no option but to sign the note, and no opportunity to inspect properly, the safer course would be to add 'goods not examined' or a similar note to the effect that you have not had an opportunity to inspect the contents to see if they are perfect.

Q *The iron I bought was faulty and I was given a replacement. The replacement is no better and stopped working within a week. The shop has refused to exchange it saying that the second iron was a gift. Is this correct?*

A No. Although you cannot insist on a replacement, if you *are* offered one it must be of satisfactory quality and fit for its purpose (pp. 28–30). There is some legal dispute over whether the second goods are supplied under a new contract, or whether this transaction is a continuation of the original contract of purchase – this precise legal point has not been tested, but the fact remains that you are legally entitled to goods of satisfactory quality.

If your goods are replaced by the manufacturer this will give rise to a contractual obligation on the manufacturer to ensure that the goods supplied are of the proper quality. Legally this creates a contract of exchange, and your rights would be governed by the Supply of Goods and Services Act 1982 instead of the Sale of Goods Act 1979 (pp. 59–60).

Q *After my new freezer was delivered I noticed a scratch on the side. Can I reject it and get my money back?*

A This will depend on how bad the scratch is. The Sale of Goods Act 1979 says that to be of 'satisfactory quality' (pp. 28–9) goods must be free from minor defects. If the scratch is very small it may be that there is no legal claim. The law will not concern itself with trifles.

Q *I've seen some clothes I'd like to buy but they are only available by mail order and I'm worried about ordering goods by post. Am I right to worry?*

A Not necessarily. In fact you may have extra protection when you buy mail-order goods:

- you are fully covered by the Sale of Goods Act 1979, so the goods must be of satisfactory quality and be reasonably fit for their purpose, and should correspond with their description in advertisements or catalogues (pp. 28–9)
- you are fully covered by the Consumer Protection Act 1987, so if something you have bought turns out to be dangerous and causes damage to you or your property you can claim against the manufacturer (pp. 46–8)
- when you buy from a catalogue or respond to an advert in a magazine or newspaper, you are probably covered by one of the mail-order protection schemes.† For example, the Mail

Order Traders' Association code of practice states that customers should be allowed at least 14 days to return unwanted goods. Not all traders are members of particular schemes. The British Code of Advertising Practice, administered by the Advertising Standards Authority (ASA), covers *all* mail-order traders: it says that consumers are entitled to return unwanted goods within seven days. So you have time to change your mind if you don't like the goods, and if you send them back within the stated time you will be entitled to all your money back. If you run into difficulty, contact the protection scheme or the ASA as appropriate†

- the trade association will usually investigate any complaint against a member, and will offer a conciliation service to you and the member free of charge
- if you have a complaint about goods ordered directly in response to an advertisement in a newspaper or journal, write to the advertising manager at the publication in which the advert appeared giving details of the date of publication, the name and address of the company, goods ordered, price, amount of money sent, and nature of the complaint
- if you ordered and paid in advance for goods from a company that goes bust you will be protected if the company belongs to the Mail Order Protection Scheme (MOPS). The MOPS logo should be displayed on the advert. There are time limits within which you have to claim, so in such cases you should contact the advertising manager for the publication in which the advertisement appeared as soon as possible. MOPS schemes are run by:
- the Newspaper Publishers' Association† – for the national dailies, and the Sunday papers
- the Periodical Publishers Association† – for most magazine and periodical publishers
- the Newspaper Society† – for most regional and local papers
- Scottish Daily Newspaper Society† – for daily papers in Scotland.

Q *The goods I bought from a mail-order company haven't arrived after six weeks. Can I cancel the contract and get my money back?*

A There is no legal requirement that goods arrive within a particular time. The law merely says they must arrive within a 'reasonable' time (p. 39). The British Code of Advertising Practice (BCAP) states that mail-order goods should arrive within 28 days of order, unless the goods are of a type that may require longer, such as plants, or made-to-measure clothing. The timescale should be stated on the advert or in the catalogue.

- if you need goods by a particular date, make this date 'of the essence' when you make your original order
- keep a note of the date (as well as the company's name and address and goods ordered) when you order goods so you know when the stated date has arrived or the 28 days are up
- if the goods don't arrive by the stated date, or within the 28 days set out in the BCAP, you can cancel the contract and recover your money
- if the trader is a member of a trade association contact it for help in sorting out your problem. If it is not a member of any particular association, contact the Advertising Standards Authority (ASA).† The ASA administers the BCAP, and although this has no legal force, it is a good indicator of what length of time is 'unreasonable'.

Q *Can I prevent mail-order traders from passing my name and address on to other traders? I'm fed up with receiving junk mail and offers for things I don't want.*

A In theory you can, but in practice the law may be of little help. The Advertising Standards Authority (ASA), administrator of the British Code of Advertising Practice (BCAP), governs the use mail-order companies can make of your personal data. Traders must tell you if they might pass your name and address on to other companies and must give you a chance to tell them if you don't want your details used in this way for other traders' promotions.

If you want to reduce the volume of unwanted goods you receive write to the Mailing Preference Service.† The BCAP says that any company using a mailing list to send out goods must refer to the MPS register and exclude people who appear on it.

Unfortunately, there is no legal obligation on traders to follow the provisions of the various codes, but the ASA† will help sort out any problems you have.

Q *I ordered a hair-dryer by mail-order. It was delivered in a battered box and when I opened it the plastic casing of the dryer was smashed. Do I still have to pay for it?*

A In practice, mail-order companies which belong to trade associations generally agree to replace damaged goods free of charge. But there may be no protection if the company is not a member of a trade association and therefore does not subscribe to a code of practice. In such circumstances your rights will depend on whether the supplier can prove that the goods left its premises in perfect condition.

If it is clear that the goods were damaged in transit, you have a claim against the carrier. In the case of the Post Office, you should complete form P58 (available at any post office) and send it to the Head Postmaster. Remember to keep a copy of what you write. If you can show that the parcel was damaged in the post, you are entitled to compensation on a sliding scale, but it may not cover the actual cost of the item.

The Sale of Goods Act 1979 says that once goods have been handed over to a carrier (this may be the Post Office or a delivery company) they become the property of the buyer, who must bear the risk of accidental loss or damage in transit. This may seem harsh, but the Act also says that the supplier should make sure those goods are adequately covered by insurance during transit (by sending them by registered post, say). So if the goods arrive damaged and the supplier has not taken out any insurance protection you can refuse to accept the goods and demand your money back.

Q *I received in the post a set of kitchen knives which I didn't order. A letter arrived asking for £60 which I ignored. Now I've received a letter threatening to sue me. What should I do?*

A You should certainly not pay any money. The practice of demanding payment for unsolicited goods was made illegal by the Unsolicited Goods and Services Act 1971 (or, in Northern Ireland, the Unsolicited Goods and Services [Northern Ireland] Order 1976). As long as you had not requested the goods and they were sent to you in your private capacity (not to your business), you have two options:

- to do nothing and keep the goods safely for six months from the date of receipt, at the end of which time the goods become yours to keep. But if the supplier wants them back during this period, you can't refuse to let him collect them, nor can you refuse to send them back if the supplier pays the postage
- alternatively, to send written notice to the supplier stating that you did not ask for the goods, that you do not want them and that they are available for collection from the address to which they were originally sent; if they are not collected, the goods are yours after 30 days.

The law makes it a criminal offence for a trader to demand payment or threaten legal proceedings over unsolicited goods. As well as ignoring all demands for payment you should report the matter to the Trading Standards Department at your local council (address in phone book).

Q *We collected tokens from cereal packs, sent them off with 50 pence and waited for our 'free' gift to arrive. A letter from the company told us that they were out of stock. It's now been three months and nothing has arrived. Can we insist on being sent the goods offered?*

A Truly 'free' offers are very rare indeed. If you have to do something in return, such as collecting tokens and/or sending money, this creates a contract between you and the company offering the 'gift'. So by collecting and sending off tokens from the packets of cereal, you have entered into a contract and you are entitled to receive your gift. If the company fails to deliver its part of the bargain, the compensation you can expect to receive should put you in the same position as if the contract had been fulfilled, so you can claim the cost of buying the same item or a similar one elsewhere.

Q *What does the term* ***product liability*** *mean?*

A It means legal responsibility for the safety of goods and is generally used to describe the legal position between a manufacturer and the ultimate user of the product, the consumer. This is to distinguish it from the legal relationship between the consumer and the person who sells the product. Usually this is a different person or company. Your rights against the seller are governed by contract law (pp. 28–9). But you do not have a contract with the manufacturer. So a different set of legal principles applies if you want to hold the manufacturer responsible for losses you suffer owing to a problem with his product. Product liability laws are usually cited if the product in question has proved to be unsafe in some way and has caused either physical injury or damage to property.

Q *My parents bought us a washing machine as a wedding present. The machine burst into flames while we were out. Luckily the emergency services put the fire out quickly but the smoke and fire damage is extensive. It will cost us a good deal to replace everything we've lost and to repair the damage. Who is responsible for this?*

A As you did not buy the machine yourself you have no contract with the shop it came from and therefore cannot claim under the Sale of Goods Act 1979 (pp. 28–9). So any claim will be against the manufacturer under the Consumer Protection Act 1987 (p. 47). This allows you to claim for the damage to your house and any injury to you, but not the damage to the machine itself, for which your parents should claim from the retailer. Had you been injured during the fire you would have needed to obtain medical evidence from your GP or a specialist.

You may also be covered for the damage to the building and contents under your household insurance, so check this carefully.

Q *Do I have to prove the manufacturer was at fault to have a viable claim for injury or damage caused by faulty goods?*

A It used to be the case that to establish a claim against the manufacturer you had to prove he had been negligent. This was often very difficult without specialised technical evidence and knowledge of the company's manufacturing processes. The Consumer Protection Act 1987 changed all that. Nowadays:

- you have to prove that the product was **defective** and that it **caused** the injury or damage of which you are complaining
- a product is considered **defective** if it is **less safe** than the consumer is reasonably entitled to expect (for a successful claim, therefore, goods must be unsafe, not merely shoddy)
- the terms of the Consumer Protection Act 1987 do not remove the existing liability of retailers under the Sale of Goods Act 1979 (pp. 28–9)
- the Consumer Protection Act applies to products *supplied* after March 1988
- you cannot claim for damage to the product itself. So if, say, your car breaks down completely but does not damage you or anything else this law will not help you, although you may be able to claim against the retailer for this sort of problem under the contract of sale.

Q *I received severe head injuries following a car accident. My head hit the steering wheel in the crash and I have had to give up my job. The consultant told me that if an air bag had been fitted to the car, I wouldn't have received any head injuries. Surely it's the manufacturer's responsibility to fit safety features to products?*

A It is, although much will depend on the age of the car. The Consumer Protection Act 1987 makes manufacturers 'strictly liable' for 'defective' products (see above), so you may have a claim against the manufacturer for damages for the injury you suffered as a direct result of the lack of safety features in the car. Damage to property must amount to at least £275 (a purely arbitrary figure designed to discourage lots of minor claims against manufacturers) but even minor personal injury is covered.

Given that you have suffered a serious injury and the fact that air bags have for years been standard on cars sold in the USA, and are now found on some in Great Britain, there is a strong argument that the overall design of the car does not meet current expectations of safety (p. 47). In any claim for serious injury, you should seek the advice of a specialist personal injury solicitor. Contact the Law Society or the Association of Personal Injury Lawyers.†

Q *I've found out too late that the washer dryer that caused my house to burn down was the subject of a* ***product recall****. I never heard about this. Does the fact that there was a recall strengthen my case?*

A The recall makes it much easier to prove that there was a defect as the evidence has been provided by the manufacturers. It will be difficult for them to argue that the product was not defective if the fault that caused your house to burn down is the same as the one that prompted the recall. It may be advisable to have the appliance in question examined by an appropriate independent expert to confirm what the nature of the problem was. The manufacturer will probably also be keener to sort out problems if there has already been the bad publicity of a recall.

At present product recalls are usually advertised in the national press, and *Which?* magazine carries details of them every month. If you have such a product you should contact the manufacturers immediately. If it's already too late and the damage is done, ask the manufacturer for compensation (p. 47).

There are few guidelines for domestic product recalls. Serious faults need more urgent and widely published recalls, and some products including medicines and foods have special rules to ensure that unsafe products are taken off the market as soon as possible. But what are needed are simple procedures that all manufacturers can follow. No one can force a manufacturer to initiate a product recall although the government can make a manufacturer issue a notice warning people about an unsafe product. This is usually enough of a threat to make most manufacturers institute a recall.

Q *My motorbike broke down completely after six months, and the manufacturer is refusing to repair it or replace it. Isn't it the manufacturer's responsibility?*

A No. Product liability does not help you when goods are merely shoddy or break down. You should go back to the shop and exercise your rights as a buyer under the Sale of Goods Act 1979 (pp. 28–9). The manufacturer will only be liable if:

- the fault was such as to make the vehicle **unsafe** and you actually suffered some damage to yourself or your property (other than the bike) as a result of this
- check to see whether you received a manufacturer's guarantee when you bought the motorbike. If it has not expired, the manufacturer may put things right under the terms of the guarantee (see pp. 35–6).

Q *I bought a* ***second-hand*** *car from a garage last week and signed a form which said 'sold as seen'. It was a low-mileage car and was described as in 'very good condition'. The car broke down as I was driving along the motorway and now needs a new engine. The engineer's report says that the garage would have known that the engine was defective when they sold it to me. But they refuse to pay the repair costs. Is this right?*

A No. When you buy **second-hand** goods from a trader, the Sale of Goods Act 1979 applies, so they must fit their **description**, be of **satisfactory quality**, and be **fit for their purpose** (pp. 28–9). Obviously, a second-hand car won't be in such good condition as a new car, but it should be roadworthy, and the quality you can expect will depend on the age, the price and the description given of the car. In this case the engineer's statement shows that the car was defective at the time you purchased it so it didn't fit its description and was not of merchantable quality. It also seems likely that there was a **misrepresentation** which led you to buy the car (p. 50). Therefore:

- if you act quickly enough, you are entitled to reject the car and get your money back. If you've lost the right to reject, or if you want to keep the car, you are entitled to compensation for the defective engine. This is usually taken to be the cost of repair. In this case the engine has to be replaced, so the garage will be responsible for this, although you may be asked for a contribution if the engine it puts in is a new one and therefore better than the old one you thought you were getting (p. 64).

Q *We've just bought a car from a* ***private ad*** *in the local paper. The ad described it as reliable, and as having been serviced regularly. The lady who was selling the car said that it had been looked after well. On the first long journey the engine seized up and it's now obvious that it hasn't been serviced for a long time. Will the seller have to pay for the repairs?*

A When you buy goods from a **private seller** the principle of *caveat emptor* ('let the buyer beware') applies. There is no legal requirement that the goods are of merchantable quality or fit for their purpose. With private sales you will have redress only if:

- the goods don't correspond with any **description** you have been given (pp. 28–9), or
- the seller was guilty of **misrepresentation**, or
- the seller doesn't really own the goods (p. 28).

In this case the car was described as being reliable, in good condition, and as having been regularly serviced and looked after well. This is clearly not true and so will give rise to two possible claims:

- **breach of description** This entitles you to reject the car and get your money back, or keep it and ask for compensation (usually the cost of repair) (pp. 29–30)
- **misrepresentation** This entitles you to cancel the contract and get your money back, or keep it and ask for compensation. A misrepresentation is a statement of fact (not opinion) which is made by the seller before the contract is made. If you relied on that statement when deciding whether to buy and it turns out to be wrong, you can claim.

In any dispute where the seller has made a written or verbal statement about the goods, it is probably best to allege both misrepresentation and breach of contract.

Q *What steps should I take to avoid problems when I buy a second-hand car?*

A When buying a second-hand car, your legal rights may be limited (p. 49). It is almost impossible to protect yourself fully against hidden defects and legal problems. However, here are a few tips which should help:

- employ an engineer to check the car over and report on the car's condition. This is especially important if you are buying from a private seller (p. 50). If you are a member of a motoring organisation it may provide a vehicle inspection report if requested
- carry out a search with HP Information plc.† You can apply to HPI direct and each search will cost £15. An HPI search does not guarantee that the car you buy is OK but it will tell you whether the car is recorded:
  - to be subject to an outstanding finance agreement (pp. 53 and 130)
  - to have had a major damage-related insurance claim (p. 204)
  - to be stolen or subject to fraudulent activity (see below)
  - to have been subject to a registration plate change
- try to make a note of everything that the seller says about the car – it would be useful to take an independent witness along with you so that you have proof that any claims made were really said. Also, hang on to the advert if it contains a description of the car (p. 29)
- read the latest *Which?* report on buying a second-hand car: following the advice should help you avoid costly mistakes.

Q *Last year I bought a used car privately. I have now received a visit from the police, who inform me that it had been* ***stolen*** *the year before*

I purchased it. The person I bought the car from doesn't know anything about this either. The original owner wants the car back. Do I have to return it?

A Possibly yes, but it's a very complicated area. The Sale of Goods Act 1979 says that a person who sells goods must be the real owner (have **title**), or have the consent of the real owner to sell (pp. 28–9). Your seller had no right to sell the car, as he was not the owner himself and was not in a position to transfer the ownership to you. The original owner from whom the car was stolen remained the real owner throughout. If you refuse to return the car, he will be able to bring a civil action in the courts for 'conversion'. The court may order you to pay the original owner the value of the car at the date you bought it, or, more likely, order you to return the car to him or her.

Even if this happens, all is not lost:

- you may recover the full price from your seller, because under the Sale of Goods Act 1979 the requirement that a seller must own the goods he sells means that your seller is in breach of his contract with you (pp. 28–30). You are therefore entitled to a full refund from him. It is irrelevant that your seller was completely innocent and had no knowledge or suspicion that the car was stolen: like most of the obligations under the Act, it is a 'strict liability' on the seller to ensure that he has the rights of ownership, and hence, to sell on
- it is equally irrelevant that your seller was a private seller, as the provision as to title applies to private and trade sales alike (pp. 50–1)
- the 'market overt' rule used to allow buyers to keep stolen goods purchased between sunrise and sunset at a market or fair established by charter or custom. This very old and quirky bit of law was abolished in January 1995 and is likely to be replaced by better legal protection in an area where most consumers are likely to be affected. Stolen goods now account for most of the problems over title. In the meantime, always investigate the history of the car, for example, via the HPI (see p. 51) or the police, before buying.

Q *If I had a new gearbox put in my recently purchased car before I realised it was stolen, can I claim that money back off the true owner?*

A Under the Torts (Interference with Goods) Act 1977 you are entitled to receive compensation for the repairs and improvements you make. This Act can be used like a shield, not a sword, so if the true owner of the car takes you to court to get the car back, the court will make an allowance for the increase in value of the car which is attributable to the repairs and improvements you have made. Your position will be much weaker if you let the true owner take the car back without going to court, because then you cannot use this Act to sue the true owner for your financial outlay on repairs. So while there is a dispute park the car on your property if possible, and don't give anyone permission to take it away. Try to negotiate a reasonable payment and avoid going to court if you can. But if a court does order you to hand it over you should be able to recover the full purchase price from the person who sold the car to you (p. 52).

Q *I bought a second-hand car but, unknown to me, it was still on* ***hire purchase****. The finance company is now reclaiming the car. Should I let the company take it?*

A No. Under an HP agreement the goods are still owned by the finance company, and the hirer does not become the legal owner until he has paid all that was due under the HP agreement (pp. 129–30). Until then he has nothing more than a right to possession of the car and has no right to sell it. The Hire Purchase Act 1964 offers protection specifically where a motor vehicle which is the subject of an outstanding HP agreement is sold to a **private purchaser**. Provided you (the private purchaser) did not know about the existence of the hire-purchase agreement, or were told about it but informed that it had been paid off, you will obtain a good title to the vehicle and be able to resist the finance company's claims. So if you meet these criteria the car is legally yours to keep. The finance company will have to fight it out with the dishonest seller.

Q *What is the position if I buy goods at an* ***auction*** *and they turn out to be defective?*

A Although the Sale of Goods Act 1979 applies to auction purchases, its main conditions (pp. 28–9) may be excluded by a notice on display or in the catalogue – so beware, and check the auction house conditions before you bid. If you buy goods at an auction, your rights are against the seller, who could prove difficult to trace and, unlike in an ordinary consumer transaction where your statutory rights cannot be excluded (pp. 18–19), your rights at an auction may be limited.

Q *My car has just broken down and the gearbox needs replacing. The car is only four months old but the garage I bought it from has gone out of business. I used credit to pay for the car. What can I do?*

A It is a sad fact that when a company goes out of business the consumer often loses out (p. 25). But paying for goods and services on credit can offer some protection (pp. 132–3). The answer here depends on what form of credit you used to buy your car:

- if you entered into a credit agreement that was arranged by the garage that sold you the car, then under section 75 of the Consumer Credit Act 1974 the credit company is liable for any breach of contract or misrepresentation that the garage would be liable for (pp. 28 and 50). In this case you can claim that the car was unmerchantable, but it would be difficult to argue that you could reject the car because you are deemed to have accepted it, and have lost the right to reject it after four months' use (pp. 29–30). You would be entitled to the cost of fitting a replacement gearbox and consequential losses
- if the finance was in the form of a hire-purchase or conditional sale agreement your contract is with the finance company and not the retailer, and you have the same basic legal rights as if you had paid cash. With HP agreements these rights are laid down by the Supply of Goods (Implied Terms) Act 1973. However, when it comes to rejecting a faulty car, your rights

to claim your money back last longer. You have the common law right to reject throughout the time period covered by the HP agreement. In this case you should stop paying the instalments, write to the HP company saying that the car is unmerchantable, that you're rejecting it, and that the car is available for collection by the lender. The HP company should then arrange for collection of the car and refund any payments you have made

- if you arranged a loan through your local bank, and you use that to pay for the car, then you will not be able to pursue the bank under section 75 of the Consumer Credit Act 1974. The bank is an 'unconnected' lender and has nothing effectively to do with the purchase of the car. In this case you have only two hopes: one is that there will be some money over to pay your claim as you are one of the creditors of the garage (this is unlikely) (p. 25); the other is that any manufacturer's guarantee will cover your claim (look at the wording of the guarantee to see whether it is or not).

Q *I ordered a new car a couple of months ago, but it was badly dented and scraped while being transported to the garage prior to delivery to me. I don't like the colour and I'm upset about the damage. Can I reject the car?*

A As for a second-hand car, under the Sale of Goods Act 1979 a new car should fit its description, be of satisfactory quality and be fit for its purpose, although the standard is higher for a new car. If the car does not meet these requirements you have a claim against the dealer. You can ask for the car to be collected and for your money back. However, you must reject the car straight away because you have only a 'reasonable time' from when you get the car to reject it and get your money back. The Act doesn't say what a reasonable time is, but you should assume it is weeks rather than months (pp. 29–30). The problem with complex goods like cars is that time may have run out before you discover the fault. If you are too late to reject you will have to pursue the dealer for compensation. You are also entitled to claim compensation for any expenses you incur which were reasonably foreseeable by both you and the dealer at the time of purchase, such as the cost of alternative means of transport while your car is off the road.

Q *I purchased the car I am now trying to sell on* ***hire purchase****. I've been told that I can't do so until I've paid off all the instalments. Is that correct?*

A Yes, that is correct. The car is still owned by the finance company, and you will own it only when you have paid off all the instalments and purchased it. Your agreement is most probably a consumer credit agreement (p. 128), which means that you are entitled to settle the agreement early and to obtain a rebate on the interest charges to reflect the early repayment. If you want to do this, write to the finance company for the settlement figure, pay that off, and then the car will be yours to sell. If you do not follow this procedure you will have broken the contract with the buyer under the Sale of Goods Act 1979 and you will be liable to the finance company for wrongfully dealing with its property.

Q *A car dealer sold me a car with a recorded mileage of 45,000 miles. After I had driven the car for about five months, my garage said the engine needed a lot of work, and in their opinion it had done more than the 50,000 miles on the clock. I contacted the previous registered keeper, a company, and they told me that when they sold the car it had at least 120,000 miles on the clock. What can I do?*

A When you purchased the car it had a false odometer reading, and if you were given no warning (a sticker, for example) that the odometer was wrong you have two courses of action open to you:

- you may pursue your rights in civil law under the Sale of Goods Act 1979 (misdescription) (pp. 28–9) or under the Misrepresentation Act 1967 (misrepresentation) (pp. 50–1)
- you should report the matter to the Trading Standards Department at the dealer's local council. Simply threatening

to do so may lead to a quick settlement of your case. The Trade Descriptions Act 1968 makes it a criminal offence for dealers to make false statements about the cars they sell. The Act, which is criminal, not civil, law, cannot help you directly if you want to make a claim for compensation, but if the Trading Standards officer does decide to prosecute you may ask the court for compensation.

Q *My car broke down when the starter motor failed. A local garage fitted a new motor, but a couple of weeks later that one broke down as well. The garage manager has just told me that I will have to pay for the new work because his mechanic checked the replacement starter motor and he had no reason to think it was faulty. He said he couldn't be held responsible for manufacturing defects. Is that right?*

A No. The garage should have supplied a starter motor that was of satisfactory quality under the Supply of Goods and Services Act 1982 (common law in Scotland) (pp. 59–61). It is no defence for the garage to say that the staff were careful and had no reason to suspect that the motor was defective. The garage manager shouldn't charge you for putting the car right, and should provide a starter motor and labour free of charge. If not, you are entitled to have the work done elsewhere and ask the garage to pay the bill plus any extra expense, such as car hire while your car is off the road.

Q *What difference would it have made if the new starter motor had turned out not to be faulty but had been fitted incorrectly by an incompetent mechanic, which caused the subsequent breakdown?*

A The garage would still have to put the car right free of charge. The Supply of Goods and Services Act 1982 (common law in Scotland) states that the work should be done with reasonable care and skill. As the garage was under a duty to carry out the repair carefully, it is responsible for the incompetent and careless work of the mechanic. There is a possibility that you could have signed away your right to compensation if you signed a contract containing a clause that excluded the garage from liability for negligence. This clause must be reasonable; if it is not, it will have no effect on your rights (p. 72).

Q *I left my car at a garage for repairs. When I collected it, I noticed that the wing had a big dent in it. The garage denies any responsibility. What can I do?*

A When you take your car into a garage for repairs, the garage must take reasonable care of it. If your car is damaged while in the possession of the garage, or on the garage forecourt, for example, the garage is responsible – unless it can prove that the damage was caused through no fault on its part. This principle is enshrined in the law of bailment (p. 73).

The garage may attempt to restrict your legal rights by referring to a sign excluding loss or damage to cars in its possession. Under the Unfair Contract Terms Act 1977, notices or conditions in contracts which exclude or restrict liability for loss or damage to property will be upheld only if the garage can prove that they are fair and reasonable in the circumstances. This protection is now supplemented by new EU laws on unfair contract terms, set out in the Unfair Terms in Consumer Contracts Regulations 1994. It is very unlikely that a court would allow a garage to rely on a notice which tried to exempt it from all responsibility for loss and damage, whatever the cause (p. 72).

CHAPTER 2

Commercial Services

CALLING in a plumber, having your hair cut, getting your wedding photos developed, having your car serviced, or having kitchens, bathrooms or double glazing installed – all are examples of contracts of service. If a dispute arises between you and the person providing the service, it is the contract which dictates the legal rights and obligations you owe each other. This chapter looks at the rules involved in paying for services, and how you can attempt to resolve complaints.

Q *When I employ a trader to do work for me, what are my rights?*

A Contracts where the trader provides not merely goods such as spare parts, or materials for repairing, building or constructing something, but also the labour element, are classified in law as contracts for **work and materials**. This covers everything from large building works, to double glazing installation, to servicing a washing machine. Contracts of this type are governed by the Supply of Goods and Services Act 1982 (common law in Scotland), which imposes the following legal duty on the supplier of the service:

- to carry out the service with reasonable skill and care
- to carry out the service within a 'reasonable time' where no time limit has been fixed (p. 71)
- to make a 'reasonable charge' for the service where no charge has been agreed in advance (pp. 60–1)

- to use materials which are of satisfactory quality and fit for their purpose, as they would need to be under the Sale of Goods Act 1979 (pp. 28–9).

Q *I've just had new leather soles put on my shoes, but the workmanship is so poor that the soles started to come off the first time I wore them. I don't trust the repairer to do the job properly, but can I get them put right free of charge?*

A Yes, you are entitled get the job done properly. The **Supply of Goods and Services Act 1982** (common law in Scotland) gives you rights when you have work done. It imposes two main obligations on the person doing the work for you:

- to carry out the job with reasonable skill and care, and
- to use suitable materials of satisfactory quality.

Clearly the shoe repairer has not fulfilled the first requirement, and you are entitled to take the shoes back and ask for them to be put right free of charge. But if you have really lost confidence in the repairer, have them put right by someone else and charge the cost to the original repairer. If the shoes are beyond repair you should be entitled to compensation, which in this case would be the second-hand value of the shoes and a refund of the wasted repair charges.

If your complaint drags on, find out whether the repairer is a member of a trade association† which subscribes to the code of practice for shoe repairs; if he is, you may be able to ask for conciliation, and, for a small fee, get an independent test report to resolve the dispute.

Q *I discovered a leaking pipe in my loft, so I had to call a plumber in to do some emergency work. On the phone he said it would probably cost 'around £50' depending on the work needed. He was only here for one hour but handed me a bill for £250. Do I have to pay the extra £200? The plumber's argument is that it was an emergency and he stopped considerable damage resulting, so he can charge what he likes. Is this right?*

A If you're only given a rough guide to the cost, or if no price is agreed at all, the trader may charge only a **reasonable price** in accordance with the Supply of Goods and Services Act 1982. What is reasonable depends on how much work has been done, whether that work was done well, and the type of job that was undertaken. So the fact that the work was a matter of urgency and may well have prevented further damage does not automatically justify the trader increasing the charge except to take account of any lost business caused by dropping everything else to help you out.

If you just give blanket instructions to do whatever was necessary to repair, you must expect the final bill to cover the work actually required. But the bill must still be **reasonable.** Follow these guidelines:

- always ask for a written **exact and firm quotation** before agreeing to the work (p. 27)
- ask the relevant trade association† for guidance on charges
- after the event, get quotes from other traders as to what they would charge for the same work in the same conditions
- finally, send the trader a cheque for what you consider to be the fair price (p. 144)..

Q *I paid to have my washing machine serviced and the trader overhauled my tumble drier at the same time free of charge. The washer works perfectly but now the drier has packed up. Even though I didn't pay for the work to the drier, can I still complain?*

A Yes. The trader agreed to service both machines as part of the contract for the work and is responsible for the standard of work to both. The Supply of Goods and Services Act 1982 sets out the legal requirements of the work (p. 59). It is immaterial that the trader serviced two machines for the price of one – the work to the drier should have been carried out with reasonable skill and care, and if it wasn't, the trader will have to put the matter right: if he refuses, you are entitled to get the work done elsewhere and send the bill to the trader.

Q *I need some work done on my house. What can I do to reduce the chances of getting into a dispute over the work?*

A Follow these steps:

- problems with the price charged for work, the time it takes to do the job and the standard of the work can be reduced by finding a reliable trader: use someone recommended by a friend or relative, and look for membership of a trade association†
- be as **precise** as possible about the problem you have and ask for a clear explanation of what the tradesman proposes to do to solve the problem
- once you have agreed on what needs to be done, insist on a written **exact and firm quotation** for the job rather than an estimate
- get quotes from more than one trader: three should give you a good guide
- have a written **contract**, especially for bigger jobs such as building work (see model opposite)
- ideally, pay only when the work is complete and you're happy with it. It certainly shouldn't be necessary to make any payments until work has begun other than for materials bought on your behalf, but for more complicated work, or work of longer duration, you may have to pay in instalments during the job as stages are completed. If you do agree to this, write the stages into the contract as well as the final payment date. If you're not happy with the work done at any particular stage, then you're entitled to withhold payment for that stage until the work is done to your satisfaction.

Q *What should be included in a contract for work to be carried out on property?*

A If possible, draw up your own contract using the example opposite so you and the trader know exactly what's expected of both of you. Ideally this should include:

- your name and the name and address of the contractor

Contract

1 ______________________ **(contractor)**
of ______________________________
____
shall carry out and complete the work outlined in the attached specification and drawings in a good and workmanlike manner in accordance with all relevant British Standards and Codes of Practice, all for the sum of £_____ **plus VAT** at the standard rate.

2 The contractor shall provide all the labour, plant, materials and equipment necessary to complete the work.

3 The work shall start on ______ **(date)**
The work shall be completed by__ **(date)**

Time is of the essence with regard to this work. All work must be carried out diligently and on a regular basis. The completion date will be extended only if the contractor is prevented from completing the work by factors outside his/her control. Should the contractor, without good reason, fail to finish the work on time he/she agrees to pay the owner damages which represent actual loss to the owner of £_______[*] for every week or part of a week during which the completion is delayed.

4 The contractor shall remove all rubbish as it accumulates and all tools, surplus materials etc. from the site and leave it in a clean and tidy condition within 14 days of completion of the contracted work.

5 The contractor shall comply with all statutory requirements, local and national regulations and by-laws that relate to the work. He/she shall make all notifications, arrange inspections etc. in connection with the work.

6 The value of any variation to the contracted work should be agreed before it is carried out. Only variations authorised in writing by the owner shall be paid for.

7 The contractor shall take out all necessary insurance.

8 If the contractor's work is not of a reasonable standard, or if the contractor leaves the site without reasonable explanation for more than 4 consecutive days, the owner may terminate the contract paying only for the value of the work done, less compensation for inconvenience or additional expense.

9 Once the contract is completed the contractor shall submit a final account to the owner. This shall be paid within 14 days of receipt by the owner.

10 The contractor shall make good at his/her own expense any damage to the owner's premises caused by him/her and/or his/her agents or employees.

11 Any defects that arise due to faulty work or materials shall be put right promptly by the contractor for no further payment.

[*£50, say, or whatever sum you think is likely to reflect your out-of-pocket expenses arising from the delay.]

- a reference to the standard of workmanship ('good and workmanlike manner') and materials to be used, including a statement that the work will be in accordance with any plans and specifications. These specifications may refer to appropriate British Standards or codes of practice
- the date on which the work will start, and the date on which it will be finished. You can also agree that the contractor pays

you reasonable compensation if the work is late (while allowing give and take in the completion date due to delays caused by unusually bad weather or other circumstances beyond the contractor's control)
- a requirement that the trader should leave the site in a tidy state at the end of the work
- clarification of who (you or the trader) is responsible for applying for Building Regulations or planning permission
- agreement that any changes to the specification are to be confirmed in writing
- a requirement that the contractor must be properly insured
- provision for ending the contract, by you or the contractor
- the total cost of the work and how it will be paid – a lump sum at the end or stage payments as the work progresses
- a requirement that the contractor returns to put right any defects in the work, and any damage caused to your property, at his expense.

Some tradespeople will present their own terms and conditions in the form of a contract. If they do, read the small print very carefully and check it against the list above before signing. Make sure the trader agrees to any changes you make before you finally give the go-ahead for the work (p. 18). If he is only happy to work with lots of exclusion clauses in the contract, he is not worth hiring.

Q *We had our house rewired recently, and the electrician accidentally knocked a tin of paint over our carpet and up the walls. The trader has agreed to pay for redecoration, but says that as the carpet wasn't new he won't pay the full cost of replacement as this would put us in a* ***better position****. Is this right?*

A If someone working on your property carelessly causes damage in the process, you are entitled to claim full compensation for any losses you would not otherwise have incurred. Normally, you may not be able to recover the full cost of replacing an old item with a brand new one as this would put you in a better position as a result. If the carpet was perfectly serviceable and, but for the other party's **negligence**, would not have needed replacing for several years, you may be able to claim the full cost of replacement. If a second-hand replacement is readily available, the amount of compensation will be reduced to take account of **betterment**. But if the carpet was fitted it may not be possible to buy a second-hand carpet to fit, so, even if the damaged carpet was not brand-new, you are still entitled to the full cost of a new replacement.

Q *I'm considering having an extension built. Are there any steps I can take to* ***protect my money*** *if the work is unsatisfactory or if the builder goes bust?*

A If you have paid money in advance you risk losing it. There are three ways to protect yourself:

- if you have no option but to pay something in advance, don't pay too much: 10 per cent would be a reasonable maximum. With large jobs like this it's better to pay at certain stages of the work (p. 62)
- pick a builder who offers an **insurance-backed guarantee scheme**. To benefit from such schemes the customer will have to pay a small percentage of the total cost of the work (usually about 1 per cent) as the insurance premium. Get full documentation of the cover before you give the final go-ahead. There are several different schemes on offer and they vary in the cover they provide. For example:
  - the Independent Warranty Association†: this covers the installation of windows, conservatories, kitchens and bathrooms, and will give protection in the event of the trader going out of business. The scheme will ensure that any uncompleted work is finished, and will make sure any remedial work is carried out
  - the Building Guarantee Scheme Ltd†: this offers cover for two-and-a-half years after the completion of the job. It is available for any building work costing between £500 and £100,000, and covers disputes over the quality of that work or the insolvency of the trader
  - the Guarantee Protection Trust Ltd†: this covers treatment

for woodworm, wet and dry rot, rising damp and replacement wall tiles. If the customer has a complaint over the quality of the work and the trader has ceased trading, the insurance will pay for remedial work

- pay a deposit with your credit card if the company will accept it, or arrange with the builder for finance to pay for all or part of the work.

The credit or finance company is 'jointly liable' with the builder. So if the builder goes bust, or breaks the contract in any other way, you can also claim against the credit company who financed the deal. This protection is provided by the Consumer Credit Act 1974 for loans to buy specific goods or services where the lender has a contract with the supplier, such as credit card purchases (a general loan from your bank will not give this protection as the credit deal has to be made specifically to finance the work). It applies if the cash value of the goods or work is between £100 and £30,000 and the loan is for less than £15,000 (see pp. 54–5).

Q *When the builder had finished the roofing work he asked me to sign a note to say 'I accept that the work has been inspected by me and completed to my satisfaction'. The roof looked all right so I signed, but now it's leaking. The builder says I signed so I can't complain now. Is this right?*

A You were unwise to sign a **'satisfaction note'** of this sort. It could make it difficult to claim for defects in the workmanship later. By signing you have admitted that you inspected the work and found no problems, even though you had no idea whether the work was good or bad. If you had no option but to sign, and no opportunity to inspect, the safer course would have been to add 'work unexamined' or a similar note to the effect that you could not say whether the work was satisfactory or not. It is still worth pursuing the complaint, especially if the defect was not of the kind that an inspection by you would have discovered.

Q *The joinery of the extension I had built is appalling. The builder says that the woodwork was done by a* ***subcontractor*** *and so he is not responsible. What is my legal position?*

A The argument that the builder is not responsible for subcontractors is incorrect. He has agreed to do the work and it is irrelevant whether he does it personally or by using employees (p. 230) or by subcontracting. If the job is not done properly the main contractor, the builder with whom you made the contract, is responsible for doing the job in accordance with the express and implied terms of the contract.

The work should have been done in accordance with the technical specifications in the contract as well as any stipulations as to time and cost. The Supply of Goods and Services Act 1982 implies a condition that the supplier shall supply goods that correspond with the contractual description. If the timbers are the wrong size and do not meet this description the builder has broken that contractual condition.

Further, the work should have been carried out with reasonable skill and care. If it was not, the builder is in breach of contract on this score as well. If the builder will not put right the defects, you are entitled to call in another builder to finish the job off properly and deduct the cost from the first builder's account.

There are many trade associations for the building industry which can attempt to resolve a dispute with a member company by conciliation or even independent arbitration if you wish (pp. 238–9). Some builders who subscribe to the Building Guarantee Scheme Ltd can offer an insurance-backed guarantee to cover the quality of work, and to protect you in the event of their going out of business (p. 65).

Q *I took a day's holiday for the repairer to come and mend my television. He promised to call on Friday so I took the day off specially. He didn't come until Saturday. Will he have to compensate me for my wasted day?*

A There is certainly a breach of your verbal agreement with the trader. But whether you can recover compensation for the wasted day rests on the repairer's knowledge that you would have to take a day off work specially. He might have assumed somebody would be at home anyway. So if you didn't spell this out at the time you requested the visit, your loss may not have been a foreseeable one (see below).

If you have a complaint about a trader failing to keep to an agreed deadline, or indeed any other complaint, and the trader is a member of a trade association, such as the Radio, Electrical and Television Retailers' Association (RETRA)†, he may be bound by a code of practice that covers the situation, and the association may be able to conciliate in your dispute (pp. 238–9).

Q *My car was taken to a garage for major repairs. It took six weeks to do the job. Meanwhile, I had to hire a car from another garage, which was surprised at the delay and said the work should only have taken a fortnight. I accept that I should pay for the work, but can I recover some of the car hire charges?*

A Under the Supply of Goods and Services Act 1982 the garage should have carried out the work 'within a reasonable time'. In your case, two weeks would seem to be that reasonable time, in the view of the second garage. The extra four weeks' hire charges, therefore, were caused by the garage's delay and should be recoverable as damages for breach of contract, as long as the garage was aware that you would be hiring a car while yours was with them. The general rule is that you can recover only those items of loss which both parties could have contemplated at the time the contract was made as being likely to result from any breach. Unless you told the trader that you would need to hire a car, he might have assumed you would use public transport.

Many garages are members of one of the trade associations which adhere to the motor industry code of practice†. If the dealer is a member and you are having difficulty getting it sorted out, tell the relevant association about your complaint as soon as possible. It may be able to resolve the problem. If that doesn't work, you have the choice of going to court (pp. 245–8) or taking your claim to arbitration (pp. 239–42). The trade associations run their own schemes in conjunction with the Chartered Institute of Arbitrators.† Your case will be heard by an independent arbitrator who will study your evidence and the evidence of the dealer and make a decision, but you will not be able to go to court if you are unhappy with the result (p. 240).

Q *I asked my local garage to give my car a 24,000-mile service, according to the manufacturer's guidelines. When I went to pay for the service, the garage told me that they had also replaced the rear tyres because they were worn. This isn't part of a 24,000-mile service, and I could have got the tyres cheaper elsewhere. Is there anything I can do about this?*

A As you had a contract with the garage to service the car according to the manufacturer's guidelines for a 24,000-mile service, and no other work, you are entitled to tell the garage to remove the new tyres, put the old ones back on and reduce the bill accordingly. Practically, it might be easier to try to get the garage to reduce the bill for the tyres in accordance with the price of the cheaper tyres mentioned, and you keep the tyres.

Q *I have to have my car repaired soon, and the garage is not quite sure what is wrong with it, so they don't know how much the work is going to cost. I can't afford a really big repair bill at the moment. Is there anything I can do to limit the cost of the repair work?*

A When you ask a garage to do some work on your car, you only have to pay for the work that you've authorised. So, be clear about what you have agreed before allowing the garage to carry out any work, preferably by putting things in writing. If no fixed price is agreed, the law says that you are obliged to pay a 'reasonable price' for the work (pp. 59–61). This depends on how much work has been done and the type of repair or service undertaken. If you feel that the price you are charged is too high, you will have to show that the price is unreasonable. You can do this by getting evidence from other garages or motoring organisations, if you are a member.

As you have not yet entered into a contract you could ask the garage to give you an estimate once the problem has been diagnosed. Instead of just asking the garage to put your car right, ask whether the work is going to cost more, for example, than £100. If you are forced to pay as a condition of recovering your car, you should make it clear in writing that you are paying **under protest** and **without prejudice** to any legal rights you may have against the garage (p. 20). This means that you can pursue the matter further when you have your car back.

Q *I ordered double glazing. The order form stated a delivery period of '10–12 weeks' and stated that 'time for delivery is not of the essence of the contract'. After 14 weeks nothing had happened. I rang to cancel the order, but was told that the windows had been made and if I did not take delivery the company would keep the deposit and sue me for the balance of the price? Could they really do that?*

A Yes, because time was expressly stated to be 'not of the essence'. And there appear to be no special circumstances which made the delivery date vitally important to you. So, although the company did not meet the delivery date, this did not entitle you to cancel the contract:

- if the goods are not delivered and the work is not started within a 'reasonable' time, you should write giving the company reasonable notice of a deadline – if, say, the windows were not supplied and fitted within two weeks at the latest you would regard the contract as terminated
- in the absence of a notice imposing a strict time limit in that way, you were legally obliged to continue with the contract and let the double-glazing company complete the job
- assuming the windows were in fact ready for fitting the following week and you refused to let the work proceed, you would find yourself saddled with considerable expense: as the windows had been specially made for your house, it is unlikely that they could have been sold to another customer and you would have been liable for the total contract price less the small value of the glass and other materials left on the company's hands
- if you wish a trader to do a job on or by a particular date and to be able to cancel otherwise, you must ensure that the

agreed date is seen to be of importance by stressing that delivery or completion of work take place precisely on time, by, for example, making 'time of the essence'.

If you run into difficulties, contact the Glass and Glazing Federation or any other relevant trade association.†

Q *I asked a builder to build an extension to my house, but we did not agree a starting date. Whenever I manage to speak to him he tells me he is very busy and will fit it in when he can. When can I call it a day?*

A Where no date is fixed for work to be done (or goods to be delivered, see p. 39), the contract contains an implied term that it will be done within a **reasonable time**. Contracts for a service are governed by the Supply of Goods and Services Act 1982 (common law in Scotland). It is always difficult to determine what a reasonable time actually is in any particular case. But what is clear is that there is no excuse for the supplier to justify his delay on the grounds that he is busy.

It would be reasonable for you to expect work to begin within a few months of making the agreement. In spite of the long delay, you should not cancel the contract without first giving notice by setting a deadline, making time of the essence, by which work must commence: a month hence would seem long enough. If nothing happens by this date, you will be released from the contract as a result of the builder's breach. You could then claim from him any additional cost of placing the building contract elsewhere (p. 67).

Q *Last week when I went to collect my trousers from the dry-cleaners, I was told they couldn't find them. The cleaners are now refusing to pay me any compensation. Can they do this?*

A Under the Supply and Goods and Services Act 1982, dry-cleaners are under a duty to take reasonable care of your possessions. The fact that they have lost your clothes whilst they were in their care and can provide no explanation as to what happened is evidence that they were negligent. In the circumstances you are entitled to compensation. You should start off by claiming the cost of replacing the lost item but you may find that you have to accept less to take account of wear and tear.

Q *I recently took a silk suit to the cleaners, pointing out a particular stain that needed to be removed. When I got the suit home I noticed that the stain not been removed and the colour of the suit seemed to have faded in certain parts. I complained but they pointed to a notice which said, 'We cannot accept responsibility for loss of or damage to goods howsoever caused.' Can they rely on this notice?*

A The Supply of Goods and Services Act 1982 (common law in Scotland) entitles you to have articles cleaned with reasonable care and skill, and if they are not you are entitled to claim compensation. However, it is very common in business contracts, particularly contracts for services, to find terms which attempt to limit or exclude liability. These are commonly called **exclusion** or **exemption clauses**. The Unfair Contract Terms Act 1977 and the new EU Unfair Terms in Consumer Contracts Regulations 1994 control these and allow suppliers to hide behind them only if the clause is fair and reasonable. What is fair and reasonable depends on the circumstances of each case. Factors that may be taken into account are the bargaining position of both you and the cleaners, whether you could have got the service elsewhere on different terms, and whether you had ever used that cleaners before. So don't be put off pursuing your compensation claim just because of the sign. Each case depends on the individual facts.

To avoid problems with dry-cleaners follow these guidelines:

- if the garment is stained, point out the stain to the cleaner stating if possible what caused it and how long it has been there
- take the garment to the cleaners as soon as you can: in some cases the longer you leave a stain the more difficult it is to remove
- examine the item at the cleaners to check that it has been cleaned properly.

If there *is* a problem:

- take the item back as soon as possible and complain
- if you get nowhere put your complaint in writing, explaining the problem and what you want done
- if the dry-cleaner does not respond or you cannot reach a settlement and the cleaner is a member of the Textiles Services Association† (TSA), ask the TSA for a list of independent labs which will consider the problem to try to decide who is at fault. You will initially have to pay a fee but if the TSA finds in your favour the cleaner will be asked to refund you the lab costs as well as paying you fair compensation
- if you don't want to go to arbitration (pp. 239–42), or if the cleaner is not a member of the TSA, you will have to go to court in order to get compensation. You can make a claim of up to £1,000 under the small claims procedure (£750 in Scotland) (pp. 245–8).

Q *When I arrived at a hotel the attendant parked my car for me in the hotel car park. I didn't use it all weekend but when I went to collect the car on leaving there was a large scratch on one of the doors that certainly hadn't been there before. Can I get the hotel to pay for the repairs?*

A Since the hotel took possession of your car, it was under a duty to take care not to lose or damage it. This is known as the law of **bailment**. Where goods are lost or damaged, the law assumes that the bailee (in this case, the hotel) has not taken care of them, so it is up to the hotel to prove that the damage was caused through no fault on its part.

If the attendant had parked the car sticking out on a dangerous corner, you would be entitled to compensation for the cost of repairing the car. Even if there had been a notice saying 'The hotel accepts no responsibility for loss of or damage to customers' cars', you could challenge this (p. 72), particularly as the attendant parked your car for you and the notice was not brought to your attention.

Q *I sent my holiday photos off to be developed. Later, the photoprocessing company wrote to me a letter saying they had lost the photos; they offered me my money back and a free film. I challenged this but they pointed to a statement on the envelope which said, 'In the event of loss of or damage to films, the company's liability is limited to the cost of processing and a replacement film.' Am I entitled to compensation?*

A Yes. As you have a contract with the photoprocessing company, the Supply of Goods and Services Act 1982 (common law in Scotland) gives you rights in the event of the photoprocessing going wrong. If your photos were of a once-in-a-lifetime holiday, say, or of an unrepeatable event, such as a wedding or other special occasion, you are entitled to compensation for the value of the film and for the upset, disappointment and loss of enjoyment arising from the loss or damage. The amount of compensation depends upon the importance of the photos to you – so, if it was your wedding, you would get more than for those of a distant relative's birthday celebration. Some recent awards have been for as much as £500.

To have any legal effect on your claim, the term in the small print which attempts to take away or limit your rights must be fair and reasonable, as laid down by the Unfair Contract Terms Act 1977 (p. 72). Many photoprocessors now use small print which offers alternative sorts of service, such as insurance, to cover films that are more valuable to you than the average snaps. Whether this makes the term reasonable depends on the size and legibility of the small print, whether every reasonable effort was made to bring it to your attention, and whether the insurance cover, say, is sufficient and easily obtainable.

Q *Last month I went to a new hairdresser for a perm. The salon owner used a perm solution which reacted with my scalp and within a few days I had a bald patch on the top of my head. The owner blamed it on a bad batch of solution. Can I expect any compensation?*

A The hairdresser was providing a service and so should have used reasonable skill and care when perming your hair (pp. 59–61).

When using chemicals a competent hairdresser should carry out a patch test on a small section of the scalp or on some strands of hair to test for any adverse reaction. If the hairdresser fails to do this and you suffer injury as a result, you will have a claim for compensation.

Even if there was something wrong with the batch of perm solution, the Supply of Goods and Services Act 1982 (common law in Scotland) puts the hairdresser under a strict liability to supply materials suitable for your particular hair and scalp. You should complain immediately in writing, bearing in mind that:

- you will need medical evidence concerning your injuries and the cause, so visit your doctor and, if necessary, a member of the Institute of Trichologists†
- if the hairdresser is a member of the Hairdressing Council, you may be able to take advantage of this trade association's conciliation and arbitration schemes, designed to deal with complaints against members†
- if you cannot reach an agreement with the salon, and the hairdresser is not a member of the Council, your only option will be to go to court.

Q *I complained to the Hairdressing Council about the hairdresser I used. They say he's not registered with them. Isn't registration compulsory?*

A No. Anybody can set up a salon and cut hair without any training or experience. In fact this is typical of many services offered to the public. It is wise to choose a trader who can demonstrate the necessary competence to do the job. The Hairdressing Council is the trade association which provides state registration of hairdressers. Under this scheme members must have at least two years' training and expertise. Some salons train their staff, but unless a hairdresser is state registered, you have no easy way of knowing if he or she is competent.

Q *I made an appointment for a haircut at a busy salon. I decided I didn't have time to get there so I didn't bother to turn up. The salon now wants compensation from me. Do I have to pay?*

A Probably. When you make an appointment with a trader, you are making a contract under which you agree to turn up at the appointed time and the trader agrees to provide whatever services he offers. If you don't turn up the trader can claim reasonable compensation for loss of business if he is unable to fill the appointment. Traders must prove that they made reasonable efforts to get a replacement customer, and if they did manage to fill the gap they will have suffered little or no loss, so they cannot make a charge.

If you have made an appointment but cannot keep it, tell the trader as soon as possible to give him the chance to find another customer. If not, you may be legally obliged to pay what you would have spent if you had turned up.

Q *I am in dispute with a garage over charges for repairs. The garage won't let me have my car back until I pay the bill. Can it do this?*

A Yes. If a garage has carried out repairs and improvements to your car, it has what in law is called a **repairer's lien** over the goods. It is legally entitled to hold on to the car until it is paid for the work. This can create problems, particularly as you may need to get another garage to look at the car in order to get evidence to challenge the bill, or the quality of the work. Check whether the trader is a member of a trade association†, and try to enlist the association's help in getting your car back. If that fails, you may have no option but to pay the bill **under protest** in order to recover your car – do this in writing, on the back of the cheque, say – and this will leave you free to claim back the disputed amount later (pp. 188 and 263). Again contact the trade association, and consider the options of arbitration or taking the matter to court (pp. 239–48).

Q *We moved home recently. When the removal company delivered our belongings to the new house, many items of china were broken and some items just didn't turn up. The removers also damaged the wallpaper when they were bringing furniture in. What rights do we have?*

A Removal companies must carry out their services with reasonable skill and care, as laid down by the Supply of Goods and Services Act 1982 (common law in Scotland). It is clear that this company did not carry out the service properly and is in breach of contract (pp. 59–61). Therefore you are legally entitled to claim against the firm for the loss and damage resulting from its lack of care – this will include the cost of repairs to your possessions, if indeed they are repairable, the cost of replacing the missing items, and redecorating the damaged areas of wall. Note that:

- small print attempting to limit or remove your rights is common in removal contracts, so check this very carefully. You will often find a term limiting liability to a small sum, £20 say, but offering additional insurance cover if you want it (p. 74). If such insurance is offered and you fail to take advantage of it, the courts might well consider that a clause limiting a removal company's liability to £20 is reasonable under the Unfair Contract Terms Act 1977 (p. 72)
- always make a full inventory of your possessions before the company packs and transports or stores them, so you can identify the missing items
- it is better to let the company's staff pack your belongings so there can be no argument that your packing was inadequate
- make sure you have up-to-date valuations on your possessions to help you assess your claim precisely
- the British Association of Removers† is the trade association for removal firms and provides a conciliation service to resolve disputes with its members. If both parties agree, the Association can appoint an independent arbitrator to give a decision which is binding on both of you (pp. 239–47).

Q *Is it possible to take over woodworm and similar guarantees when work was done for a previous owner of my home?*

A Almost always, guarantees for all types of specialist treatment to property can be taken over by purchasers, but a guarantee issued by a company is worthless if the company goes bust, unless there is some form of insurance backing for the guarantee (p. 65). Guarantees are issued following timber treatment, damp treatments, roof sealing and so on. Although many of these guarantees are for impressively long periods, some for up to thirty years, experience shows that not every company that offers such a guarantee itself survives that long. In strict legal terms the guarantee forms part of the original contract for the work between the previous owner and the specialist company, so in every case you have to check the guarantee form:

- it may be necessary to inform the company concerned of the change of ownership, and possibly pay a small registration fee
- it may also be necessary to have a formal written 'assignment' of the guarantee at the same time as the purchase of the property, so check with your conveyancer when you buy
- when you are offered a property with the benefit of one of these warranties, check that the company is still in business, as you will have no benefit at all if it has gone out of business unless the guarantee was backed by insurance.

Q *While my car was in the car wash the water stopped, but the brushes continued revolving and badly scratched the paintwork. The garage manager pointed to a sign stating: 'The garage is not responsible for damage to customers' cars, however caused.' Should the garage pay for repairs?*

A You must prove that the garage failed in its duty to act with reasonable care when providing the service, so you will need to discover why the water stopped. If the breakdown occurred because the garage had failed to have the equipment maintained and serviced properly, that would be evidence enough – but the garage would not necessarily be to blame for the failure of the water supply. You may be able to challenge the exclusion clause under the Unfair Contract Terms Act 1977 (p. 72).

Q *If I* ***hire*** *goods, am I protected regarding their quality, safety and so on in the same way as if I'd bought them?*

A Yes. The law governing contracts of hire, often called rental or leasing agreements, is clear:

- the Supply of Goods and Services Act 1982 says that a hire company has to supply goods which are of **merchantable quality**, **fit for their purpose**, and **as described** – these are comparable with the provisions in the Sale of Goods Act 1979 (pp. 28–9)
- before hiring, you must explain just what you intend to do with the goods and listen to the hire company's advice. That way you'll be in a stronger position if the goods turn out to be not up to the job and will be able to demand a refund of the wasted hire charges and any extra expenses
- it is a criminal offence, under the Consumer Protection Act 1987, for hirers to supply unsafe goods, or goods without appropriate instructions and safety warnings (pp. 46–9). If you hire goods which you feel are unsafe, contact the Trading Standards Department at your local council offices.

CHAPTER 3

DOMESTIC SERVICES

OVER recent years the whole structure of the domestic supply industry has changed from nationalisation to private ownership. The imbalance of power between public utilities and the consumer has lessened with the introduction of regulatory bodies, such as the Office of Water Services (OFWAT), the Gas Consumers Council (GCC), the Office of Electricity Regulation (OFFER), and so on. Privatisation has brought improvements in the nature of the relationship between the supplier and consumer, and introduced new legal obligations. The **Competition and Service (Utilities) Act 1992** provides for standards of performance to be set for the gas, electricity, phones, water and sewerage industries, and establishes procedures for dealing with complaints. All the domestic supply companies now have codes of conduct incorporating these standards, and most offer fixed compensation payments in the event of standards not being met.

Q *Our boiler broke down, so I made an appointment for the British Gas engineer to call. I waited in but he didn't show up. I made an appointment for two days later and the repairs have now been done. I'm annoyed that I had to wait in all day. I've read about* ***fixed compensation schemes****. Is my situation covered?*

A Your situation is certainly covered under the British Gas 'Commitment to Customers' charter, which sets standards of service. If British Gas fails to meet its targets you can in many cases get fixed compensation for the inconvenience caused. However, while this scheme provides for guaranteed compensation in certain circumstances, it does not prevent you claiming if you suffer additional financial loss (see p. 68). The guaranteed compensation scheme includes:

- **missed appointments** You receive £10 compensation if British Gas fails to turn up for an appointment, unless you were given 24 hours' notice of cancellation
- **interruptions in the gas supply for safety reasons** British Gas promises to put the gas back on within one working day. If you are still without gas after a day compensation of £20 will be paid for every extra day or part of the day you are without gas
- **special treatment for older, disabled or vulnerable customers** £10 compensation is payable if British Gas cuts off the supply to an elderly, disabled or otherwise vulnerable customer and leaves him or her without adequate heating and cooking facilities.

Full details of the scheme are published in the booklet *Commitment to Customers*, which can be obtained free from your local gas showroom or district regional office (address on your gas bill).

Q *I'm having some problems with the gas company. How can I get help?*

A If you want to complain about a gas bill, an appliance or a service, initially you should write to or phone your local gas showroom or British Gas office (address on back of bill). If you are not happy with the reply contact the Customer Relations Manager at the regional head office.† If you're not happy with the way British Gas responds to your complaint, contact your regional Gas Consumers Council (GCC) (address on bill), which can not only comment on all aspects of work done by British Gas but can persuade it to respond and provide evidence to back up its arguments. But the GCC's decisions cannot be enforced. To ensure that British Gas complies with its statutory obligations, the GCC refers cases which need this sanction to OFGAS.† However, OFGAS can only investigate complaints about the supply of gas (including payment for supply and disconnection) and gas bills, not those concerning appliances (p. 85), or appliance servicing (p. 84).

Q *I'm disputing a bill and have sent the details to my local GCC. Can British Gas cut me off if I don't pay the bill?*

A Yes. British Gas is legally entitled to **disconnect a supply** for non-payment of a gas bill, and this could mean the extra cost of disconnection and reconnection fees on top of the bill. When you disagree with a bill, or even if you have trouble paying it, contact the company immediately:

- British Gas must allow 28 days from the date when the original bill was sent, and must then give another seven days' notice before disconnecting
- before disconnection it must offer you alternative payment methods – for example, a pre-payment meter – and allow your past debts to be repaid as part of your future bills
- if you have a genuine dispute, contact your local GCC (address on bill)
- it may be worth paying the proportion of the bill you think is right while your complaint is considered
- cases of hardship should be dealt with by British Gas reasonably and sensitively.

While your complaint is subject to investigation by the GCC you are unlikely to be cut off. But if you have failed to contact British Gas, or the GCC, or if you cannot reach agreement with British Gas, you could be disconnected. Disconnection, incidentally, is not a way of avoiding the original bill as you will still be liable to pay it and could be taken to the county court if you fail to do so.

Q *My gas bill is far too high. I was on holiday for a month during the period the bill covers so I didn't use much gas. How can I check whether it's right?*

A If you think your bill is wrong, follow these steps:

- check whether the amount was **estimated**. As you were away the estimate may be higher than the actual usage. Take your own reading as soon as possible after receiving the bill and phone or send the reading to the gas company. It will then send an amended bill
- if the bill has been **assessed**, check back over past bills: the previous one may have been underestimated, so you may have been charged for more than one period
- the meter itself may be inaccurate (see below). Turn off all your gas appliances, including pilot lights. Read the meter and wait as long as you can before turning anything back on. If the meter changes during this time, tell British Gas immediately
- contact the GCC: it will help you calculate your gas usage and will assist with your complaint to British Gas.

Q *How can I get my meter checked?*

A If you disagree with British Gas about whether your meter is working properly, you can request a meter examination by the Department of Trade and Industry. Your meter and the gas supply will be tested and the meter may be removed for further tests. If the meter is found to have been over-reading you will be compensated for your over-payment, but if the meter is found to be operating correctly you will have to pay a test fee of about £20.

The examiner's decision is final, so if no fault is found you will have to pay the outstanding bill.

Q *I had central heating installed by a gas engineer. It doesn't work properly. What can I do?*

A You have the same rights as you would have with any other contractor. Under the Supply of Goods and Services Act 1982 (common law in Scotland), you are entitled to expect the work to be carried out with reasonable skill and care, using materials of merchantable quality (pp. 59–61). If the work or materials are not up to scratch you should contact the installer and ask him to put the work right free of charge. If he refuses or fails to do this, or if you have lost all confidence in his ability to do the work competently, you can employ another gas installer to do the work and send the bill to the original trader. Make sure you get all the evidence you can to prove that the original work was done badly. Additionally:

- you can refer the dispute, if necessary, to your local Gas Consumers Council (OFGAS cannot investigate complaints about an appliance or appliance servicing)
- if the work was done by a fitter who is a member of a trade association, it may be worth complaining to this organisation†
- complaints about the safety of appliances or services should be immediately referred to the local GCC, which has access to technical experts and can, if necessary, provide a report. Alternatively, if the trader is registered with CORGI (the Council for Registered Gas Installers†), you can refer safety issues to them
- if the matter remains unsettled your only option will be to claim through the courts. If the amount claimed is below £1,000 (£750 in the sheriff court in Scotland), you can use the small claims procedure in the county or sheriff court (pp. 245–8).

Q *The gas cooker I bought last week from a high street store has broken down. What are my rights?*

A When you buy goods from a trader, your rights are set out in the Sale of Goods Act 1979. You should complain to the shop straight away (pp. 28–30). If you fail to reach an agreement, contact your local Gas Consumers Council†, which will help with any dispute over gas appliances and services, wherever you bought them. It will put pressure on the trader and can give an opinion on whether the case is worth pursuing (through the small claims court, for example).

Q *I came home to find that British Gas had entered my premises without my permission. They say there was a gas leak and they had to investigate. Can they do this?*

A If there is a gas leak or some other emergency, British Gas employees can break in at any time – they don't need your permission. But they must leave your property reasonably secure. However, they do need your permission to enter for non-emergencies like reading your meter, inspecting fittings like the meter, or disconnecting the supply for unpaid bills. If you don't give permission, they can get a warrant to enter your property. The warrant allows them to use reasonable force to get in, and they must show that you were given at least 24 hours' notice that they were coming, and that they have been refused entry or your house is unoccupied. Entry must be at a reasonable time. They can also get a warrant if they suspect that you are tampering with the meter.

Q *Under what circumstances may an electricity company* ***disconnect*** *a meter?*

A An electricity company may not cut you off without warning. If the problem is an unpaid bill, the company must first try to find out the reason for non-payment:

- if the unpaid bill was an estimated reading you may not be disconnected: owing to the fact that the meter has not been read, there is no precise sum 'due'
- you may not be disconnected if the bill was left unpaid by mistake (because, for example, you failed to sign the cheque)
- you may not be disconnected if the unpaid bill is the subject of a genuine dispute and negotiations are in progress (p. 187)
- if you genuinely cannot afford to pay, the electricity company must first offer you a payments plan that is tailored to suit your individual financial circumstances, rather than simply cutting you off
- where it is safe and practical to provide one, you may be offered the option of having a pre-payment meter

- even if no agreement can be struck, the company should not disconnect you until 20 days after the date of the first bill
- you should always be given at least 48 hours' notice of disconnection
- if the company does not try to make alternative arrangements for payment or does not give you the required notice, you should take up the matter with OFFER.† OFFER has powers to make an electricity company change its decisions in its dealings with customers
- even if you have been disconnected you remain legally responsible for the unpaid bill, and the company can still take you to court to recover the amount outstanding.

Q *I live on my own and have gas central heating. My latest electricity bill is almost twice the usual amount. How can I challenge this?*

A All meters are checked before installation, and are replaced at regular intervals. The electricity company therefore assumes that the meter is working properly and that the reading, and hence the bill, is correct. The bill will tell you if the electrical usage figure was an **estimated** or an **actual reading**. So, as for any other meter reading, check the bill first. If it is based on an actual reading, check the meter reading against the bill: mistakes and misreadings do happen. Ask the company to come back and take another reading if you spot an error. If the bill and the meter match, there are two ways of challenging the charge:

- you may be able to show that what you regard as an abnormally high reading is caused by a 'leakage to earth': to do this, turn off all appliances which use electricity; if the meter is still recording usage, tell the electricity company immediately
- ask the company to check the accuracy of the meter. You will have to pay for this (between £20 and £50) but you will be refunded if the meter is faulty.

If you are not happy with the outcome of your complaint, refer the matter directly to the industry regulator OFFER† (the Office of Electricity Regulation) via one of its 14 regional offices, and tell the company that you are doing so. OFFER will nominate an independent meter examiner to test your meter and send his conclusion and report to OFFER. If you are still unhappy with OFFER's decision, you will have to pursue the matter in court. The small claims procedure in the county court (pp. 248–9) is a useful way of doing this, but you will have to prove that the meter examiner's report is incorrect, which will be virtually impossible.

Q *What do '**guaranteed standards of performance**' mean in the context of electricity services?*

A Following the privatisation of the electricity industry by the Electricity Act 1989, OFFER has instituted performance standards with which the electricity companies must comply. If they do not, fixed amounts must be paid to compensate for the inconvenience, whether you would have a legal claim or not. Specifically:

- electricity company engineers must keep their appointments: if they fail to, you, the customer, will be entitled to £20
- the company must reply to a billing or voltage complaint in ten working days: if it does not, you will be entitled to £20
- the company must give you five working days' notice if it plans to interrupt the electricity supply (for example, to carry out maintenance work): if it does not, you will be entitled to £20
- following an unplanned cut in the supply you should not be left without power for more than 24 hours: if you are, you will be entitled to £40, plus £20 for each additional 12 hours you remain without electricity (p. 89).

All the companies must send their customers details of their standards at least once a year. Most payments are automatic and are usually made by reducing the next bill. Some electricity companies also offer rebate and voucher schemes, so check by writing to the address on your bill.

For Northern Ireland, contact your local Northern Ireland electricity office (in the phone book). If you are not satisfied, contact the General Consumer Council for Northern Ireland.†

Q *I keep experiencing* ***power cuts****. I live in a rural area and sometimes have to cope without electricity for long periods. Am I entitled to compensation?*

A If you suffer a power cut for a **continuous period of 24 hours** or more, you are entitled to £40 compensation, plus £20 for every further 12 hours without power, but only if:

- the power cut is the result of a technical breakdown or negligence on the part of the company – *not* when severe weather is the cause
- the power cut is **continuous**, so even if you are frequently without power for long periods you can claim only if the power goes off for 24 hours or more each time. Frequent shorter cuts are not eligible for compensation.

If you suffer loss and damage as the result of a power cut due to the negligence of the electricity company, your claim for compensation is not limited to the guaranteed £20. So if the food in your freezer is ruined, say, you can claim from the electricity company.

Q *I bought a washing machine from my local electricity showroom and had it installed through them. There's something wrong with it but they won't sort it out. Can I complain to OFFER?*

A No. OFFER cannot consider disputes over faulty products or defective electrical services. It can deal only with disputes over electricity supply and billing. The Sale of Goods Act 1979 sets out the responsibilities of the retailer, who is liable if the goods sold are defective (pp. 28–9).

Consider referring the matter to the relevant trade association†. If that fails to resolve the dispute you will have to consider whether it is worth starting a claim under the small claims procedure (pp. 245–8).

Q *If I don't pay the electricity bill, can the electricity company come into my home to disconnect the meter?*

A If you do not pay your bills, the electricity company can take various steps to make you pay up (pp. 86–7). Disconnection should be its very last resort. However, ultimately the company can get a warrant which allows it to use reasonable force to enter premises and disconnect the meter. The circumstances which would allow electricity company employees access to your home are the same as for British Gas employees (p. 86).

Q *What level of service can I expect from my local water supply company?*

A Following the Water Act 1989, each water company in England and Wales must have a **code of practice** setting out the services offered, charges, what customers should do in an emergency, how the complaints procedure works, and what to do in the event of a leakage or a disconnection. Leaflets on the code of practice are available from your local water company. Water companies are also legally obliged to operate a **Guaranteed Standards** scheme and customers are entitled to a fixed amount of compensation (£10) if those standards are not met. Under this scheme each company:

- must keep appointments made, or give at least 24 hours' notice of cancellation
- must respond to your complaint or enquiry within 20 working days of receiving your letter
- must respond to complaints within ten working days, or 20 if detailed investigation, such as a site visit, is required
- must restore the water supply, in the event of planned interruption, on or before the date specified
- must restore the water supply, if the interruption was unplanned, within 24 hours.

Q *I was without water for two days, but I'm not happy with the water company's response to my complaint. Whom can I contact?*

A If you cannot get satisfaction from the water company, write to the regional Office of Water Services' Customer Service

Committee (CSC) for your area (address in phone book under Office of Water Services). Ten regional CSCs deal with the water and sewerage companies in their locality. The CSCs will liaise between you and the company concerned and can force it to provide information. The CSCs do not have power to force the water companies to abide by their decision, but, where the company refuses to accept a CSC decision, they can refer the complaint to the Director General of OFWAT, the Office of Water Services.†

The water supply is provided in Scotland by the regional and islands councils and in Northern Ireland by the Department of the Environment Water Service. Neither is regulated by OFWAT, therefore rights and complaints procedures are not as strong as those described above. Contact your local water supplier for details.

Q *The water from my tap was yellow and smelled fishy. I complained to the water company and it was cleared up quite quickly. But I had to buy bottled water for a couple of days. Can I reclaim the cost of this from the company?*

A The Water Act 1989 says that water companies must maintain a supply of **wholesome** water. The quality of water for domestic purposes is also controlled by regulations which reflect the requirements of the European Community. If you incur extra expense because the water does not seem clean and healthy to drink, or worse, if you are made ill by it, you may be able to recover this from the water company, if the company was to blame for the problem, or could have prevented it. However, if the cause was a problem with your own water pipes, say, the company would not be liable. If you had any doubts about the water you were right not to drink it and to tell the water company immediately. And if you have trouble getting your claim sorted out, you should follow the complaints procedure (see above).

It is an offence for a water company to supply water that is 'unfit for human consumption', so any quality problems should be immediately reported to the water company and OFWAT.

Q *There is a leak from the water supply pipe under my front garden and the grass is always sodden. The water company says it's my responsibility. Is this right?*

A The water company is legally responsible for keeping the following pipes in good order:

- the water main in the road
- that part of the service pipe from the mains up to a point at or near the boundary of your property, at which location, underground, there will usually be a stop tap; and
- the stop tap itself.

The rest of the supply pipe which goes from the stop tap into you property is normally your own responsibility (or that of the landlord or freeholder), so you are obliged to keep it in good repair. This is so even where that pipe runs under a neighbour's land before it reaches your property. As the leakage is from your pipe, it is your responsibility to have it repaired. The water company may ask you to repair it, and, if you fail to do so, may carry out the repair and charge the cost to you. If your water is metered, you will have to pay for the water lost through the leak.

Q *In what circumstances may a water company disconnect a water supply?*

A A water company may disconnect your supply:

- if it is necessary to carry out repairs to the water system; except in an emergency, the company must give you reasonable notice of the repair work and must pay compensation if it fails to do so, or fails to reconnect the supply within specified time limits (p. 90)
- if you fail to pay your water bill, in which case the water company must give you seven days' notice that you will be disconnected; if you do nothing in reply to the notice, your water can be cut off, but if you dispute the bill you should follow the complaints procedure described above (pp. 90–1):

if that fails to resolve the matter, the company may disconnect you only after obtaining a court judgment against you.

Q *Do I have to allow officials from the water company to come into my home?*

A Water officials may enter your home with your permission to install, read or repair meters, inspect fittings, or test or alter your supply. If you refuse to let them in they can apply for a warrant, which allows them to use force to gain entry. To obtain a warrant for entry the water officials must have shown that they have given you notice, that entry is necessary to carry out the work, and that you have refused to let them in or that the house is unoccupied. Water officials can also enter in an emergency or as a last resort (with a court order) to disconnect your supply.

Q *My phone bill is far too high. What should I do?*

A The first step is to contact the local office of the telephone company concerned (British Telecom or Mercury or whatever), at the address on the bill. The company will then usually test its meter and check the readings (which are recorded on film) to trace any inaccuracy. It will also check for any recently located faults in the network that could have affected the metering. If you are not satisfied with the response, consult the area office of the National Advisory Committee (address in phone book). If you are still not happy, write to OFTEL† (Office of Telecommunications), the regulatory body covering all telephone-operating companies. It can insist that the company reply to your complaint and provide evidence for its claims. It can also force the company to abide by OFTEL's decision on complaints.

Should you still be dissatisfied, you have to choose between court or arbitration. Most claims would be well within the small claims limit of £1,000 (£750 in Scotland) (pp. 245–8). Alternatively, the Chartered Institute of Arbitrators, which is totally independent, provides a fixed-cost arbitration service. If you use this service:

- all the evidence is submitted in writing, so you will not have the chance to argue in person (if you use the small claims procedure you will have to give evidence in court)
- the decision of the arbitrator is legally binding on both you and the company, so you cannot start legal proceedings if you do not agree with the decision. The small claims judgment is also binding and rights of appeal are limited (p. 253).

Q *I was without a phone for a while due to a fault, which I reported to BT. Should they have repaired it within a specified time?*

A Yes. BT is committed to providing **guaranteed standards** of service, and you will receive compensation if it misses its targets. BT will make a payment of one month's rental for **every day** you are without a service:

- if you report the fault to BT and it fails to repair the faults on the line by the end of the next working day
- if you make an appointment for a phone line to be installed but BT fails to stick to it.

BT will pay up to £1,000:

- if you can show that you have incurred a financial loss as a result of BT missing a target, but you must have proof that you have suffered the loss.

Q *I am disputing my bill. Can BT cut me off?*

A Your bill becomes payable as soon as you get it. The practice is for reminders to be sent out 21 days later, but before disconnection BT must send you a final notice, giving you seven days to pay:

- if you do nothing in reply to this notice, your phone may be cut off

- if you dispute the bill you should follow the complaints procedures above (p. 93), but you should pay the portion of the bill that is not disputed (say, an estimated amount based upon previous bill). If you do not pay anything while the dispute is being considered, BT may disconnect you.

Q *Can BT officials enter my home without my permission?*

A No. When you rent a telephone line from BT you agree to let its employees enter your home at all reasonable times to check that the line is working correctly. This does not mean they can come in without your permission, but if you do not give them reasonable access you will be in breach of your contract with BT, and that will allow BT either to claim compensation or to terminate its contract with you and cut you off.

CHAPTER 4

LEGAL SERVICES

YOU are unlikely to buy something in a shop without having first ascertained the price and decided whether it is reasonable. Therein lies the main difference between buying goods and hiring commercial or professional services. With services (particularly advice from a professional) you may not know how much the service will cost in advance, and you may have little opportunity to shop around. And unlike goods that don't work properly, any defects in what you are buying may not be obvious until it is too late.

Q *I'm looking for somebody to do the conveyancing on my house. How can I find a competent professional?*

A There are never any guarantees that the person you choose will do the work competently, but all professional conveyancers, whether solicitors or licensed conveyancers, must meet minimum standards in training and competence. Mistakes can still happen, however. If you do have reason to complain about the services offered by a solicitor or conveyancer, contact the relevant professional body or complaints bureau, then the Legal Services Ombudsman (p. 101).

The most effective way of finding a lawyer or conveyancer is by personal recommendation. Failing this, contact the Law Society† or the Council for Licensed Conveyancers† for a list of practitioners in your area, or visit your local library, which should have a regional directory of solicitors indicating the sort of work undertaken by each practice.

Q *What questions should I ask before hiring a lawyer?*

A Whatever the nature of the problem, the object of the initial interview is to establish what has to be done and lay down the ground rules for doing it. Solicitors must supply a copy of their terms of business, known as the **client care letter**, and clients must agree to these before work starts. Further to this:

- as lawyers tend to charge by the hour, you should if possible obtain a written estimate of the likely number of hours' work involved
- set a ceiling on the costs charged and find out whether other costs will be involved, such as search fees and barristers' charges
- ask to be billed at regular intervals so that you can keep tabs on mounting fees and decide as necessary whether or not to carry on
- ask for a clear timetable showing when you will have to pay
- make sure any advice given to you is confirmed in writing and take notes of what is said at the meeting. Also ask for copies of all letters that go out on your behalf.

Q *My solicitor was handling my dispute with a builder. He failed to start court proceedings on time and I've just discovered that the claim is* ***statute barred****, so it's now too late to sue the builder. Surely the solicitor was negligent?*

A Complaints about solicitors generally fall into three categories:

- **negligence** – where you have suffered loss as a result of the actions or omissions of the solicitor
- **shoddy work** – where the work may be inadequate, slow or generally substandard, causing inconvenience or distress, but no financial loss (p. 101)
- **professional misconduct** – where the solicitor is in breach of the professional code of conduct (which may or may not cause you loss).

Solicitors are paid to do a good job for you and you have every right to complain if they let you down. As for any other service under the Supply of Goods and Services Act 1982 they are obliged to exercise the care and skill to be expected from a reasonably competent professional. So the solicitor should give such advice and take such action as the facts of that particular case demand. Negligence arises when your solicitor fails to exercise that care and skill and you suffer financial loss as a result.

Your solicitor's duty is to protect your interests. Failure to take certain actions which a reasonable solicitor would do, and which causes damage as a result, constitutes negligence. By failing to start a claim against the builder within the legal time limits (pp. 20–1), thereby losing you the chance of taking that claim to court and recovering compensation, your solicitor has been negligent. However, if you want financial compensation your only option may be court action. There are some alternatives and whichever course you take it is as well to get some detailed advice on your legal position first:

- if your financial claim does not exceed £1,000 you will have the benefit of the small claims procedure in the county court (£750 for the sheriff court in Scotland). If you are claiming more than this there will be a formal hearing in the county court (pp. 245–8)
- if you cannot find another lawyer with experience of negligence work to help you contact the Solicitors' Complaints Bureau† and insist on seeing a member of the Law Society's Negligence Panel, who will give you up to an hour's free advice. The SCB limits this service to those who genuinely cannot find their own solicitor, but many consumers who face a possible claim against their solicitors will not want to spend more money on another solicitor, so it's important to find out whether your case is worth pursuing (in Scotland the Law Society will appoint a solicitor called a 'troubleshooter')
- an alternative to court action is referral to the Solicitors' Arbitration Scheme. For a small fixed fee the case will be considered by an arbitrator, independently of the Law Society, appointed by the Chartered Institute of Arbitrators. However,

both you and the solicitor must agree that the claim should go to arbitration; you cannot insist if the solicitor in question doesn't agree. If your case does go to arbitration the decision is binding, and you can't then decide to take the matter to court if you're not satisfied (p. 240). Details and application forms are available from the Solicitors' Complaints Bureau†, the Law Society† or the Chartered Institute of Arbitrators.†

Q *I wasn't happy with the work done by my solicitor and decided to change to another, but the old one is refusing to hand over my papers until his bill is paid. Can he do this?*

A As a general rule, a client can change solicitors whenever he wishes to do so. If you are already involved in court action, there may be formalities involved which your new solicitor should complete for you. But if you do owe a solicitor any fees for work done, he has the legal right to hang on to your property if it came into his possession as part of his professional employment, and that includes all documents, money, deeds, etc. The principle is the same as the right of a garage to hold on to your car if it has done work for which money is owed (p. 76). There are circumstances in which you can get the papers back without paying the disputed bill:

- the Law Society can recommend that the papers should be released subject to a satisfactory undertaking on your part to pay the outstanding fee
- your new solicitor may agree an undertaking with the original solicitor as to payment once the dispute is resolved
- it may be possible to make a payment of the disputed amount into an 'escrow' account, which will only be paid out, in part or in full, when the dispute over the bill is settled (pp. 102–3)
- if the papers are vital for your case and you would be prejudiced by the solicitor withholding them, you may get a court order for their release: your new solicitor should advise on this.

Q *My solicitor never returns my calls. He has taken three months to prepare my will. How can I speed things up?*

A All firms of solicitors are required to have a system for handling disputes of this sort and to nominate a senior person to deal with complaints, so write to the senior partner of the firm. If that doesn't solve the problem, you should send a brief account of your complaint to the Director of the **Solicitors' Complaints Bureau** (SCB).† The SCB cannot deal with complaints of negligence (although it can refer you to a negligence solicitor); it limits itself to complaints of incompetence or **shoddy work**, that is, work which has caused you frustration, inconvenience, annoyance or distress, but not financial loss (p. 98). The SCB provides a system aimed at sorting out disputes quickly and informally and will contact the solicitor on your behalf in an effort to solve the problems you are experiencing. If appropriate the Bureau can take **disciplinary action** against the solicitor, and also has powers (under the Courts and Legal Services Act 1990) to award compensation of up to £1,000.

In Scotland you should contact the Law Society of Scotland†, which has powers broadly similar to those of the SCB, although it cannot award compensation.

If you are still unhappy with the way the complaint has been handled by the solicitor or by the SCB, or if you are unhappy with the decision reached, you can then ask the **Legal Services Ombudsman**† to investigate on your behalf. But you must have exhausted the complaints procedure of the SCB. You must complain within three months of the SCB reaching its decision. The ombudsman can recommend that the solicitor or the SCB pay you compensation, and there is no limit on the amount he can award. Awards are not strictly binding, so the solicitors or SCB may not have to abide by the decision. In Scotland contact the Scottish Legal Services Ombudsman.†

Q *The lawyer who represented me in court didn't put all the evidence forward. He seemed totally unprepared and didn't ask the other side's witnesses the right questions. As a result I lost my claim which I'd been told I'd win. What can I do?*

A Very little. If you receive negligent service from a solicitor, barrister or licensed conveyancer which causes you financial loss, then you can claim compensation (pp. 98–100). But if the negligent act which causes the loss takes place during court proceedings, the lawyer is **immune** from any claim by you.

This much-criticised protection of legal professionals means you cannot make a claim for compensation for work done badly in court. It may be worth referring the facts to the Law Society† or Council of the Bar†: if the lawyer's work was bad enough it may amount to **professional misconduct**, which could mean that the lawyer is banned from practising law.

Q *I have just received a bill from my solicitor. It seems unreasonable and is way above the original estimate I was given. How can I* ***challenge the bill?***

A You cannot rely on an 'estimate' as a guarantee of the final bill. But a solicitor's bill must be **fair and reasonable**, although it is not possible to calculate solicitors' fees exactly as there is no set scale of costs and much will depend on the time spent on the matter. If you feel the charges are too high, write to the head partner of the firm setting out your reasons for dissatisfaction. If that doesn't work there are formal methods for challenging a bill, but how you go about it depends on the type of work done – that is, whether it was classified as **non-contentious** or **contentious**.

Contentious work is any for which court proceedings have been started (even if you never actually got to court):

- you should request a **detailed breakdown** of the bill. The solicitor is obliged to provide this under section 64 of the Solicitors Act 1974
- if you're still not happy, you can apply for the costs to be **taxed** by the court. This means that a special bill is drawn up and the court decides whether each item is fair and reasonable. 'Taxation' can be expensive – not only will you have to pay a fee to the court to have the bill assessed, but if the bill is reduced by less than one-fifth, you will lose the court fee and

have to pay the solicitor's costs of going to court as well as your own.

Non-contentious work is any work done where the case does not involve court proceedings, like conveyancing:

- ask the solicitor to apply to the Law Society for a **remuneration certificate**. This states whether the bill is fair and reasonable, and, if it is not, suggests another sum that would be reasonable. This procedure is free
- if you feel that the certified amount is still too high, you still have the right to apply for the costs to be **taxed** by the court (as above).

The complaints system for solicitors' charges is broadly the same in Scotland. However, there is no procedure for a remuneration certificate, so regardless of whether there have been court proceedings you will have to go for taxation.

CHAPTER 5

PROPERTY

BUYING a home is the single biggest purchase most people ever make, so getting it right is crucial. You may spend a lot of time and money travelling to see properties which don't match up to the estate agent's prose. And when you find your home, you may find more problems than the surveyor pointed out, with disastrous consequences. So what are your rights when buying property? This chapter looks at the law relating to estate agents and surveyors, at the guarantees that come with most new houses, and at the new legislation allowing leaseholders the right to buy their home.

Q *I'm thinking of buying a house and I'll need a mortgage. Do I have to pay for a structural survey?*

A No. But you will probably have to pay the mortgage lender (the building society or bank) for its valuation survey or report (p. 107). You are not obliged to have any other type of survey done, but if you decide to do so the options available are as follows:

- **valuation report** This is carried out on behalf of the lender and is simply an assessment of what the property is worth. It is based on a purely visual inspection and takes into account only the age, size and type of property, the location and amenities, the construction and general state of repair. Even if you buy a new house, if you rely on the scant information

in a valuation report you'll be taking a gamble. The valuation is not an indication that the house is structurally sound. The report is addressed to the lender, not to you, and gives you very little protection (p. 107)
- **home buyer's report** This is carried out on behalf of the purchaser. It gives more information than a valuation, on standard forms from the Royal Institution of Chartered Surveyors† and the Incorporated Society of Valuers and Auctioneers†, but it does not include details of every minor defect. Major faults, such as damp and signs of subsidence, should be included, but the report will cover only parts which are reasonably accessible and visible. So the surveyor may not lift carpets or inspect the loft if access is difficult (pp. 107–8).
- **full structural survey** Carried out on behalf of the purchaser, this is the most thorough (and expensive) type of survey. It should cover all the main features of the property from the roof to the foundations, commenting on the wiring, plumbing and central heating as well as garden fences and problem trees. This type of survey will give you extra protection, and is particularly useful with older houses. If the surveyor has been unable to lift carpets etc. then this should be stated in the report.

A survey is a form of insurance. If it shows major defects you may not want to go ahead with the purchase and will be thankful to have been saved the headaches of dealing with such problems. If there's nothing alarming to report, you are paying for peace of mind. When the position is somewhere in the middle, with defects that need attention but may not be severe enough to put you off, a survey is a useful way to negotiate a reduction in price. If you don't have your own survey done then you may have no basis for a compensation claim if the property turns out to have serious defects: you will not be able to claim against the seller (pp. 16 and 109). However, if it becomes clear that the surveyor has missed some defects that should have been spotted then you could have a claim against the surveyor (pp. 107–8).

Q *The building society gave me a copy of its* ***valuation report****. This said there was a small damp patch in the hall wall and a rotten* *end on a joist in the cellar ceiling. It also said that the cellar was relatively dry. Six weeks after I moved in the cellar floor and walls were covered with mushrooms and mould. I've been quoted up to £10,000 to put it right. Can I claim this from the building society which carried out the valuation?*

A A valuation report is for the benefit of the lender (the bank or building society offering the mortgage), not you. It helps the lender to decide whether the property is good security against the mortgage. But never confuse a valuation with a survey (p. 105). Many defects will not affect the value or the lender's decision to grant a mortgage, but if a major defect is overlooked which is bound to make the valuation unreliable, it is possible to claim against the building society surveyor in some circumstances. It doesn't matter if you paid for the report or not, although nowadays most valuation surveyors do charge. What is important is that you relied on it, went ahead with the purchase and found you had been misled.

If in making the valuation the surveyor has missed something of importance, like a major structural defect or severe damp, which should have been apparent from a visual inspection, you can sue for compensation (see below). You can also complain to the banking or building societies ombudsman† (p. 243).

Q *I bought a house after having a full structural survey done. Now I find that there is serious trouble with the roof which will be costly to repair. I've written to the surveyor and he says that he didn't manage to inspect every part of the property. I've now got a letter from his insurers saying that I have no claim. How can I get the surveyor to pay for the repairs that are now needed?*

A Your surveyor must exercise **reasonable care and skill** in carrying out the work. If he does not and you suffer loss and damage as a direct result then you have a claim for compensation. Some surveyors' reports contain such phrases as 'we do not inspect areas that are covered or are not readily accessible' and 'we could not move the items stored in the roof void and therefore cannot report'. Such attempts to limit the surveyor's responsibility have to be fair and reasonable. If they are not, they will be invalid under the Unfair Contract Terms Act 1977 (p. 72). If you think that your surveyor has been negligent you will need to prove that he failed to see the faults or the tell-tale signs in the property that would have revealed trouble to an observant and knowledgeable surveyor, so you may have to get a report from another surveyor, concentrating on what the first surveyor could have seen and what he should have mentioned in his report.

But even if you can prove your case you cannot claim the cost of repairs. The test is *not* 'how much will it cost to put matters right?' but rather 'how much less might I have paid for the house had I known of the defects?' (the **difference in value**). As some defects will have little or no effect on the market price of the property there may be no claim for compensation even though the repairs may be expensive.

Don't be put off by the surveyor's insurers – it's their job to look after their clients' interests. If the surveyor (or his insurance company) disputes your claim, you may have to go to court. Negligence cases are often costly and complicated, particularly if your claim is for more than the small claims limit of £1,000 (£750 in Scotland) (see p. 247), so you may have to go to a solicitor. The Royal Institution of Chartered Surveyors† has an arbitration scheme run by the Institute of Arbitrators† covering allegations of negligence arising in England and Wales. Its great advantage is that for a small fixed fee you can get an independent decision on a claim against your surveyor without all the hassle and possible costs of a lengthy court case. If you win, the decision is binding on both parties, and you may get the fee back, plus compensation. If you lose you cannot refer the same case to the courts (p. 240). But your surveyor has to agree to take part. If he does not you will have to go to court instead.

Whichever way you get the complaint dealt with you will need all the evidence you can get concerning whether the surveyor should have spotted the defects and the effect the missed defects have on the value of the house. For more information contact the Chartered Institute of Arbitrators, or the Professional Practice Department at RICS.†

Q *I sold my house to someone who didn't have a survey done. There has been a long-standing subsidence problem but I didn't disclose this to the buyer. I've now had a letter from the buyer demanding compensation from me. Everything was handled by my solicitor. Do I have to pay up?*

A No. The principle of **caveat emptor** ('let the buyer beware') applies to property purchase. That is why the burden is always on the buyer to make any inspection and enquiry that seems necessary, hence the riskiness of buying a property without having a structural survey done first. The standard form of contract normally used for selling houses states specifically that the buyer takes the property in the state and condition it is in – so if he didn't do all he could to check that state and condition himself, he can't claim against you.

There is only one situation where you might be responsible. If the buyer (or more usually the conveyancer or solicitor) asks a straight question about the state of repair, or whether something is in working order, you must either give a truthful answer or simply say that the buyer should find out for himself (the usual response is 'make your own enquiries'). If you do mislead the buyer, and that causes him loss, you will have to pay compensation. This means that if you are selling a house you must be careful to be scrupulously accurate. If the prospective buyer asks about something you do not know, do not guess, because if you are wrong you could be held liable.

Q *The new house I have just bought has many problems. Can I claim the cost of repairing the defects as the house is not of merchantable quality?*

A No. There is no legal requirement that a new house should be of merchantable quality – the Sale of Goods Act 1979 does not apply to property (p. 23). Fortunately, however, almost all new homes are covered by a **warranty scheme** which guarantees that they have been built to certain standards and that, if they were not, problems will be put right either by the builder, or, if the builder will not co-operate, or has gone out of business, by the warranty company. It is very unlikely that you would be able to borrow money for a new home that does not have warranty cover of some sort (see below).

Q *I've just seen a* ***newly built house*** *I'd like to buy. The developer says it has housing warranty cover. What is this?*

A When you buy property you do not have the same rights as when you buy goods and there is no implied term that the property will be of merchantable quality. So it is important to carry out your own investigations and some form of survey on the structure is advisable (p. 105). Even with a new house there's no guarantee that it was built properly. So look for a house that is covered by a warranty which guarantees that it was built to certain standards. The notable warranty schemes for new homes are the National House Building Council† (NHBC) 'Buildmark' scheme and Foundation 15 operated by Zurich Insurance, which people not covered by the Buildmark scheme can choose to have applied to their property. Both of these offer similar cover whereby during the first two years after purchase the builder undertakes to put right any defects which result from the failure to comply with the minimum standards of workmanship stipulated. For the next eight years with the NHBC, and the next 13 years with Foundation 15, any major defects in the load-bearing structure of the property will be put right free of charge.

Q *What* ***fixtures and fittings*** *will I have to leave behind in my house when I sell it?*

A What you leave behind and what you take with you is completely a matter for agreement between you and the purchaser. If the matter is dealt with in the formal contract of sale, you can spell out in that what you have decided. However, in practice it is difficult to deal with each and every item, so if nothing is said about particular items:

- what are properly called **fixtures** automatically go with the property, and should therefore be left behind – a fixture is something that is firmly attached to the building or the land and not simply put up for display (a light switch is a fixture, but many light fittings are not)
- to avoid a dispute over what constitutes a fixture, list all the items which the purchaser will have seen fixed in place when he viewed the property but which you specifically want to take with you, then give the list of items to the conveyancer and ask him to add it to the contract of sale
- if you do leave things behind which are not normally considered fixtures – curtains, carpets, cooker, say – it is up to you to decide whether to ask a separate price for these or to include them in the selling price.

Q *Are there any legal controls over what estate agents can do and say? And how can I complain about their work?*

A The legal controls which govern agents' work are various:

- breach of contract (pp. 112–14)
- breach of agency obligations (pp. 114–15)
- Estate Agents Act 1979. This is designed to make sure that agents act in the best interests of their clients and that both buyers and sellers are treated honestly and fairly (pp. 114–15)
- Property Misdescriptions Act 1991 (pp. 116–17).

Some agents may be members of professional associations, such as the National Association of Estate Agents, Royal Institution of Chartered Surveyors or the Incorporated Society of Valuers and Auctioneers.† These operate codes of practice governing how their members work. The relevant body can reprimand member agents and also take disciplinary proceedings against them. They risk being thrown out of the association, but you're unlikely to get compensation.

Check whether the agent belongs to the Estate Agents' Ombudsman† Scheme. This is operated by the large agency chains run by banks, building societies and insurance companies, so many thousands of smaller estate agents are not covered by the scheme. For complaints about scheme members the Ombudsman can order the agent to pay up to £1,000 compensation. If your estate agent is not a member of the scheme your only option is to pursue your claim for breach of contract of breach of agency obligations in court (see pp. 113–15).

Q *Although I used estate agents I feel my house was sold largely through my own efforts. Someone saw the 'For Sale' sign and called in, and I persuaded him to buy. The agents did virtually nothing. Do I still have to pay them their full commission?*

A You probably do. If you instruct an estate agent to sell your home, your legal position is governed by the law of contract. If estate agents abide by the promises they make in their contracts, you have to abide by your promise to pay them. However, agents do not generally make promises about exactly what they will do to sell your house. Instead, many agreements just state that *you* will pay *them* if they 'introduce' a buyer to you. So, if you found a buyer because of the agents' sign, even if putting up the sign was all they did, they are entitled to their commission. On the other hand you do not have to pay if no buyer is found, however much they do, unless the agreement says you must pay a certain amount, or that you will pay, for example, for marketing costs, such as advertising.

Some estate agents' contracts are different (see p. 113), and an agent may specify that he will do or not do certain things, or will charge for specific items, such as advertisements, even if the property is not sold. If an agent breaks the contract by not doing what he agreed to do, you would, strictly speaking, be entitled to compensation for any loss you suffer. But if you either pull out of the contract before paying or you do actually sell the house through the agent, then you probably won't have suffered any loss. However, if the agents were to incur costs without your authorisation, they would have no right to make you pay for them.

Q *I'm thinking of selling my house. When I've instructed an estate agent, can I pull out of the agreement and sell the house privately or through another firm if I decide the agents are not getting the job done?*

A This may be difficult as there are no hard and fast rules about what an agent actually has to do to find a purchaser. Whether you can pull out of the contract depends on the agreement you have, so check the terms and conditions carefully:

- if you chose a no-sale, no-fee deal, you are liable for commission only if the agent introduces you to someone who actually buys your home
- many agents' contracts say that you will have to pay the fee 'in the event of our introducing a purchaser who is **ready, willing and able** to complete the transaction'. Under this arrangement you could end up paying a fee if your home was not sold because you took it off the market or if you found the eventual buyer yourself
- normally you can pull out and will owe the agents nothing except any agreed costs such as those incurred for advertising in the local press, *provided* you do not go on to sell to a buyer who was 'introduced' to you as a result of their efforts (see p. 112)
- some agents now agree to a programme of action for you, and may expect to be paid something at the outset. With that sort of agreement it may not be so easy to pull out and pay nothing, but if the agents have done little or nothing of what they agreed to do, you may have a legal case in this instance for suing for the return of your payment, whatever the terms of the agreement say.

Q *My estate agents want me to sign an agreement giving them '**sole selling rights**'. If I do, I will pay less than I would if I were to use other agents as well. Isn't this the same as '**sole agency**', so if I sell the house by my own efforts I won't have to pay the commission?*

A These two arrangements are very different:

- **sole selling rights** means that however your house comes to be sold, even if you come to a private agreement which has nothing to do with the agents, you will have to pay them their commission. Never agree to sole selling rights unless you are sure you will not find a purchaser through your own efforts

- **sole agency** leaves you free to sell privately by your own efforts without paying any commission, but not through other agents. You can instruct other agents, but if they sell the house, you have to pay commission to the original sole agents *and* the agents who have sold the property.

Other types of agency arrangements you can opt for include:

- **joint agency**, whereby you instruct two agents. Both have to agree to this, and on who gets the commission on the sale
- **multiple agency**, whereby you instruct as many agents as you like: the one who comes up with the buyer earns the commission. The fee for this type of arrangement will normally be the highest of all the options available.

Whether sole, joint or multiple agency is best for you depends on circumstances – for instance, what charges are to be made, the merits of the firms involved, how quickly you wish to sell, etc. If you instruct more than one firm of agents, you will generally pay higher commission levels to whichever of them may ultimately sell the property, but you have the advantage of more than one agency being at work on your behalf. On the other hand, a sole agent may have more incentive to sell, and may use subagents without any extra charge to you, thus giving you the same advantage at no extra cost.

Q *I heard by chance that a couple were interested in buying my house and had got as far as trying to make an offer for it. Yet the offer was never passed on to me by my estate agents. What is more, it was higher than the offer I actually accepted. Surely that can't have been right?*

A It certainly wasn't. Your agents owed you a legal duty to find the best available sale for you – it sounds as if they were in breach of that duty. Furthermore, under the Estate Agents Act 1979 it is an 'undesirable practice' for agents to fail to pass on offers (or to misrepresent them) or in any other way to discriminate against one potential buyer in favour of others. Agents can be banned from their profession if they are found to have engaged in 'undesirable practices'. You should certainly tell your local Trading Standards Department about this situation (at your local council offices; in Northern Ireland contact the Department of Economic Development†).

What happened here could of course have been simply poor service. But it could also be more disturbing. It may be that the potential buyer of whom you heard was not interested in arranging finance through the agents and was put off by them in favour of someone else who was. Agents can make large sums of money in commission on arranging mortgages for purchasers. That is why the Estate Agents Act obliges an agent to tell you in writing, in advance, if he is going to offer services such as arranging mortgages for people who express an interest in buying the house you have placed with his firm. This does not mean that if agents offer such services your interests are bound, or are even likely, to be prejudiced. But it is as well to be aware of the possibility of a **conflict of interest**.

Other examples of 'undesirable practices' and matters which should be referred to your local Trading Standards Department are as follows:

- failure to disclose promptly and in writing any **personal interest** in a transaction: for example, if the estate agent wants to buy the house himself he may not encourage other offers
- failure to tell the client if a prospective purchaser is seeking financial or other services from the agent.

Q *I put an offer down on a house, had a survey carried out and arranged a mortgage, then the seller pulled out leaving me with a lot of wasted expense. I believe he did this because the estate agents found him a better offer. Do I have any redress against them?*

A This is what is known as **gazumping**, which tends to be common in a booming property market. It is rarer when houses are difficult to sell. In a buyers' market the boot is more likely to be on the other foot, with buyers refusing to go ahead at the last minute unless the price is dropped (sometimes called '**gazundering**').

Unfortunately, there is no legal redress for gazumping and gazundering. A contract for the sale and purchase of a property (for example, a house) is not binding unless it is in writing and signed by both parties. (N.B. Contrary to popular opinion, this is *not* true of most contracts – land, or property, is an exception; see pp. 17–18.) That means that until both parties have signed a contract for the house, either can withdraw without the other having any right to compensation, whether an offer has been made and accepted 'subject to contract' or not.

Buyers who are gazumped and blame the agent should remember that the agent acts for the seller, and is paid by him or her, and therefore has a legal duty to get the best deal possible for the seller (p. 114). Agents don't owe any such duty to buyers. If a buyer with a better offer comes along after an offer has been accepted subject to contract, it is actually the agent's legal duty to pass that offer on to the seller and to recommend that the seller accepts that offer, leaving the first purchaser 'gazumped'.

The opportunities for gazumping and gazundering could be reduced, for instance by speeding up conveyancing in England, Wales and Northern Ireland. However, in Scotland the whole system of land purchase is different and there is less opportunity for problems of this nature to arise, because once an offer has been made, and accepted by the seller, a binding contract exists, which prevents buyer and seller alike from withdrawing before exchange of contracts.

Q *I was interested in buying a house described in the agents' particulars in glowing terms – deceptively spacious, immaculate, located in a quiet cul-de-sac close to all amenities etc. When I went to see it, it turned out to be small, in only fair decorative condition, and though the cul-de-sac was quiet, the motorway on the other side of the house wasn't! Also, there was a long trip to the shops, because they were on the other side of the motorway. Wasn't this a breach of the Trade Descriptions Act?*

A No – the Trade Descriptions Act 1968 doesn't cover sales of land. But the Property Misdescriptions Act 1991 fills that loophole. It sounds as if there certainly has been a breach of this legislation.

The test under the Act is whether the description (verbal or written) would **mislead** a reasonable person. If it would then the agent has committed an offence. It is doubtful whether 'deceptively spacious' would be misleading, so that phrase is probably not a breach of it. Descriptions of decorative condition tend to be subjective and are not covered by the Act. But the other two descriptions you mention sound very misleading, even though they may not have been literally false. If an agent's description of a property (verbal or written) misses out some crucial fact which means that what he has said is misleading, then he has committed an offence. Here, it would have been quite reasonable to assume that the house was in a quiet location, and that the shops would be a few minutes away, neither of which was the case. This is a matter for Trading Standards officers (at your local council offices; in Northern Ireland contact the Department of Economic Development†).

Q *I live in a flat, and I've always felt at a disadvantage having a leasehold rather than a freehold. The landlord hasn't maintained the building satisfactorily, and I'm worried about my flat falling in value as the lease starts to run out. Am I right in thinking it's now possible for me to buy the freehold to my flat from my landlord?*

A If you and your neighbours in the building *own* your flats – i.e. you bought them on long leases, rather than renting them on short tenancies – then you and they may well soon have the right to get together to buy the freehold of your block. This is called **enfranchisement**. But the legislation will put some hurdles in your way.

First, you must be the owner of an **eligible long lease**, which means (among other things) paying only a very low ground rent, if you are to join in an enfranchisement. Moreover, you cannot just buy the freehold of your own flat: freeholds of blocks cannot be split up – they have to be bought as a whole.

Secondly, therefore, your **block as a whole must be eligible**. At least two-thirds of the leaseholders must have eligible long leases, so if you have several neighbours who rent you may well not qualify. A block can also be ineligible if more than a small part of it is given over to use as shops, offices, etc., or if it is a small 'conversion' (not purpose-built as flats) and you have a resident landlord. Moreover:

- if a block is eligible for enfranchisement, at least **two-thirds of the eligible flat-owners** will have to sign a written proposal to buy the freehold. This document will commit those who have signed it to coming up with the full cost of purchase, or paying the landlord's costs if the deal falls through. That will start the enfranchisement process
- at least half of those who sign must have lived in their flats for a year or more
- those who sign must represent at least half of all the flats in the block (whether eligible or not)
- most leasehold house-owners *already* have the right to enfranchise (p. 119).

Q *How much will enfranchisement cost?*

A The prices of freeholds will be determined by negotiation between the flat-owners who are seeking to buy and the landlord. If agreement can't be reached, a price will be set after a hearing by a Leasehold Valuation Tribunal, a body resembling an informal court.

Enfranchisement will not be cheap: the legislation lays down that a landlord will be paid:

- all that he would have got if he sold the freehold on the open market, plus
- at least a half-share of any special value that it has for the flatowners as opposed to anyone else (called 'marriage value' because it arises from the marriage of leases with the freehold), plus
- compensation for any loss which the sale causes him to suffer, and

- all the landlord's costs.

In areas where property values are high, and especially where there are fewer than 60 or so years left on flat-owners' leases, then the special 'marriage value' mentioned above could be many thousands of pounds per flat. Enfranchisement will also be expensive if flat-owners have to buy any shops and offices, and/or the rented units, in their block. And where less than 100 per cent of the flat-owners take part in the enfranchisement (N.B. at least 67 per cent must participate), the costs per person will be proportionately higher because they will be shared amongst fewer people. Where all these factors work together, enfranchisement may be very expensive indeed.

But, by the same token, in a straightforward suburban or provincial block, with leases that still have 90 years or more to run (as many do), where there are no renting tenants or shops, then the cost should be only a small percentage of what you paid for your flat in the first place – especially if everyone joins in the enfranchisement bid.

Q *We want to enfranchise but can't, under the rules in the new legislation. Are we just left out in the cold? Won't that affect the value of our flats?*

A If you have an eligible long lease, you will have an individual right to buy an extension to that lease from the landlord, provided you have lived in your flat for at least three years (or three years out of the past ten). This will leave him in control of management, but should help to avoid the problems which can arise when the lease starts to run out (problems which can start as early as 60 years or more before the end of the lease).

It is not certain whether flats which remain on unextended leases will end up worth less than flats sold with a share of the freehold or with new, longer leases. But it is quite likely that they will, especially if the right to enfranchisement and extensions is widely taken up.

Q *What will happen if, although eligible, I don't join in an enfranchisement bid, but it still goes ahead?*

A You will end up with a new landlord – your neighbours. Otherwise, nothing will change: you will have the same lease, the same rights and duties, and the same rules to comply with as before. Note that you might be able to join in the enfranchisement at a later date if those who have already enfranchised agree.

Q *Where can I get advice to help me and my neighbours enfranchise?*

A There will be leaflets, books and advice at Citizens Advice Bureaux to start you off, and it is likely that an advice agency will be set up to ensure information is readily available. But once you decide you may be eligible and you seriously want to go ahead, it will be essential to have the advice of both a solicitor and a surveyor or valuer. Enfranchisement will be a difficult and complex process, like conveyancing but with far more potential pitfalls.

Q *Is enfranchisement the same as* **commonhold?**

A No. Enfranchisement gives you some of the basic advantages of commonhold, such as control of your property, and will be a necessary first step to commonhold, but it is not the same thing.

Enfranchisement brings about one simple, but crucial, change: you buy out your landlord. You still have leases and the law of leasehold still applies to you. You still have a landlord – the only difference is that the landlord is now you and your neighbours (usually, it is in fact a company owned by the flat-owners). **Commonhold**, when it is introduced, will create a whole new way of owning flats, tailor-made for collective ownership and management of blocks of flats by those who live in them. Where it applies, it will do away altogether with leases and landlords, and there will be no need for flat-owners to set up companies.

The government plans to introduce commonhold in the near future, but it is likely to be an option only in enfranchised blocks, and where everyone in the block wants to set up a commonhold.

CHAPTER 6

FINANCE AND CREDIT

CREDIT is a means of borrowing money, and a particularly useful facility for buying expensive items such as cars and washing machines. This chapter explains, among other matters, what rights you have if a purchase you make on credit is not up to scratch; what to do if a cheque of yours, or credit card, falls into the wrong hands; how to complain if your bank or building society provides bad service; and what options you have if a company you are dealing with goes out of business.

Q *What is the procedure for buying on credit or hire purchase?*

A The procedures are defined in the Consumer Credit Act 1974:

- the consumer signs a credit/hire purchase application form or the credit agreement itself (usually at the bank or the finance company's premises, or in a shop) and retains a copy of the document signed. The creditor then checks the creditworthiness of the applicant – for example, by making enquiries with credit reference agencies (pp. 125–6). If all is satisfactory, the creditor will agree to grant the credit and will then sign the contract. The creditor must deliver to the applicant a *second* copy of the agreement form, signed by both parties, within seven days of the creditor signing
- if the customer signs at a bank or in a shop, and the creditor signs at the *same* time, the agreement becomes legally binding

there and then, and the customer is entitled to only *one copy* of the completed agreement

- where the form is signed by the consumer at home (or anywhere other than the trader's or creditor's place of business) following face-to-face discussions between the customer and the trader, the situation is similar but the customer has a right to cancel the agreement (see below) during the 'cooling-off' period.

Most contracts become legally binding as soon as they are made, even if they are entirely verbal (p. 17), and you cannot get out of them simply because you have changed your mind (p. 19). However, a credit or hire agreement must *always* be in writing.

Q *I've just signed a credit agreement for some new furniture. I now realise I can't afford the payments. Can I get out of the deal?*

A Broadly, the answer depends on *where* you made the agreement and whether it was signed by the trader at the same time you signed:

- if you signed at the furniture store and the trader signed the credit agreement at the same time you cannot cancel (see above)
- some credit agreements do not come into force as soon as you have signed since the company also has to sign before the agreement becomes binding. The trader may want to run credit checks on you to see whether you are a good loan risk before he goes ahead (pp. 125–7). So if you change your mind you may be able to get out of the deal even if you signed the contract at the trader's premises. Tell the trader as soon as possible that you are withdrawing, before he has completed his credit checks and signed the agreement himself, then you should have no problem
- if you signed face to face with the trader, say, at your home or a friend's, you have a right to cancel. But you must act quickly. The **'cooling-off'** period lasts for five clear days. Note that:

- when you sign up for credit you must be given a **notice of your cancellation rights** along with a copy of the credit agreement, and you have five days in which to send your cancellation in writing
- the five days does not start to run until you receive the *second copy* of the agreement from the company with a notice of your cancellation rights
- both copies of the agreement must mention the right of cancellation
- the second copy must be delivered *by post*. The countdown to the fifth day of the cooling-off period does not begin until the debtor has *received* the second copy and does not include that day
- if the trader fails to comply with the formal procedures set down by the Consumer Credit Act 1974 the credit agreement cannot be enforced by the company.

To cancel you must give written notice to the creditor or an agent who conducted the negotiations, such as the salesman. If you mail the cancellation it will take effect as soon as it is posted, so make sure you get a certificate of posting from the Post Office. The effect of cancellation is to bring the whole agreement to an end and to absolve you from any future liability. If you have paid a deposit, that must be refunded to you. (For cancelling after the cooling-off period, see p. 128.)

Q *How do lenders decide whether to lend money or enter into credit agreements?*

A When you apply for a loan, or for any other kind of credit, including a credit or store card, whoever puts up the money bears the risk that you might not pay it back. So lenders often use their own system of **credit scoring** and/or a **credit reference agency** report to sort the mass of credit applications they receive into good and bad risks, or they may simply use their own judgment.

- **credit scoring** The answers you give on an application form will be given marks from a score card. Lenders keep their

scoring systems secret to prevent cheating. However, it is common knowledge that indicators of personal stability, such as being at the same address or in the same job for a long time (over three years, for example), tend to score highly
- **credit reference agencies** Lenders may use these to obtain information on your credit history (see below).

The final decision will be made, on a commercial basis, by the lender.

Q *I applied for a bank loan but I've been turned down. Can I find out why this has happened?*

A No one has a legal right to credit and lenders are not obliged to tell you why you have been turned down. But you do have a right to see any information from a **credit reference agency** file on which the lenders may have based their decision. However, the vast bulk of the credit industry is bound by the Finance Houses Association† code of practice, which states that customers who feel they have been refused credit unreasonably have a right to go to a senior official for a final decision. Although there is no way of discovering the basis for the first ruling, if you think you have been refused on the grounds of race or sex, or marital status, complain to either the Commission for Racial Equality, or the Equal Opportunities Commission.†

It is possible that there has been a mistake on your **credit reference agency** file. The Consumer Credit Act 1974 gives you a right to know what information agencies hold on you. To find out:

- write to the credit company within 28 days of refusal, asking for the names and addresses of any agencies they used
- if the credit company confirms that it used agencies, you are entitled to see a copy of your file(s); to obtain this, write, enclosing the fee of £4, with your full name and address and any previous addresses over the last six years. Within seven working days of receiving your request the agency must send you a copy of your file and a statement of your rights

- if the file contains incorrect information you have the right to ask for its removal or amendment. If the agency does not reply within 28 days, or refuses to alter the file, you have 28 days in which to write a notice of correction
- the agency must place the correction on the file and may send a copy of the correction to other credit reference agencies and anyone who consulted it about you within the last six months
- unfortunately the correction on the file does not guarantee that you will be given credit: this is still at the discretion of the lender (see pp. 125–6), but once the correction has been made you can re-apply for credit
- if the lender (your bank) is still refusing you a loan despite your having written to a senior official, contact the Data Protection Registrar, or the Office of Fair Trading.†

Q *What does 'APR' mean and how can this information help me decide on taking out finance?*

A **APR** stands for **Annual Percentage Rate**. Comparing the costs of different types of credit is not easy. The aim of the APR is to give you a yardstick by which to compare the cost of one type of credit with another so you cannot be fooled into thinking you have a really good deal by confusing figures and different rates. A flat interest rate is no basis for comparison because it takes no account of the different ways in which interest can be charged (for example, daily or monthly), which will affect how much you actually pay, and it ignores one-off charges such as arrangement fees. The APR, which must be quoted for most forms of credit, provides a better basis for comparison than the flat rate because all lenders are required (in theory) to quote credit costs in the same way. It takes into account the size, number and frequency of repayments you make, together with one-off costs. It's not a perfect tool for comparing the costs of credit, but if it's used in conjunction with the **total charge for credit** (which shows all the interest and other costs payable when you borrow) it will provide an indication of the deals to consider and those to avoid.

Q *Last year I took out a* **personal loan** *from a finance company to buy a new car. It was repayable over a four-year period, but I now want to pay it off early. Can I do this?*

A Yes, but with a fixed-term loan you are still liable to pay some of the interest you would have paid had you kept the loan up for the full term. The Consumer Credit Act 1974 gives the debtor two related rights:

- the right to pay off all amounts due *at any time* during the agreement, and
- the right to a *rebate* of the credit charges to take into account the earlier receipt of the money by the creditor. The rebate is calculated in accordance with formulae set out in regulations made under the Act. A word of warning: repaying a loan does not simply mean paying off the outstanding capital. The creditor would have received the capital plus all the interest charges over the full loan period, and in a sense the early settlement is a penalty rather than a rebate in its ordinary meaning.

The most common way to exercise your right of early settlement is to send **written notice** to the creditor. The creditor is obliged to send a statement, free of charge, setting out the amount required to pay off the loan after taking into account the rebate allowable. The statement must set out the basic calculations involved in arriving at that sum. You can then pay off all you owe under the agreement, less the rebate. Alternatively, you can work out the amount to pay using the formula in the booklet available from the OFT† or your local Citizens Advice Bureau. You may then send this amount with your notice of settlement.

Q *I recently took out a loan. I checked my bank statements and discovered that I'm also paying for insurance. It seems this is to cover the repayments should I fall sick or become unemployed. But I didn't ask for insurance. Can the lender do this?*

A When filling in any application form, especially for a long-term commitment such as a loan, always read it very carefully.

Insurance policies of this sort are often sold through **negative option tickboxes** – this means you are said to have agreed to buy the insurance unless you tick a box saying you do not want it. Although this is unfair, it is perfectly legal.

Q *I bought a second-hand car on* ***hire purchase*** *three months ago. The car has broken down three times now but when I complain to the garage where I got the car they just fob me off. I'm fed up with the car. Can I get rid of it?*

A When you buy on HP your legal rights are against the finance company which lends you the money, *not* the retailer with whom you originally dealt. This is because in effect the retailer sells the car to the HP company and it then sells the car on to you. The goods will not legally become yours until you have paid all the instalments. However, if you have been sold faulty goods:

- you have the same basic rights as if you had paid cash. For HP these rights are laid down by the Supply of Goods (Implied Terms) Act 1973, which states that goods supplied on HP, like goods sold in the normal way, must be of **satisfactory quality**, **fit for their purpose**, and correspond with any **description** given of them
- your rights in the event of faulty goods last longer if you buy on HP than if you buy for cash: on HP you have the common law right to reject faulty goods *throughout* the duration of the agreement
- to reject the item(s), tell the finance company that the goods are unmerchantable, that you are rejecting them, and that they are available for collection by the company
- you are then entitled to be refunded any instalments you have paid and you do not have to pay any more
- you are not *compelled* to reject the car: if you want to keep it, but would like a free repair, say, write to the finance company explaining what is wrong, what you want done about it, and that you will continue paying only 'under protest' until the faults have been put right

- you are entitled to claim compensation for any expenses you incur which were reasonably foreseeable by both you and the company at the time when you entered the HP agreement: for example, the cost of alternative means of transport while your car was being repaired.

Once you have paid all the instalments on your goods, your rights become the same as if you had paid cash.

Q *I have a motorcycle on hire purchase. Do I have to pay all the instalments before I sell it, or can I sell before I finish paying?*

A No. The motorcycle is still owned by the finance company, and it will not become your property until you have paid all the instalments and thus purchased it. You have only the right to use the motorcycle until then. If you do sell, you will automatically be in breach of your obligations as a seller under the Sale of Goods Act 1979. That Act says that you must have title to the goods (i.e. own the motorcycle) before you sell (pp. 28–9). You would also be liable to the finance company for wrongfully selling its property (p. 53). The situation is different where you have bought goods on credit using a loan or credit card, as you will become the owner of the goods as soon as you start paying.

If the amount of credit is £15,000 or less, your HP agreement is a consumer credit agreement regulated by the Consumer Credit Act 1974. This gives you the right to settle the agreement early and to obtain a rebate on the interest charges to reflect the early payment (p. 128). So, if you want to sell, you must pay off the outstanding instalments first.

Q *I paid for my stereo TV on credit. Now I can't keep up my repayments. Could the company come round to my house and take it away?*

A No. Only certain people have the right to enter your home, and may do so only for specific reasons (p. 235). You should contact the finance company straight away, explaining your circumstances and asking for your repayments to be rescheduled. If it will not agree new terms or you cannot afford to pay anything, you can be taken to the county court. However, the court may allow you time to pay.

If you break the credit agreement by not paying, the finance company has to serve a 'default notice' on you before taking any action to enforce the agreement. This notice must say what you have done wrong and what you must do to put things right, giving you at least seven days in which to do so. The finance company is not allowed to increase the rate of interest on the amount owed. If you do not comply with the notice or get in touch to sort things out you could be taken to court.

If you are buying on HP and you have paid more than a third of the total price the finance house may not recover the TV without a court order and has no right to recover the goods. If the TV was not bought on HP or being rented, but you just arranged a loan to pay for it, then the TV is legally yours. But you can still be taken to court by the loan company for defaulting on loan repayments. If you do find yourself in financial difficulties, contact your local Citizens Advice Bureau or Money Advice Centre.

Q *I lost my wallet with my credit card in it. Will I have to pay if the finder or thief uses the card?*

A You should notify the credit card company of the loss immediately:

- you will not be liable for any loss arising *after* you have notified the company
- you must confirm any oral notice by giving written notice within the following seven days
- if you are quick enough to contact the credit card company before the thief has had time to use the card, you will have no liability at all
- under the terms of the Consumer Credit Act 1974 you will in any case be liable for no more than £50, even if you fail to notify the credit card company or the thief is quick off the mark (see also p. 136).

Q *I bought goods on my credit card which I've tried to reject because they are faulty. The retailer has gone out of business and I'm told that there is unlikely to be any money to pay my claim. Is the credit card company responsible?*

A Whether you pay for faulty goods or services in cash or by credit card, your rights are against the seller (pp. 28–9). However, the Consumer Credit Act 1974 provides added protection where you buy goods or services on credit card, as long as the price of the individual item purchased was over £100 (pp. 54–5). Note that:

- the credit card company as well as the retailer is also liable for any breach of contract. So you can claim for faulty goods or services against the retailer, the credit card company, or both. If you are making a claim for faulty goods bought on credit, write to both parties. You will not get two lots of compensation, but you will increase your chances of getting the problem sorted out
- if the retailer goes bankrupt your claim against him is unlikely to result in any return of your money, or compensation, for the faulty goods or service. You will remain an unsecured creditor (p. 25). But if you paid by credit card this allows you to claim against the credit card company. This cover is particularly useful if you have paid a deposit in advance to a company that subsequently closes down.

Q *While on holiday in Italy I went to pick up the hire car which I had paid for by credit card in the UK. I was asked to sign a blank voucher in case of fines or damage to the car. After protesting I agreed to leave a signed blank voucher. What happens if the car hire firm processes it with unjustified amounts?*

A Avoid signing blank vouchers if possible and always remember to complete the totals box on the credit card slip. Usually if a voucher you have signed is processed you'll have no comeback on the amount that goes through since you will have authorised the transaction. If a voucher has been processed for something you were not warned about or for an expense that is not yours, complain straight away to both the credit card company and the car hire firm. The card company should take things up with the car hire company, although things may not be sorted out for some time since the disputed incident happened abroad.

If you do make credit card payments abroad, you should be protected by the Consumer Credit Act 1974 (pp. 132–3) (this principle has never been tested in the courts).

Q *I used my credit card to buy a computer. It hasn't been delivered, but the trader has gone bust. Have I lost my money?*

A You can try to recover your money from the trader as part of the bankruptcy or liquidation process, but it's very unlikely that you will get anything back (see p. 25). You can get your money back from the credit card company, provided the price of the item is more than £100 but less than £30,000, and the credit advance up to £15,000. The credit card company, along with the trader, is liable for any breach of contract such as non-delivery of an order. But this protection doesn't apply to **charge cards**, **debit cards** and most **gold cards**. Credit cards give you the facility to pay by instalments rather than settling the whole balance at the end of each month. Charge cards do not give you this facility, so there is no credit element.

Even if you pay only part of the price by credit card (and the rest by cheque, say) and even if that part-payment was less than £100, you can recover the whole amount from the credit card company as long as the total price is £100 or more.

Q *I closed my credit card account six months ago and I've just received a statement for a purchase I made when on holiday last year. Do I have to pay?*

A Yes. Although you 'closed' the account you are still legally obliged to settle up for:

- transactions that were authorised during the life of your account, and
- any 'continuous authorities' on that account – for example, if a book club has your old card number and you authorised it to charge your subscription to the card account, it can do this unless you stop the arrangement and pay by another means. Such payments are the credit card equivalent of direct debits, regular payments that you have authorised a company to take from your card. But unlike direct debits the card issuer will carry on paying them and sending you statements *after* you have closed your account, unless and until you contact the individual companies direct to cancel them.

So if you do not pay up, the credit card company can charge you interest on the outstanding amount. Pay up now and check that you have not authorised anyone else to take out annual subscriptions or payments from that account.

Q *My mother was sold a loan by a doorstop salesman. The interest seems incredibly high. Is there anything she can do?*

A It is illegal for lenders or credit brokers to call uninvited to offer loans *unless* the loan is for goods and services that they are also supplying. Even then, if your mother did not ask for a visit from whoever sold her the loan, or she didn't sign the loan on their premises, she is allowed five full days after receiving a copy of the agreement in which to change her mind and cancel the loan (pp. 123–5).

If she is committed to the loan, because she signed at the trader's premises, say, and it seems a complete rip-off, she *may* be able to get a court to change the terms or set the loan aside altogether. But she must be able to convince the court that the loan is in some way 'extortionate'. There is no legal definition of this since the court assesses how expensive the loan is in relation to the risk to the lender that the loan may not be repaid. The court would also consider your mother's financial know-how, and whether the lender somehow took advantage of her – for example, by asking her to sign a blank application form.

But be warned, court action can be slow and expensive. If you have financial problems contact your local Citizens Advice Bureau or Money Advice Centre.

Q *I paid for some repairs to my car by cheque and now the car has broken down again only two days after the servicing. I told the bank to* ***stop the cheque*** *and now the garage is threatening to sue me. Can it do this?*

A It is dangerous to stop a cheque, especially if you are not sure, as in this case, that the garage is at fault. So the golden rule is, in most cases, not to do it. If you give someone a cheque the courts will not generally intervene – it will be assumed that since you gave the cheque to the garage you did owe it the money. This means the garage can take you to court for the value of the cheque and will win simply by saying that you paid for the work by cheque and then cancelled it. You will only be able to challenge the garage if you have clear evidence that the garage's repairs were substandard. Since you do not know whether the car broke down because the garage failed to do its job properly or for some other reason, it is unlikely that you will be able to challenge the garage if you are taken to court. So get the car inspected by an independent mechanic who can back up your suspicion that the garage did something wrong. If you cannot get such back-up, pay up by sending the garage another cheque and investigate the cause of the problem later (pp. 59–61).

Q *I've got a* ***multi-purpose plastic card*** *– debit, cashpoint and cheque guarantee card in one. A few weeks ago I bought a computer by mail order giving my card details over the phone. The company has not delivered the computer, though the payment of £900 has cleared. I cannot get any response from the company. I've heard that if you pay by plastic you can get your card company to sort things out or even to refund money if the seller has done something wrong. Does this apply to me?*

A No. Debit cards, like Switch or Connect, are like paperless cheques, not credit cards. If you give your debit card number the money comes directly out of your bank account, so there is no credit involved. You don't get the same protection as you would if you had paid by credit card (pp. 132–3). Write to the company requesting delivery within a specific time limit, say, 14 days, and make this time 'of the essence' (p. 39).

Q *What rights do I have when dealing with banks and building societies?*

A When you open a bank or building society account you are making a contract, and all the usual rules governing contracts to supply a service apply (pp. 59–61). The Supply of Goods and Services Act 1982 states that the bank or building society must carry out the contract with reasonable skill and care.

A **code of practice** (pp. 237–8) was introduced in 1992 to improve the service offered by banks and building societies. The main areas covered are:

- **fair conduct** Banks and building societies should always act 'fairly and reasonably' in dealings with customers
- **no 'charges on charges'** If your current account goes into the red purely because of the charges that have been taken from it, you should not incur a second lot of charges
- **plastic cards** For any type of plastic card – credit card, cash withdrawal, debit card and so on – the maximum liability for money taken without your agreement before the card issuer has been informed is £50, or nil if the card is lost or stolen before it reaches you in the post. You will lose this protection only if you have been 'grossly negligent' (by, for example, writing your Personal Identification Number – PIN – on the card), and it would be up to the bank or building society to prove that this was the case
- **confidentiality** Your personal financial details will not be passed to separate 'non-banking' companies in the banking group, such as its insurance or investment arm, without your consent (but check that such use of information was not made a condition of opening the account)
- **complaints** All institutions must have proper complaints procedures.

If you have a complaint, write to the branch or area manager of the bank or building society. If this proves unsatisfactory, take your complaint further by writing to the head office, then to the Banking or Building Societies Ombudsman†, as appropriate (pp. 243–4):

- the **Banking Ombudsman Scheme** includes all the major banks and most types of bank business normally conducted through their branches. The ombudsman can award customers compensation of up to £100,000. The bank must abide by the ombudsman's decision, but the consumer has the choice of accepting *or* pursuing the matter further
- the **Building Societies Ombudsman Scheme** covers all societies and can recommend awards of up to £100,000.

Q *I've just checked my bank statement and I dispute a couple of the* ***cash card withdrawals****. The bank says that the cashpoint machine definitely paid out the money to me and that there is no mistake. How can I convince the bank that I didn't make these withdrawals?*

A If your bank statement shows a cash dispenser withdrawal which you know you have not made, and you have not given anyone your PIN (Personal Identification Number), informing the bank is the first priority, so you were right to tell yours immediately. Since the **banking code of practice** came into force in 1992 subscribing banks (which include all the major high street banks) have had to show that the withdrawal was made by the card-holder or someone authorised by the card-holder. If, in this case, the bank insists that you made the withdrawal, that its technology is infallible, and it will not make any sort of refund to you, you will need evidence to back up your claim that it was not you. So make sure you can remember where you were at the time of the **'phantom' withdrawal** and if possible try to prove that you had your card with you at the time. Statements from friends who were with you at the time could help.

If the bank accepts what you say you should get back all the cash taken. If the bank does not accept that there was a phantom withdrawal, you can complain to the banking or the building societies ombudsman† (see pp. 243–4).

Q *Are cheques a safe way of paying?*

A If your cheque book is stolen, provided you let your bank or building society know of the theft as soon as possible, you will not be liable for a penny in the event that someone forges your signature: the cheque would be invalid and the bank has to bear the total loss. But if your cheque guarantee card is stolen at the same time, you may fall foul of your contract with the bank, which requires that you keep the cheque book and the card separate, so you may be held liable for the loss.

If you have written out a cheque which then falls into the wrong hands, it is possible for the thief to forge the signature of the person to whom you were paying the money (the '**payee**') on the back of the cheque, pay it into his own account and, when it clears, withdraw the money and disappear. All cheques are transferable, and even if it had been a crossed cheque, you would have no redress against either the bank where the cheque was paid in or your own bank which paid the cheque.

The Cheques Act 1992 states that if you write the words '*Account payee*' or '*a/c payee*' with or without the word '*only*' on the face of a crossed cheque, you are protected against the cheque being transferred to a thief's account. If the bank where the cheque is paid in negligently credits an account other than that of the payee named on the face of the cheque, it will have to make good your loss. Many banks and building societies now issue cheque books with the protective words already printed on them. If yours does not, ask your bank to supply these.

Q *My current account balance was a bit low last month because I hadn't been keeping an eye on my spending. I knew that I had a direct debit due to go out on the 26th so I paid in a cheque for £100 on the 25th from my savings account to make sure I would have enough money to cover the direct debit and other outgoings. To my horror I got a* *statement from the bank saying that there had been insufficient funds to meet payment of the direct debit so it had been refused. The bank is also charging me for an unauthorised overdraft of £20 from the 26th to the 28th. Why should this have happened if I'd paid in the money on time?*

A Banks and building societies require at least three days (and in some cases a week) for cheques to clear. So unless you take this into account when paying in money you could get into trouble. If you go overdrawn without agreement, it may be worth writing to the bank manager explaining the circumstances and asking for the charges to be withdrawn since you had no intention to go overdrawn without authority. If you have kept your account in credit previously the bank may refund the charges if you're lucky, but it is not obliged to do so.

If you know that you are going to overdraw, always get your bank's agreement beforehand. If you do so, you'll pay lower charges.

Q *I've lost out on some investments I made, in my view because I was badly advised by my financial adviser. How can I complain?*

A Anyone who carries out investment business must be authorised to do so under the Financial Services Act 1986 (and carry a statement to this effect on his or her letterhead), which means that checks will be made on whether the individual is 'fit and proper' to do business. Anyone offering investment advice must be regulated by a self-regulating organisation (SRO), or by the Securities and Investments Board (SIB), or a recognised professional body like the Law Society. The main SROs† are:

- the Financial Intermediaries, Managers and Brokers Regulatory Association (FIMBRA) and the Life Assurance and Unit Trust Regulatory Organisation (LAUTRO). The work of both these bodies is now being taken over by the Personal Investment Authority, which has set up its own PIA Ombudsman Scheme.

- the Investment Management Regulatory Organisation (IMRO), which is concerned with firms specialising in investment management and some independent intermediaries.

Under the Financial Services Act 1986 intermediaries must tell you whether they are independent or tied (i.e. effectively an agent for one particular company) and also to which regulatory body they or their company belong. The intermediaries should also ask you for detailed information about your circumstances since they must recommend only suitable investments. Independent advisers should also tell you whether they receive a commission for selling a particular product: those who do are unlikely to give the most impartial advice.

So if you feel you have been badly advised and cannot agree a solution with your intermediary, send the details to the appropriate regulatory bodies; the Insurance Ombudsman Bureau† deals with investment complaints for member companies.

Q *A builder did some work for me which wasn't up to scratch. He is still trading but says that when I had the work done he was the director of a company that has now gone bust. He says I can't take him to court as it was a limited company. Is this true?*

A This is generally correct. But what action you take depends on whether you made your contract with a company or with the builder personally. When you deal with a limited company or a plc (public limited company) this usually means that your contract is with the company, not the individual directors who run it. So if you have a compensation claim the company will pay you out of company money. The director's personal money is not generally involved or at risk. So when a company goes out of business you may lose out on any compensation claim.

If the trader is not a limited company and your contract is with a partnership, firm or one-man band, the trader's personal money is at risk if you have a compensation claim, and you may be able to pursue him.

So check your paperwork to see whether the contract was made with the limited company or with a firm or partnership, or sole trader. If it was with the company check with Companies House† to find out whether the company has gone out of business. If it has you have probably lost out even though your builder is still trading on his own account (p. 143).

Q *I've just received a statutory demand from someone who lent me money. What does it mean?*

A If you owe more than £750 and the debt is not a secured loan (like a mortgage, say) you can be bankrupted, at the instigation of the creditor, if you do not pay up and the bankruptcy court believes you cannot repay the money. So if you get a statutory demand you should pay any debt you owe to avoid bankruptcy proceedings. You generally have three weeks from the date on which the statutory demand is served to pay up or arrange for payment. If you do not or cannot pay, the person or business you owe can present a bankruptcy petition to court.

If a bankruptcy order is made, a trustee in bankruptcy is appointed by the court or the official receiver is appointed to manage your property. The trustee or receiver will take over the running of your financial affairs and can sell off your property to help clear your debts. As an undischarged bankrupt you will be deprived of the ownership of your property. But you can keep some things such as your clothing and tools of your trade. Generally the bankruptcy is automatically discharged after three years. On discharge you are no longer responsible for bankruptcy debts.

Q *I've got a court judgment against a builder who made a mess of fitting my kitchen. I've been chasing him for the £700 compensation I was awarded by the court. He now says that he's* ***bankrupt****. Does this mean I've lost my money?*

A To check whether he is telling the truth telephone the **Bankruptcy Search Room** (a section of the official receivers department†) to obtain the name and address of his trustee or receiver. You can then send the trustee or receiver information about the money you are owed. Any funds that are collected will be distributed according to a 'pecking order'. This means that preferred creditors (often banks and the Inland Revenue) will get all their money before you. Only if there is anything left after the preferred creditors have been paid will you get anything. So if the builder *has* gone bankrupt it is likely that you will lose out.

Q *When I paid for a new rug the sales assistant put a label on it with my name and address. It hasn't been delivered yet although I know it was at the warehouse. I've just heard that the store has gone bust. Will I get my money or my carpet?*

A When a business collapses and cannot pay all its debts, there is a strict order of priority for creditors. As an ordinary customer, you are an 'unsecured creditor' and unfortunately you come at the back of the queue behind other creditors such as the bank, the Inland Revenue and company employees who are owed salary. You'll miss any chance of getting your money back if you do not get in the queue quickly, so contact the receiver or liquidator straight away. Often there is not enough money to go round so you could end up getting less than you paid or nothing at all.

Always make sure you know where your goods are if you are not taking them away with you, and insist that they are marked with your name. If they are clearly labelled as yours go to the shop or warehouse and try to collect them. But if they haven't been marked as yours you cannot insist on collecting them.

Q *What is the difference between* ***receivership*** *and* ***liquidation****?*

A When a company is in receivership one of its big creditors – a bank, say – has put its own employee in to run the company. It is the receiver's job to collect enough money to pay off the debt owed to the bank. This could mean that any money you have paid to the company (as a deposit, for example) goes straight to the bank. But you are still entitled to your goods or cash, and should eventually get them if the company does not subsequently go into liquidation.

If an administrator is appointed instead, you could be better off in the long run: a serious attempt to save the company might be under way.

When a liquidator is put in charge the company is going to be wound up completely (liquidation). If any cash is left at the end of this process you might get something back, but you will be with all the other unsecured creditors at the back of the queue. So it is unlikely you will get anything (p. 25).

Q *Is the **guarantee** on my recent re-roofing work worth anything now that the builder has gone bust?*

A When a company goes bust its guarantees generally aren't worth the paper they're written on. But if another company buys out the failed business and agrees to take over its liabilities your guarantee should be honoured. Also, check to see whether you paid for your guarantee to be backed by insurance. If you did pay a premium when you agreed to have the building work done then the insurance should cover the cost of any work that needs doing if the builder did a bad job (p. 65).

Q *A year ago, I lost a lot of money when I paid a deposit to a firm that went bust. The same people have now set up again using the same name. Is this allowed?*

A It is against the law for those involved to set up again using the old name (or a similar name) of a liquidated company for five years following the liquidation. If anyone who was a director of the old company is taking the important business decisions at the new one, even if not officially a director (i.e. a 'shadow' director), he or she is breaking the law. You should report this to the Companies Investigations Division of the Department of Trade and Industry.†

Q *The garage that was restoring my classic car didn't do the work properly. A couple of months ago, after much wrangling, I was offered £1,500 in* ***'full and final settlement'*** *of my claim. I accepted the money, but now discover it will cost £3,000 to put the work right. Can I claim some more?*

A No. When you agree to accept compensation in 'full and final settlement' you cannot go back and ask for more at a later date. So if you are unsure of whether an offer is fair get advice and do not be pressured into accepting less than you are entitled to. If, during negotiations:

- the other side hassles you, write saying that you are seriously considering the offer but are seeking expert or legal advice before you finally decide whether to accept. Most traders will be reasonable and will understand that you need time to make a decision. However, you should remember that an offer can be withdrawn at any time before it is accepted, so don't leave it too long before getting back to the other side
- you receive a cheque in 'full and final settlement', don't bank it, as to do so may be interpreted as acceptance. You should either hang on to it or return it with a letter rejecting the offer.

CHAPTER 7

HEALTH

HOW do you change doctors? What are your rights when your treatment in hospital goes wrong, of if your dentist doesn't provide an acceptable level of service? This chapter explains the legal duties of doctors, opticians, dentists, pharmacists, dentists and alternative practitioners.

If you opt for private treatment – in a private hospital, or by a private dentist, GP, optician or pharmacist – the avenues for complaint may be limited (pp. 146 and 155).

Your rights, and the correct complaints procedure to follow, will also differ if your complaint:

- is about a failure in the provision of a whole range of hospital services, or
- concerns the 'clinical' judgment of an NHS dentist, GP, etc. (pp. 148–9), or
- concerns the 'clinical' judgment of a hospital doctor (pp. 149–50), or
- results from the professional misconduct of the medical professional (p. 155), or
- arises from the injury you suffered as a result of medical negligence (p. 151).

There can be few consumer services as important as the National Health Service. But the NHS is a bewilderingly large organisation, and it may be difficult to know where you can turn if you experience problems. This chapter explains your rights and the procedure for complaining. You can always seek help from your local **Community Health Council**, listed in the phone book under 'Community' (Local Health Council in Scotland, Health and Social Services Board in Northern Ireland).

Q *If I have a problem concerning medical treatment, to whom should I complain?*

A Whatever your complaint, and whether the treatment received was NHS or private, follow these golden rules:

- clarify the situation with the person responsible for the treatment – this might prove the simplest and quickest way of getting things put right
- try to resolve your complaint informally, if possible, but once you decide to start a more formal complaint, act quickly – delay could cause difficulties with evidence and may lead people to doubt the seriousness of your grievance
- keep copies of letters and other written records concerning your complaint
- seek advice, at any stage, from a Community Health Council (Local Health Council in Scotland) or other organisation or pressure group which might be able to help
- be persistent, and prepared for a process which may prove both frustrating and time-consuming
- be sure in your own mind about the **subject** (GP, dentist, hospital nurse, etc.), the **substance** (wrong kind of treatment, or rude and uncaring behaviour on the part of a health professional), and the **object** of your complaint (do you hope to receive an apology, a change of treatment, financial compensation, or simply to make sure that what happened to you will not happen to others?)
- what makes the greatest difference is whether the treatment you are complaining about was from medical staff in hospital ('hospital medical care') or from medical practitioners out of hospital ('community medical care'), by dentists, GPs, opticians, pharmacists, etc. There is a different process for each category (see pp. 148–51).

Q *Is there an* **ombudsman** *for the NHS who can look at my complaint?*

A Yes. His official title is the **Health Service Commissioner.**† He is independent of the NHS and the government and his services are free. Although he cannot award compensation, he can ask the NHS authority or trust to remedy or compensate for any injustice or hardship suffered.

Before making a complaint to the ombudsman you must first take it up with the appropriate NHS authority (p. 148). You need to show that the failure in service or maladministration has caused you injustice or hardship. Complaints may be about the attitude, as well as the actions, of a member of staff. It is up to the ombudsman to decide whether to investigate a complaint – the decision will depend on its merits. The main purpose is to ensure that you receive an apology and that the NHS authority agrees to change policies or procedures to prevent the problem happening again. If you have any doubt about whether he can deal with your complaint, contact the ombudsman first.

The ombudsman has the power to investigate complaints that an NHS authority or trust:

- has not provided a service which it has a duty to provide
- has failed to provide service of sufficient quality, e.g. late arrival or non-availability of ambulances (p. 152)
- is guilty of **maladministration** in any action it has taken or authorised – such as not following proper procedures, not explaining the care being given to a patient, or giving wrong information, or carrying out an unsatisfactory investigation into your original complaint.

The ombudsman *cannot*:

- investigate complaints concerning a clinical decision about the care or treatment of a patient (see pp. 149–50)
- investigate complaints about 'community medical care', that is, services provided by family doctors, dentists, opticians or pharmacists (p. 148)
- award compensation for any harm or inconvenience suffered.

Q *I feel that my NHS dentist is rather off-hand and impatient with me and on one occasion recently he was downright rude. Is there anything I can do about this?*

A If you're not happy with the treatment you or your family have received from the NHS, misunderstandings may be resolved by complaining directly to the person concerned. If you do not get satisfaction or you would rather not discuss the problem with the person face to face, your local **Family Health Service Authority** (FHSA) should be able to help you (Local Health Council in Scotland; Health and Social Services Boards in Northern Ireland). FHSAs deal with complaints about GPs, dentists, opticians, pharmacists and their staff.

You will have to decide whether to make an **informal** or a **formal** complaint. Both District Health Authorities and FHSAs have informal complaints procedures intended to deal with less serious allegations, for example, about a rude doctor, or a practitioner who is always late.

The **informal complaints procedure** involves conciliation – a lay conciliator (not employed by the FHSA) will discuss the problem with you, and try to reconcile any differences between you and the person you have complained about.

Q *Two weeks ago my son developed severe abdominal pain during the night. Our family doctor didn't think it was serious enough to warrant a visit. I took my son into casualty the next morning and acute appendicitis was diagnosed. I am very unhappy about the GP's attitude and wish to make a formal complaint. How do I go about it?*

A Family doctors (GPs), dentists, opticians, and general pharmaceutical services from your chemist are all independent of the NHS, but offer NHS services under a contract with the local **Family Health Service Authority** (FHSA). A family doctor must treat you with reasonable care, which would include visiting you at home if necessary. If practitioners do not fulfil their terms of service the FHSA can take action.

A complaint about the services provided by any of these health professionals should be made in writing to the General

Manager of your local FHSA (address on your NHS medical card and in the phone book). Where the matter is serious, as in this instance, involving an alleged breach in a professional's terms of service, make a **formal complaint** and ask for a formal investigation to be carried out. Note the time limits, however:

- complaints about doctors must be put in writing to the General Manager of the FHSA no later than 13 weeks after the event which caused it
- complaints about dentists must be made within six months after the end of the treatment which caused the complaint or 13 weeks after the cause of the complaint came to your notice, whichever is sooner
- if you are the subject of the complaint and were too ill to complain at the time, write to the FHSA. Late complaints can be dealt with in certain circumstances. You can appeal if the FHSA decides it is too late to investigate your complaint
- **formal investigations** are carried out by a 'service committee' made up of a lay chairperson and equal numbers of lay people and practitioners from the same profession as the person you have complained about
- you might have to attend a hearing and give evidence
- the committee can recommend that the FHSA takes action, usually by imposing a financial penalty, against the person you have complained about
- the FHSA cannot award you financial compensation for any harm you or your relative have suffered. For compensation you would have to claim through the courts (see pp. 150–51 and Chapter 13).

Q *I had to undergo hospital treatment recently. I don't think it was carried out properly and this gave rise to complications in my condition. What can I do?*

A In hospitals, complaints which involve clinical judgment – for example, if you think a doctor gave you the wrong treatment, or a nurse or other health service medical professional gave you the wrong medication – are dealt with under a special **clinical complaints procedure**. What you should do is:

- talk to staff involved or their manager as soon as you feel there are grounds for a complaint
- make your complaint as soon as possible so that the matter can be looked into quickly
- if your initial discussion has not resolved the matter, you should write to the General Manager of the hospital or clinic (the Chief Executive if it was an NHS trust†) and send a copy to the General Manager of the District Health Authority. Give your name and date of birth or hospital number. Also give the date of the incident, the names of the staff involved or a description of them, and the main points of the case, stating clearly what points you want investigated
- specify what you want to happen as a result. This may include:
  - action by staff to help sort out your immediate problem
  - an apology
  - improved services for others
  - an explanation or more information about what happened
- if they are relevant, ask to see your medical records (see pp. 160–2).

If you are not satisfied and the clinical complaint is serious, the General Manager or the consultant may refer the complaint to the Regional Director of Public Health for a review by two independent consultants who were not involved with your case.

Q *If I want to try for compensation, do I have to follow the 'clinical complaints' procedure first?*

A No. In fact if you want to claim compensation these procedures may not be open to you. But they are a useful first step *before* you decide whether to claim compensation later. The clinical complaints procedures against hospital practitioners and community health practitioners (pp. 148–50) will not help you obtain compensation, but you can seek guidance on pursuing the claim from AVMA (Action for Victims of Medical Accidents)† or a specialist medical negligence lawyer (see below).

Q *The operation I had done recently has left me in an even worse condition. I'm not satisfied with the explanation I've received from the consultant in charge of my case, and I feel I'm entitled to some sort of* **compensation**. *What should I do?*

A Pursuing a **medical accident** or **negligence** claim is certainly not something to be undertaken lightly, even if you qualify for legal aid. Besides being expensive and protracted, such cases are notoriously difficult to prove. Your lawyers will have to show that the doctor was negligent rather than just making a professional misjudgment. They will also have to show that this negligence caused your subsequent medical problems. In medical negligence cases, proper legal advice from a specialist lawyer is essential to ensure you obtain all the evidence you will need and to negotiate the best settlement terms. So, if you want to claim compensation:

- before going to a solicitor, seek advice from your local Community Health Council (see p. 146) or AVMA (Action for Victims of Medical Accidents).† AVMA can give you free basic legal and medical advice, and, if appropriate, refer you to a solicitor with substantial experience in such cases
- your solicitor will take a statement of what happened and discuss legal aid and costs with you. If the case seems worth pursuing (and if you have the financial means to proceed, or are eligible for legal aid) your solicitor will obtain the medical records, identify the issues and then send them to a medical expert so that a report can be prepared. The report may then be sent with your statement and records to a barrister for advice as to the strength of your claim and on how to proceed
- if your case is a strong one, the health authority (or other defendant) may be willing to settle your claim without the need to go to court. If it is necessary to start court action, the solicitor must do this within three years of the date when you first realised you had suffered damage (pp. 20–1).

Q *What rights does the Patient's Charter give me?*

A The government's Patient's Charter† sets out **rights** and **standards**. Your **rights** under the Charter are:

- to be given a clear explanation of any proposed treatment, including risks and alternatives
- to choose whether to take part in medical research or student training
- to have access to your health records or notes (see pp. 160–2)
- to be given information on local health services, including what to expect, and maximum waiting times
- to be guaranteed admission for treatment by a specific date no more than two years after being put on a waiting list by a consultant
- to have complaints investigated, with prompt full replies.

The national **standards** set out under the Charter which the government expects the NHS to achieve include:

- respect for privacy, dignity and personal beliefs
- all emergency ambulances should arrive within 14 minutes in urban areas and 19 minutes in rural areas (p. 147)
- at a hospital casualty department you should be assessed immediately
- out-patients should have a specific appointment time and be seen within 30 minutes of it.

If you think you're not getting any of your Charter rights as an NHS patient, raise the matter with your local health services; or complain to the NHS Chief Executive at the Department of Health.†

Q *Is there anything I can do to shorten the time I have to wait for treatment on the NHS?*

A You could ask your GP about finding a shorter waiting time at a hospital in another part of the country. Otherwise:

- try to find a shorter waiting time yourself: contact the College of Health helpline† and pass the information to your GP

- tell the hospital you are willing to come in at short notice if there is a cancellation.

Q *I don't feel I have a good rapport with my GP. Can I change to another, and if so how do I go about it?*

A You are allowed to change your GP for any reason – because you're moving, you want a certain kind of GP, such as a woman, or even because you don't like your current doctor. Just turn up at the new doctor's surgery and register (providing it is willing to take you). You do not need permission from the old doctor. You need not take pot luck either as you can find out about GPs before choosing by:

- getting **personal recommendations** (or warnings) from friends and neighbours
- looking at **practice leaflets**. All NHS GPs are required by law to produce a leaflet for patients which describes their practice. These include details of the doctor's sex, the year he or she qualified, surgery hours, other practice staff (for example, nurses), and services provided (for example, antenatal care). You can get leaflets from practices or read them at the local Family Health Service Authority offices
- looking at **Family Health Service Authority (FHSA) lists** of doctors. All FHSAs are required by law to produce a directory of all local GPs. These detail the doctor's sex and age or date of qualification, services the practice provides and who works there. Contact your local FHSA for a list of GPs in your area. Some give information over the phone. You may be able to see the whole directory at the authority's offices or a local library
- getting a **pre-registration interview** with the GP. Some GPs may be willing to meet and discuss your needs and see whether you both get on before you register. GPs are not obliged to give these interviews, and there is a risk that such a meeting could be used by the doctor to vet you. If you have a long-term condition that may take up a lot of the practice's time or money, it is possible that the doctor will not accept you

- contacting the local **Community Health Council** (CHC). Your CHC (Local Health Council in Scotland) may have information about GPs in your area.

Q *I feel my GP is uncertain about his diagnosis of a medical problem I've been experiencing recently. Do I have the right to be referred to a specialist?*

A You don't actually have the *right* to a second opinion. All you have is the right to ask for one. Many doctors would probably agree that a second opinion is justified if:

- your symptoms persist, and you cannot get a diagnosis
- a diagnosis has been made, but the treatment is not working
- you are worried about the risks or side effects of a treatment that has been proposed, or would like more information about it
- you want to know whether there is any alternative to major surgery or other proposed treatment
- you simply feel the need for specialist confirmation that the proposed treatment is right for you
- you are not confident that your doctor knows enough about your condition.

Since you do not have an automatic right to a second opinion, it could be counter-productive to go into the surgery demanding one. You may simply put the doctor's back up. Here are a few tips for how to go about it:

- write down the points you want to make before you go to see the doctor. Remember to say why you feel you would like to see someone else
- if it is true, say that you are not questioning your doctor's judgment, you'd just like the reassurance of having it confirmed
- listen to what your doctor says. There may be good reason for suggesting that you don't need a second opinion, or that you should wait a bit longer before seeing one – for example, to see whether changes in your lifestyle will help solve the problem

- try to be assertive but not aggressive if the doctor refuses.

Q *I've discovered that my GP has been talking about my personal medical problems to his other patients. I think it's very unprofessional. Is there anything I can do?*

A The relationship between a medical professional and a patient is a confidential and intimate one, governed by ethical principles set out in the rules of conduct of the professional regulatory bodies. A practitioner found guilty of a breach of professional conduct may have his right to carry on practising withdrawn. Whether you are complaining about a private or a NHS practitioner, complaints about **professional misconduct** are dealt with by the following bodies:

- General Medical Council† for doctors
- General Dental Council† for dentists
- General Optical Council† for opticians.

Q *What difference does it make to my claim if the treatment was private rather than on the NHS?*

A All NHS hospitals and most private ones have procedures for dealing with patients' complaints. But the informal and formal complaints procedures (see pp. 148–9) apply only to complaints about treatment from doctors, dentists, opticians and pharmacists within the NHS.

All complaints are best dealt with as amicably as possible, but if you cannot get a satisfactory response, and if you wish to claim compensation, you will need to take legal advice with a view to possible court action (see pp. 150–1).

Within the NHS you could sue the hospital or health authority. In the private sector you have to sue the practitioner personally because doctors, dentists etc. are rarely employees of private hospitals and clinics: they tend to work independently using such facilities on a private basis. If you feel strongly that your private treatment was unsatisfactory, you could try to withhold payment. If you are in a private insurance scheme you could ask the insurance company (before you receive any treatment) whether it is prepared to send the payment cheque to you rather than to the hospital or doctor concerned.

However, if you do consider withholding payment or starting court action you will have to establish that the treatment provided was negligent and/or that there was a breach of contract (pp. 59–61 and 151).

Q *I've been asked to go into hospital for tests to investigate a lump in my breast. I'm worried that if it's found to be malignant the surgeon may remove my breast without my express* **consent**. *Could he lawfully do this?*

A Without your permission doctors aren't even allowed to touch you. Consent does not have to be given formally – rolling up your sleeve for a blood test can be enough. But if, as in this sort of case, an invasive form of treatment like surgery is planned, you'll probably be asked to sign a consent form, to provide evidence of agreement. The type of forms currently in use aim to ensure that patients know they are entitled to full information concerning their medical condition.

The consent form will probably ask you whether you have made known to the doctor or dentist any procedure you do not want carried out straight away. If the standard form does not adequately deal with this make a written amendment to the form before signing it, stating, for example, that you do *not* want the breast removed. If the doctor or dentist were to disregard an express prohibition by the patient, he or she would be committing the offence of 'assault and battery' and would be liable to pay compensation for negligence, unless the procedure could be justified on the grounds that it was immediately necessary to preserve the patient's life or health.

Q *How much does my doctor have to tell me about the* **drugs** *he's prescribed for my arthritis?*

A Even if you have agreed to take a particular course of drugs, or to undergo some other procedure, the doctor will be responsible if he or she has failed to give you adequate information about the treatment, possible side effects and so on. You will not receive compensation for any injury you suffer as a result unless you can show you would not have agreed to that type of treatment had you been given additional information. Deciding how much information you are entitled to is a tricky issue, and if other doctors are prepared to say that you were told enough, the doctor will not be liable.

Q *I am suffering from a heart condition and my doctor has asked me if I would be willing to take part in a* ***drug trial****. He has told me something about it but I'd really like more detailed information before agreeing to take part. Would I be able to pull out if I wanted to during the trial and would I be entitled to know the results? I'm concerned about confidentiality too.*

A If you do agree you should know that there are some safeguards:

- adequate information: you have the right to know all about the trial before you start. Don't agree to take part in the trial until you are satisfied that your questions have been answered. Make sure you are aware of all known risks. Ask your doctor about what type of side effects to look out for
- pulling out: you have a right to pull out of a trial at any time without giving a reason. You should not have to worry that your future health care might suffer. It is however wise to find out beforehand whether pulling out of the trial early could have any adverse effects on your health
- results: you should be able to see a copy of the results of the trial. But you may need to be patient, as production of a research report can take years
- confidentiality: your case details and clinical data should remain confidential. In practice this may be difficult since a drug company monitor or official auditor may also be involved. If you are concerned about confidentiality make it clear to your doctor that you would like your records to be seen by as few people as possible and made anonymous.

Q *Can I influence local NHS policy?*

A Community Health Councils (CHCs) (Local Health Councils in Scotland) are probably your best point of contact if you have strong views about the way local services are run. CHCs are supposed to act as a watchdog on what is happening in local health services (for example, hospital closures) and have the right to meet District Health Authorities and Family Health Service Authorities once a year. So make your suggestions known.

Q *I'm seriously considering trying some form of* ***alternative medicine****. How do I know what is on offer and whether the person I choose is competent?*

A Doctors, nurses and certain state-registered professionals (for example, dentists and physiotherapists) must by law have a certain minimum training before they can practise. **Alternative** or **complementary medicine** includes therapies which are not usually taught at medical schools. However, note that:

- anyone can set up as a complementary practitioner or therapist
- there are no government requirements for training in complementary medicine
- some complementary practitioners choose to join registering bodies which require certain levels of training, but there may be several organisations for any one therapy, all of them claiming to register practitioners
- for many therapies there is no agreement on the training needed to be a competent practitioner, and some practitioners are not registered with any organisation
- if a practitioner is not properly trained the treatment could injure you, or he or she may not spot a problem which should be brought to a doctor's attention.

Letters after a practitioner's name could mean that he or she has had many years of training *or* has been on little more than a weekend course. Consult the organisations listed in the address section to find out what the various qualifications actually mean. And if you want advice on finding practitioners in other therapies, or information on other registering bodies, you can get information from the British Complementary Medicine Association or the Institute of Complementary Medicine.†

Q *I've suffered from back trouble for several years and recently it's got worse. My GP doesn't seem able to help. I'd like to try an osteopath. Is it possible to be referred to an alternative therapist on the NHS?*

A It is for the individual GP to decide in the case of each individual patient whether an alternative therapist offers the most appropriate treatment for that patient's condition. Any GP may employ a complementary therapist to offer NHS treatment within his practice.

It is probable that osteopathy will soon be subject to statutory regulation, providing for the registration of approved practitioners with a general council. Steps have not yet been taken to regulate other complementary therapies in this way. In the meantime, if you want to try complementary ('alternative') medicine always check the following:

- is the practitioner registered with a governing body? (see above)
- what qualifications does the practitioner have, if any?
- what was the training that led to the qualifications?
- how many years has he/she been practising?
- does he/she have professional indemnity insurance? Without it you might not be able to get any compensation if the practitioner is negligent (see pp. 141–2).

Once you have established whether the practitioner belongs to a registering body, check whether that body is professionally managed by asking if it has:

- a code of ethics specifying the professional conduct required of members
- disciplinary procedures for practitioners who break the code
- a complaints scheme for dissatisfied customers.

Q *Am I entitled to see a copy of my hospital records?*

A Yes. The Access to Health Records Act 1991 gives you a legal right to see your paper medical records (i.e. those not held on computer) written after November 1991. The Data Protection Act 1984 also gives you the legal right to see any records held on computer (p. 232). To get a copy you should write to the holder of the records – the health authority (health board in Scotland and Northern Ireland) for hospital records, your GP or dentist for non-hospital health records, for example. For records of private treatment, write to whoever it was that treated you.

Q *The doctor who treated my teenage son is refusing to let me see my son's medical records. As a parent, can I not insist?*

A No, you can only insist on seeing your own records. Children can normally see their own records, but a parent can see his or her child's records only with the child's consent, or, should the child be too young to give consent, if the holder thinks it is in the child's best interest to show the record to a parent.

Q *Three months ago I wrote asking to see my medical records. How long do I have to wait?*

A The record holder must give you access to your records within 40 days or, if fresh information has been recorded in the last 40 days (because you've been treated during that time, say), you must be shown the information within 21 days of your application. You can choose either to go and inspect them in person, or to be sent a copy. If your records have not arrived it may be easier to pay a visit.

Q *I don't think the records I saw were complete. Am I entitled to see* ***all*** *of my medical records?*

A No. Parts of the record can be withheld if the holder thinks seeing them would seriously harm your or another individual's physical or mental health.

Q *My GP let me view my medical records, but they refer back to records that were made several years ago. Am I entitled to request those earlier records too?*

A You have no legal right of access to information recorded before the start date of 1 November 1991 (p. 160), so you can only insist on seeing records made after that date. If your GP thinks that you need to see earlier records to make sense of those made subsequently, he may be persuaded to disclose them.

Q *Can I see health records written by other health professionals as well as my doctor?*

A Yes. As long as the records relate to you, you are legally entitled to see records held by a wide range of health professionals – dentists, opticians, pharmaceutical chemists, nurses, midwives, health visitors, chiropodists, dieticians, occupational therapists, orthoptists, physiotherapists, clinical psychologists, child psychotherapists, speech therapists, art or music therapists employed by a health service body, and scientists employed by a health service body as head of department. If you have any doubt whether you are entitled to see records held by a health professional, contact your local Community Health Council (Local Health Council in Scotland).

Q *My optician has charged me £20 to see my records. Do I have to pay?*

A If you ask for a copy of any paper record made within the last 40 days, this must be provided free of charge (p. 160). For older records the holder is entitled to charge up to £10 (the maximum charge is the same for access to computer records). You may also be charged if you have photocopies sent.

Q *I've just been shown my medical records, and there is an entry in them that is wrong. Should the holder alter the records?*

A If your medical records are incorrect, misleading or incomplete, you are entitled to apply to your GP for a correction to be made. If the GP thinks that the record is inaccurate he should correct it. If he disagrees with you and believes it is accurate, he should make a note in the records saying why you feel it is inaccurate. In either case he should send you a copy of the correction or note free of charge. If in doubt contact your local Community Health Council (local Health Council in Scotland, Health and Social Services Board in Northern Ireland).

CHAPTER 8

HOLIDAYS AND TRAVEL

HOLIDAYS are meant to be enjoyed but enjoyment is an extremely subjective concept. A noisy, sleepless night for one person is a lively evening in the hotel disco for someone else. Similarly, a pleasant, quiet hotel for some guests will seem deadly boring to others. The same can be said of most of the facilities provided by a typical tour operator; it all depends on your own personal tastes and, most important, your expectations.

But wherever we take our holidays and whatever their duration, holidays are a special treat for many of us, so we do not want anything to spoil them. When your booking is accepted by the hotel, tour operator or airline, a legally binding contract is made between you and the company providing the accommodation, holiday package, air transportation or indeed any other travel arrangements. For most package holidays abroad, your contract is with the tour operator. The contract is *not* with the travel agent, although travel agents are under a legal obligation to do their job with reasonable skill and care, and you will have a claim if they do not (p. 171).

However, things can and do go wrong. The descriptions in the holiday brochure may not be accurate, the accommodation may not be of the standard you expected, you may not get the room with the view that you requested, the flight may be delayed or your luggage may not turn up. This chapter explains your rights in dealing with hotels, airlines and tour operators, in Britain and abroad, and answers the questions most frequently asked by consumers.

Q *What can I do to protect myself against problems arising when I book a holiday with a tour operator?*

A You cannot guarantee that problems won't crop up, but to reduce the risks as far as possible, follow these tips:

- make sure that any special requirements which you consider important (such as disabled access or en suite facilities) are noted on the confirmation invoice. If all it says is that these items are a 'special request' the tour operator may say you have no entitlement to such facilities (p. 171)
- consider paying at least part of the cost by credit card. Then you will have rights against the credit card company if something goes wrong, provided the holiday cost at least £100 (pp. 132–3 and 180). Make sure the payment is made to the tour operator, not to a travel agent
- choose a tour operator which is **bonded** – preferably ABTA-, IATA- or ATOL-bonded. This affords you greater protection if the company goes out of business
- always take out a good travel insurance policy at the time you book, so that if you or someone close to you becomes ill before the holiday, you are covered in the event of cancellation (pp. 212–13)
- make sure the policy provides adequate medical cover, especially if you are visiting a country where medical bills can be very high, such as the USA (pp. 212–13)
- take your policy with you, and if anything goes wrong whilst you are away read the conditions of the policy and make sure you comply with them, especially time limits
- if something goes wrong on your holiday, complain to the tour operator's rep as soon as possible. Ask to be moved if your accommodation is unacceptable (pp. 172–3)
- if possible, take photos or get the names and addresses of your fellow holidaymakers to help establish your allegations
- when you get home, write to the company's head office without delay, quoting your holiday reference number, and seek compensation (p. 172)
- be polite but firm in your dealings with the tour operator. Do not be deterred by its first letter, which is likely to refuse

you compensation. If you have a good legal case, it is worth being persistent

- take legal advice if you feel unsure of your legal position
- correspond with the company, sending your letters by recorded delivery, and keep copies
- if correspondence fails, consider either arbitration (pp. 173 and 239–42) or legal proceedings in your local county court (sheriff court in Scotland). Claims of £1,000 and less (£750 or less in Scotland) qualify for the quicker and cheaper small claims procedure (pp. 245–8).

Q *What is the difference between a* ***charter flight*** *and a* ***scheduled flight****?*

A For **charter flights** a tour operator will charter, or hire, a plane from an airline. The whole plane is usually reserved and it is up to the operator whether he fills all the seats. Whether you book a complete package holiday or just buy the flights from the tour operator, if things go wrong you need to direct your complaint to the relevant organisation. In the case of lost baggage your rights are against the airline (pp. 166–7 and 170–1). But if the tour operator changes your flight your claim is against the tour operator (check the booking conditions in the brochure first, however). See p. 170.

For **scheduled flights** it is the airline which sells the seats and the airline's sole responsibility to make sure your seats are available, and that you arrive on time (see below and pp. 167–8).

Q *Our flights to New York were fine but, coming back, we were held up by over 12 hours. Does the airline have to compensate us?*

A Under the Warsaw Convention, airlines are obliged to compensate you if they fail to get you to your destination within a reasonable time of your scheduled arrival. On long-haul flights, a 'reasonable' time is usually considered to be about six hours. But the strength of your claim depends on what causes the delay: if your flight was delayed due to an event outside the airline's control, such as bad weather, for example, you are unlikely to be able to claim substantial compensation. However, a reputable airline should offer you meals during any lengthy period of delay, and should keep you reasonably well informed about the delay. If you were delayed overnight, it ought to provide you with accommodation.

It is worth taking out **holiday insurance** which provides cover for flight delays, although the amounts provided are rarely high. Check your travel insurance policy, and if cover is provided make a claim as soon as possible (pp. 212–13).

Q *I recently flew to the USA, but my expensive suitcase went missing and was never returned to me. What can I claim against the airline, and what against my travel insurance company?*

A The Warsaw Convention (incorporated into English law by the Carriage by Air and Road Act 1979) governs the liability of airlines for luggage which is **lost, damaged or delayed** on all international flights (scheduled or charter). Compensation for lost luggage is very low because claims are settled according to weight rather than value of the case and contents. This limitation applies whether your case is full of expensive designer clothes or old T-shirts and jeans:

- at present you are entitled to a maximum of £13.62 per kilo of checked-in baggage, so for a standard baggage allowance of 20 kilograms the maximum claim would be £272.60
- to make a claim, you must report any loss or damage to the airline whilst you are still at the airport, by filling out a **Property Irregularity Report (PIR)**. Keep a copy of the PIR and your baggage stubs (which are attached to your tickets on check-in)
- you may also be able to claim from the airline for essential items such as toiletries and underwear (p. 167)
- the limits set by the Warsaw Convention are low, so it is important to see whether your travel insurance policy covers baggage problems. Many policies do provide cover for lost, damaged or delayed baggage. Again, make a claim on the policy as soon as possible, but remember that you cannot

claim twice over for the same loss, so the insurers will only agree to pay out for loss of damage which comes within the policy cover, and which is not adequately covered by the Warsaw Convention limits. Send a copy of the PIR with your luggage stubs to the insurance company.

Q *My luggage was delayed on my recent trip to Florida. It didn't arrive until four days into the holiday. I had to buy clothes and toiletries to keep me going. From whom should I claim the cost of these purchases?*

A As long as you reported the baggage missing and filled in a Property Irregularity Report (see above) before you left the airport, you should be entitled to claim against the airline for the essential items you had to buy to tide you over until your luggage arrived. In fact, many reputable airlines will make an interim payment. For a delay of between 12 and 24 hours an amount of up to £75 is normally acceptable, so don't rush out and replace all your clothes and jewellery – the baggage may turn up and you will lose out.

- if the airline will not pay up in advance, keep the receipts for your purchases and claim a refund later
- if the bag does not turn up later, the amount paid for the essentials will be deducted from your final compensation claim for the lost luggage of £13.62 per kilogram (p. 166)
- if the essential items cost you *more* than the maximum, look at your holiday insurance policy to see whether it provides cover for delayed baggage. If so, put in a claim.

Q *We booked* ***scheduled flights*** *to Spain. When we arrived at the airport, we were told that our flight was already full due to* ***over-booking****. We had to wait 14 hours before there was room on another flight. Can the airline do this?*

A Airlines deliberately overbook some scheduled flights to take account of what they call 'no shows' – people who have a ticket that is refundable or transferable and choose not to travel on the flight they have booked. Using previous flights as a guide, airlines try to match seats to passengers. When they get it wrong and too many passengers turn up, somebody has to be **bumped** off the flight:

- under European Community Regulations covering scheduled flights from European destinations, if you check in on time and are **bumped**, you will be entitled to a full refund or a seat on the next available flight to your destination. The airline must also offer you immediate cash compensation of £120 for flights up to 3,500 kilometres, and £240 for longer flights
- these amounts are halved if the airline can get you to your final destination within two hours (or four hours for flights over 3,500 kilometres) of your original scheduled arrival time
- you must be given a free telephone call to your destination, meals during your wait, and overnight accommodation if necessary
- as it was a scheduled flight your claim is against the airline.

Q *I saw an ad in a travel agent's window for two weeks in Venice for £160. When I went in they told me it was no longer available and offered the same holiday for £250. The ad is still there two weeks later. Can I insist on paying only the price advertised?*

A No. You cannot insist that any trader sells goods and services to you at the price marked (p. 24). But it is an offence knowingly to mislead consumers about the price of goods or services on offer. If an advertised holiday is no longer available, travel agents should remove all material promoting this holiday from their windows and not use it to entice customers into the shop. You should report the matter to the Trading Standards Department at the local council offices (in Northern Ireland, the Trading Standards branch of the Department for Economic Development†).

Q *I recently booked a holiday, but the tour operator is now demanding another £100. Can he do this?*

A Check the tour operator's booking conditions to see if they mention **surcharges**. Some brochures boast 'no-surcharge guarantees', which they must honour. Operators must explain what the surcharge is for (usually the reason is changes in exchange rates or increases in fuel prices), and may not impose one less than 30 days before your departure.

The tour operator should absorb increases up to two per cent of your holiday cost, but may pass on amounts above this. If the surcharge represents a 'significant' change in price (over ten per cent according to the ABTA code of conduct for its members) you are entitled to cancel, and are entitled to a full and prompt refund.

Q *When a holiday company goes bust what sort of protection do its customers have?*

A The protection you get when a tour operator or airline goes bust depends on the type of travel arrangements you made. Bonding schemes are financial guarantees intended to prevent you losing your money, or being stranded abroad, in the event of a travel agent, tour operator or airline going out of business. Look for one of the established bonding schemes:

- all members of ABTA (the Association of British Travel Agents†) have to lodge a bond guaranteeing their solvency. So if the tour operator or travel agent goes bust holiday-makers abroad will be brought back at no extra cost (in most cases at the end of their holiday) and people who have booked and paid for their holidays or flights but have not yet travelled will receive a full refund. But there are significant holes in the umbrella of cover that this offers to the holidaymaker. Even when you buy from an ABTA travel agent, you may be buying holiday components that are not covered by a bond: for example, there is no compulsory bonding for holidays within the UK, for scheduled flights, or for services such as car hire or hotel accommodation booked as part of an independent holiday
- tour operators who are members of AITO (Association of Independent Tour Operators†) are also covered by bonds to

protect against the insolvency of member companies. They also have a new scheme for settling customers' disputes with its members, run by an independent mediator

- if you book a **charter flight** the person selling the seats must be covered by an Air Travel Operator's Licence (ATOL)†, backed by a financial bond, but sometimes non-bonded travel agents sell ATOL-holders' holidays, and if the travel agent goes bust while holding your money you are not covered. Make sure your contract is with the ATOL-holder, whose name should be given, and licence number quoted, on your booking confirmation and invoice
- there is no ATOL-like scheme to protect you if a scheduled airline goes bust, so if you book a scheduled flight and the airline goes bust, you are unlikely to be refunded
- as an extra source of protection, if your flights or holiday cost more than £100 each, and you book using your credit card direct with the tour operator or airline, you can make your claim against the credit card company. But you must make sure your credit voucher is made out directly to the airline or tour operator, as appropriate (pp. 132–3).

Q *Our holiday plans were changed by the tour operator after we had booked. Can the tour operator do this?*

A Most booking conditions and the ABTA code let operators make changes they consider small without paying compensation (check the conditions in the brochure). But if the change is 'significant', the operator must tell you as soon as possible. If you are not happy, you can cancel and get a full refund, or opt for compensation (often on a scale set out in the brochure). **Major changes** include moving you to a different resort or altering your flight time by more than 12 hours. If it involves extra expense, such as booking into a hotel to catch an early-morning flight, accept **under protest** and **reserve your rights**. Then write to the operator for additional compensation (p. 172).

Q *Can I challenge the tour operator's decision to change my flight to an early-morning one?*

A If your tour operator changes your flight, or any other aspect of your holiday arrangements, check the booking conditions in the brochure: unless the conditions allow such changes, the tour operator is not entitled to make them. Most booking conditions, and the ABTA code of conduct, do allow minor changes to flight times.

Any attempt by the tour operator to limit your right to complain, or to make changes to your holiday arrangements after booking, must be fair and reasonable, otherwise you may have a claim under the Unfair Contract Terms Act 1977 (p. 72).

Q *I asked for a hotel room with a sea view. When I arrived I found the room overlooked the car park. What can I do?*

A It is not generally enough to fill in the 'special request' box on the booking form because the tour operator will only be agreeing to *try* to provide you with a room with a view. But if the operator knew of your requirement and guaranteed it before you booked, it will be part of the contract. So you must ensure that it was shown on your confirmation invoice. If it was guaranteed but was not provided, and things were not put right when you complained, claim compensation (p. 172–3).

Q *We booked a holiday via the travel agents in the high street. We also asked them to arrange car hire for the week, with the car being picked up on arrival. When we arrived the car hire had not been arranged. It was high season and so we had to pay more to hire the car. Can we claim this from the agent?*

A Even though you do not have a contract with the travel agents, they are legally obliged to perform their job competently. If they fail in this duty, and you suffer loss as a direct result of their negligence, you can claim compensation from them. The agents' duty is not only to pass on your holiday booking, but also to make all the other arrangements on your behalf. If it costs you more to hire the car on arrival (because of lack of availability etc.) than you paid by booking in advance, then you are entitled to recover the extra from the agents.

Q *We've just returned from a dreadful package holiday abroad. The first few days were a nightmare, but after complaining to the representative we enjoyed the rest. Our letter to the tour operator produced an offer of £50. But the holiday cost us £600. How do we assess the amount of compensation?*

A A tour operator is legally obliged to provide the type and quality of holiday booked, taking account of the price paid, the description in the brochure and any specific requirements. However, the booking conditions may allow for changes of hotel or resort (p. 170). The amount of compensation you can expect to receive following holiday dissatisfaction depends largely on how much the problems affected your enjoyment. Assessing disappointment is not an exact science, however, and if your claim has to go to court you may not be able to recover what you consider a reasonable sum.

None the less, there are three basic components of holiday compensation, so add together:

- **loss of value** – the difference between the value of the holiday you got and the one you paid for. If, for example, you were put into a cheaper hotel for the first week because the one you booked was full, work out what a week in the cheaper hotel would have cost. You must also take account of the cost of those parts of the holiday that were *not* affected by the problem, such as flights and sightseeing tours which were included in the price. If it was only the room that was unsatisfactory, and you were on the beach or out exploring most of the day, the effect will not have been so great. So, if three days out of a total of seven were totally ruined, or if there was a continuing problem which partially spoiled the whole of the holiday, the amount in this instance might be about two-thirds of the cost of the accommodation (after deducting the cost of flights, tours etc., as above)
- **out-of-pocket expenses** – the refund of any reasonable expenses you incurred as a result of the tour operator's breach

of contract, such as taxi fares incurred because the replacement hotel was farther away from the resort attractions

- **loss of enjoyment** – to compensate you for the disappointment and frustration of your holiday going wrong, and for the hassle involved in trying to sort it out. You must ask yourself whether the holiday was a complete disaster as a result of the tour operator's breach of contract, or OK apart from the unpleasantness of the room, plus the inconvenience of moving to the new hotel. This is the hardest part to assess in any claim as it is highly subjective, but the courts are allowing quite a reasonable level of compensation for this element.

You must complain to the representative when the problems arise, and write as soon as you return (pp. 178–9). If you do not get a satisfactory result, you can either take the tour operator to court, using the small claims procedure if the amount of your claim is below £1,000 (below £750 in Scotland), or, if the tour operator is a member of the Association of British Travel Agents† (most are), use ABTA's arbitration scheme. You cannot do both, and you cannot go to court later if you are unhappy with the ABTA arbitration (p. 240).

Q *The food at our hotel in Spain was very disappointing – lukewarm, burnt or tasteless. After the first week, we decided to eat out every night. Can we claim this cost from the tour operator?*

A In a package tour which includes meals, there may be a specific promise about food standards in the tour operator's brochure. If so, the tour operator will be in breach of contract if this promise is not kept. And even if no specific promises are made, there is an implied term in your contract with the tour operator that food should be of a reasonable standard, in accordance with the type and price of the holiday. But complaints about food are very subjective. You can certainly argue that your costs of eating out should be reimbursed, but you will have to prove that the food on offer was of a sufficiently poor quality to justify your decision to eat out. Photographic evidence or supportive evidence from fellow holidaymakers may help you win the argument, but cases about poor food are notoriously difficult to prove.

Q *The holiday brochure described our Italian villa as 'peaceful and secluded'. When we got there, it turned out to face directly on to a busy main road, with a big supermarket opposite. Do we have a valid complaint?*

A Yes. When you book a holiday from a tour operator's brochure, the Supply of Goods and Services Act 1982 says that the accommodation and facilities must be as represented in the brochure, in both the words and the pictures. The tour operator should notify you of any significant changes. If you do have any sort of complaint:

- tell the tour operator's representative immediately so that, if at all possible, the problem can be put right on the spot. The representative may be able to move you to a quieter hotel
- make sure your complaint is recorded in writing to show that you tried to get something done at the time, and ask for a copy of the complaint form
- note the names and addresses of other holidaymakers who can back up your complaint, and take photographs if you think they will be helpful in showing what was wrong
- as soon as you get home, write to the tour operator, setting out the ways in which the hotel failed to deliver what the brochure had led you to expect
- ask for compensation for disappointment and inconvenience, and for reimbursement of any additional expenses incurred (pp. 172–3)
- report the tour operator to the Trading Standards Department at the local council offices. Under the Trade Descriptions Act 1968 a tour operator who publishes a brochure which makes untrue representations is guilty of a criminal offence: this will not in itself earn you any compensation but it will encourage the company to be more accurate in future.

Q *We picked what the tour operators described in their brochure as a '3-star' hotel. But it was shabby and dilapidated and had no restaurant. We complained to the tour operators but they said that* they *had rated it as 3-star, and that was the end of the matter. Can they get away with this?*

A The problem with star ratings is that they vary between countries, even within the European Community. Therefore many tour operators choose to use their own rating system to assess the accommodation they offer. This means that a claim against the tour operator based on the star rating system alone is difficult to argue, unless you can prove that they failed to meet even their own criteria in assessing the accommodation.

However, you may still have a viable claim for compensation, based on the fact that the accommodation was not of a reasonable standard in view of the price paid and/or the descriptions given in the brochure (pp. 172–4).

Q *We booked a last-minute trip to the Greek islands – five days before departure – at a bargain price. We were not told where we would stay, only that it would be at a 2-star hotel. The hotel was extremely simple. There were no en suite facilities and our room was cramped and dingy. It didn't deserve even one star. The tour operator has come up with a letter from the Greek tourist authorities, assessing the hotel as 2-star. What can we do?*

A For a last-minute cheap booking your expectations must reasonably be lower than for a more expensive booking made in advance for a particular hotel on the basis of its brochure description. You cannot base your complaint against the tour operator on the question of the hotel's fitness for a 2-star rating, since it is clear that it was in fact locally rated as being 2-star. Nevertheless, you can argue that the hotel was not of an acceptable standard and that you should be compensated for your loss of enjoyment.

The European Community Package Travel Regulations 1992 state that brochures must include the following information:

- the type of accommodation, its location, rating or degree of comfort and the hotel's main features, and
- where the accommodation is to be provided within an EC member state, its approval or tourist classification under the rules of that member state. So the official tourist category must normally be given (although that does not prevent the tour operator from also using its own rating scheme).

But for last-minute bookings (made within 14 days of departure) an organiser or agent need not give full details to the client before the contract is made. This exemption has been included to enable telephone bookings and 'square deals' like your own to continue.

Q *We'd booked a 4-star hotel as part of our family package holiday to Spain. We chose the hotel for its numerous facilities and pools. When we got there the hotel was full. The tour operator took us to another hotel, but it was of a much lower standard with no children's facilities. We complained at the time, but nothing else was available. Did the tour operator have the right to do this?*

A Accommodation should not be overbooked. When a tour operator confirms your booking for a specific hotel, it is obliged to accommodate you there. If it does not, it is in breach of contract Under the Package Travel, Package Holidays and Package Tour Regulations 1992, and the ABTA code:

- if the operator knew about the overbooking before you set off on holiday, you should have been informed and given the option of cancelling or choosing another holiday
- if the problem only became apparent on your arrival, you should have been offered other accommodation of at least equivalent standard. If it is of a lower standard you are entitled to be brought home, or you may opt for compensation (pp. 172—3)
- check the booking conditions in the holiday brochure. These may contain a term which allows the tour operator to put you in a different hotel from the one booked. If it does, you can still insist on coming home, or claim compensation if the alternative was not of the same standard or had fewer facilities etc.

- if you were unhappy with the change of hotel, you were right to complain to the rep immediately and accept the cheaper hotel only **under protest**, ideally in writing (p. 188)
- when comparing your new accommodation with the original, consider convenience of location, quality of surroundings, facilities provided and any extra expense, such as increased travel costs to the beach, or car hire
- you can claim compensation for your loss of enjoyment and the disappointment and inconvenience caused (pp. 172–3).

Q *We booked our summer holiday at a hotel in Tenerife. When we got there, it was still being built. Only the wing we were staying in and one pool (out of three) were completed and only one of the three advertised restaurants was open for business. We asked to be moved, but it was high season and everywhere was full. What should we do?*

A The tour operator's brochure descriptions should be accurate, and it should warn you of any significant factors that could affect your holiday. In this case, the tour operator should definitely have warned you that the hotel was not completed, and arguably should have offered you an alternative hotel since the one offered was essentially not the accommodation you had chosen. You can certainly complain and seek compensation for the difference between the holiday you were promised and the holiday you actually got, as well as compensation for loss of enjoyment, disappointment and inconvenience (pp. 172–3).

Q *Our self-catering apartment was totally unacceptable. It was dirty, had no cutlery, and contained only one cooking ring and a tiny grill in the kitchen. The representative refused to move us, and now we are home the tour operator is refusing to pay us compensation on the grounds that it was a cheap holiday. Does it have the right to refuse?*

A However much or little you paid for your holiday, you are entitled to reasonable standards of cleanliness and adequate facilities. Obviously, your expectations of a holiday should be related to the type and price of package, and the brochure descriptions. But whatever the description your apartment should not have been dirty, and if it was advertised as self-catering there should have been enough suitable equipment for you to prepare meals.

Make sure you keep receipts for any expenses to support your claim. You were right to complain to the rep, but since she did not move you you can now claim compensation from the tour operator. If it refuses to offer compensation, consider ABTA arbitration or taking legal action under the small claims procedure of the county court, which can deal with to claims of up to £1,000 (£750 in Scotland) (pp. 172–3).

Q *The tour operator's representative for our holiday was rude, unhelpful and hardly ever available. Can we complain to the tour operator about her behaviour?*

A Yes. If a tour operator provides you with the services of a representative, he or she should be reasonably courteous and as helpful as is reasonably practicable, as well as being available to a reasonable extent. The services of the rep form part of your holiday contract, so if the rep fails to do his or her job properly you are entitled to compensation, based on an estimate of how much of your holiday it has affected. Make sure you follow up your complaint in writing (p. 174).

Q *We had no hot water for 11 out of the 14 days of our stay in a Portuguese hotel. The tour operator has refused to compensate us, saying that we should have complained to the rep at the time. Is this fatal to our claim?*

A You may have seriously damaged your right to compensation. The lack of hot water is undoubtedly a serious matter, and worthy of compensation. But there is a general duty on you to keep your losses to a minimum by complaining on the spot at the earliest possible opportunity. Had you complained at the time, the matter could quite possibly have been rectified by the rep, thus saving you several days of aggravation and saving the tour operator a substantial claim. If the tour operator did not know you had a problem, and could therefore not try to do something about it, the company cannot be held responsible for the full extent of your disappointment and distress. So even if you do succeed in getting some compensation from the operator, the amount is likely to be reduced to reflect your failure to complain at the time.

Q *I had problems with my holiday accommodation and filled in a complaint form at the time, but because of work commitments I didn't follow up my complaint for a fortnight after my return. The holiday company has pointed to a term in the booking conditions which says that complaints should be made in writing within seven days of return. Can the tour operator hold me to this?*

A Normally, the law allows you a period of six years from a breach of contract to bring a claim. Only after the six years has elapsed does it become too late to issue proceedings, so that effectively your claim is time-barred (pp. 20–1). In some circumstances a company can alter this general rule – as the tour operator has attempted to do – by putting its own time limit in its contractual conditions. This term attempts to limit your right to claim compensation, but by virtue of the Unfair Contract Terms Act 1977 such an attempt to limit or exclude liability will be valid only if it is fair and reasonable in all the circumstances (p. 72). It would ultimately be for a court to decide whether in the circumstances this seven-day time limit is reasonable.

As such a time limit for claims is quite common in holiday booking conditions, the tour operator may cite it as part of its defence and it is possible that the court will rule in the tour operator's favour. You can challenge the term (the time limit clause) as part of your claim for compensation (pp. 172–3). The moral of the story is to complain as early as possible in writing, and always to read through contractual conditions, preferably before a problem arises.

Q *My husband and I booked a holiday to Africa six months ago. We paid a 50 per cent deposit to the tour operator and were due to travel* *next month. We have just heard that the company is* ***insolvent*** *and no longer trading. The company was not ABTA-bonded, but we paid the deposit (£2,000) by credit card. Is there anything we can do?*

A Possibly. Under the European Community Package Travel Regulations 1992, *all* tour operators must be able to give you a refund, or bring you home from your holiday destination, if they cease trading. You should have been given details of the cover provided. If you have these details, contact the bonding company. However, measures taken to enforce the regulations are, as yet, totally inadequate, so there is still no guarantee of protection. Meanwhile, therefore:

- until it is shown that the new regulations work in practice, it is worth choosing a holiday company which is ABTA-, IATA- or ATOL-bonded, to maximise your protection should the company cease trading (pp. 169–70)
- if you have paid for at least part of your holiday by credit card, and things go wrong, under the Consumer Credit Act 1974 you can claim from the credit card company as well as the tour operator (though you cannot recover compensation from both). This is particularly valuable in cases where the supplier goes out of business as it means that you can pursue the credit card company for the return of your deposit (pp. 132–3). But:
  - your holiday must cost more than £100 per person
  - the credit card slip must have been made out to the tour operator, not the travel agent
  - debit cards, charge cards and most gold cards do not offer this protection.

Q *I'm always being pestered by* ***timeshare*** *touts when on holiday. The idea seems so attractive, but there must be a catch. How can I protect myself if I go to one of the presentations?*

A Timeshare reps offer inducements to attend a presentation in the hope that you will be persuaded to make an on-the-spot financial commitment, often for many thousands of pounds. And it is even more enticing when you are in a hot and sunny country away from home. Whether you are at home or abroad, follow these guidelines:

- do not go along unless you're really interested in buying
- be prepared for a long, hard sell
- **never sign anything** on the day – even if you are offered a large 'today only' discount
- always ask for copies of all the documentation – brochures, plans, terms and conditions, finance agreements – so that you can take them away and think them over after taking advice
- if you are interested in a timeshare, do some research among resale agencies to find out how easy or costly it would be to resell your timeshare later – you may find that resale agencies offer more competitive prices than developers on the spot
- if you are buying a timeshare abroad, or even one that says it is not governed by English or Scottish law, be very careful. Your rights, should anything go wrong, will be governed by the law of the country stated, so you would need to find a lawyer in that country to help you, which could prove extremely inconvenient and expensive
- if the timeshare contract is made in the UK, the Timeshare Act 1992 gives customers a right to cancel the contract (p. 19 and below) within 14 days. But with any other timeshare agreement, once you have signed you are bound by the terms and conditions.

Q *I attended a timeshare presentation and signed an agreement for two weeks at a development in Wales. I realise how foolish I was. Is it too late to cancel?*

A There are some golden rules to follow if you attend a timeshare presentation or are offered a timeshare agreement (see above). The Timeshare Act 1992 provides for a 14-day (minimum) cooling-off period in timeshare contracts provided that *either*:

- the contract is signed by either party within the UK, *or*
- where the contract is subject to the laws of the UK.

Before you make the agreement, the timeshare company must give you a notice of the right to cancel the contract at any time during the cooling-off period. It is a criminal offence for the timeshare company not to do this. Furthermore:

- a cancellation form should be attached to the notice setting out your cancellation rights
- if you cancel during the cooling-off period, you are entitled to recover any money you have paid under the contract
- the same cooling-off period applies in the case of most timeshare credit agreements in which credit is offered to pay for the timeshare, although it is not a criminal offence if the company fails to hand over a notice of your rights to cancel a timeshare credit agreement.

If you have any problems relating to timeshare, contact your local Trading Standards Department or the Timeshare Council†, the trade association which represents many British timeshare companies.

Q *Our hotel in Tunisia was very pleasant, with good food and facilities, but our holiday was marred by the building work going on across the road – a massive new apartment complex was under construction. The work started at 5 a.m. every day and we could not sit on our balcony due to the noise and dust. The tour operator is refusing to compensate us for this, claiming that it is not responsible for circumstances outside its direct control. What can we do?*

A The tour operator may be right. But you would certainly be entitled to compensation for the loss of enjoyment (and sleep!) if (pp. 172–3):

- the building work was going on within the hotel itself, in which case you could reasonably have expected at least to have been warned in advance and to have been offered an alternative hotel if the disruption to your holiday would be great
- this new complex had been under construction for some considerable time before your holiday, in which case you could argue that the tour operator, via its rep, ought to have

known about the proximity of the work and should at least have warned you.

Q *Our holiday was spoiled by the group of loud holidaymakers in the next apartment. They played their ghetto-blasters from 1 a.m. till dawn every night for a week. We complained to the rep after the first occasion, but he was only able to find us somewhere to move after the first week of our fortnight's holiday had gone by. Shouldn't the tour operator compensate us?*

A The tour operator is not liable for the activities of other guests, even those who are its own clients. However, assuming that alternative accommodation was available somewhere in the resort at an earlier stage than one week into your holiday, you could argue that the company should have responded positively to your complaint much earlier and should have moved you in the first couple of days. In addition, if the troublesome party was travelling with your tour operator, it would have been reasonable for the rep at least to have asked them to pipe down. It is worth your trying to obtain compensation for the poor quality of the first week's holiday on this basis. However, you don't have a watertight case.

Q *After booking a room in a Brighton hotel I had to cancel. I told the hotelier immediately, but he kept my deposit and wrote asking for extra compensation. Is he entitled to this?*

A If a hotel accepts your booking (whether it is made by phone, letter or in person), you have made a binding contract whereby the hotel agrees to provide the accommodation for the specified dates at the agreed price, and you agree to pay for it. If you later back out, or fail to turn up, the hotel can keep your deposit to cover its administrative costs. The hotel must try to re-let your room, but if it cannot it may claim the profit it has lost from you, and this is likely to be a high proportion of the total price.

Q *While I was staying at a hotel my video camera was stolen from my room. Is the hotel liable?*

A Hotel owners owe you a duty of care and must look after your property while it is on their premises. They are liable for any loss and damage as long as it was not your fault (your claim would be unlikely to succeed if you left the camera clearly visible in a ground-floor room with the door and window unlocked). However, under the Hotel Proprietors Act 1956, providing the hotel owners display a notice at reception, they can limit their liability to £50 per item or £100 in total. They cannot rely on this limit if the loss was caused by the negligence of their staff, although you will have to prove such negligence to make a higher claim. Check whether you are covered for your loss on the all-risks section of your house contents policy.

Q *The cottage we stayed in in the Lake District was dirty, badly furnished and dilapidated. We had paid over £400 for the week, and had expected much better. When we complained, the tour company said we should take it up with the owner, since their small print says that they act only as agents for the proprietors. Whom should we sue?*

A Strictly, the wording of the booking conditions is conclusive, as it forms part of your contract and is binding upon both parties. Therefore, be prepared to pursue the matter with the proprietor. Whatever the contract says about ownership, however, the agents are responsible for the accuracy of brochures that they publish and could be liable for a breach of the Trade Descriptions Act 1968, so report any inaccuracies to the Trading Standards Department at the council offices local to the tour company.

Q *The hotel brochure promised floodlit tennis courts. When we arrived the lawns had been neglected, the nets were down and we couldn't play. Did we have any redress?*

A Under the Supply of Goods and Services Act 1982 a hotel must provide the advertised facilities. If it fails to you can claim compensation, or ask for an appropriate reduction from your bill in respect of the disappointment suffered, which will depend on the emphasis placed on the facilities by the hotel in the brochure and the amount you intended to use them (pp. 172–3). Keep receipts for any extra outgoings incurred to make up for the lack of tennis courts. Photographs of the court would also be useful. You should also report the matter to the Trading Standards Department local to the hotel, which may prosecute the hotel under the Trade Descriptions Act 1968.

Q *When I arrived at the hotel where I'd booked a weekend break, I was told that they had made a mistake and the hotel was full. The only other hotel in the area that had room for me was a more expensive one in the next town, so I'm out of pocket. What are my rights?*

A The hotel accepted your booking and was obliged to keep a room available for you. It is in breach of contract and liable to compensate you for the additional expenses arising out of that breach – the difference in cost between what you were expecting to pay and what you ended up having to pay in the more expensive hotel, plus any extra travelling costs. You should write first to the hotel manager explaining what happened, and enclosing copies of receipts for your additional expenditure (pp. 172–3).

Q *While I was in bed in my hotel room a section of the ceiling caved in. I was shaken and slightly injured, but it could have been worse. Can I claim for the shock and injuries?*

A Under the Occupiers' Liability Act 1957 hotel owners are responsible for the physical safety of their guests (pp. 227–9). You have a claim for compensation and would be wise to seek legal advice to have it properly assessed.

Q *When I called to book a room the hotel told me it would cost more if I wanted to pay by credit card. Is this legal?*

A Yes. **Dual pricing** has been legal since 1991, and some hoteliers have increased their charges to guests who pay by credit card in order to recover the commission they pay to the card company. But to be entitled to the increased charge hoteliers must draw it to your attention when you book and indicate it on the tariff displayed in the reception. If you were not informed, contact the Trading Standards Department at the council offices local to the hotel.

Q *My hotel room was shabby and dirty with soiled towels and grubby sheets. I refused to pay the whole bill, but then the hotel refused to let me remove my luggage until I settled up in full. Was the hotel within its rights to hold my luggage hostage like this?*

A Any hotel room, whatever its price, should be clean and safe and offer a reasonable standard of accommodation for the price paid. As yours failed to do so it is reasonable to seek a reduction in the bill. However, the hotel does have a right to hold on to your luggage until the bill is paid.

It is probably easier to pay up in full but give written notice that you are paying **under protest** and are reserving your right to seek compensation in the courts (p. 188).

CHAPTER 9

RESTAURANTS

HEALTH and **hygiene** are important issues in restaurants. What are your rights if the meal makes you ill, or if the food is not properly cooked? And whether it's called a '**tip**', '**optional gratuity**' or '**compulsory service charge**', are you legally obliged to pay extra for having your meal brought to your table? What if you book a table and don't turn up, or turn up and find there is no table for you? This chapter explains where you, the customer, stand.

Q *We recently had* ***appalling service*** *at a restaurant – the waiter was rude and took ages to serve us. We complained at the end of the meal but felt we were under pressure to pay the bill. Does this mean we can't get our money back?*

A Possibly, yes, although it is still worth writing to the manager of the restaurant to ask. You should always try to speak to the manager or head waiter at the time, and if you fail to reach an agreement you can deduct a suitable amount from the bill.

The bill is made up of two main parts – a charge for the food and drink, and a charge for the service (with VAT on top). If the food and drink are acceptable but the service is not of a reasonable standard, you can deduct a reasonable sum from that part of the bill, and leave your name and address with the restaurant (p. 193). It will then be up to them to claim against you for the rest if they do not agree with the deduction:

- if the service charge is **compulsory** and automatically **added** to your bill, you are legally obliged to pay it unless the service was unreasonable, in which case you can deduct all or part of that charge
- if the service charge is not added because the prices **include** service, again you are legally obliged to pay. But you can deduct a reasonable sum, say 15 per cent, from the total bill for the service element if it is not up to scratch
- if the service charge is not included and not added, and is entirely **optional** or **at your discretion**, there is no legal obligation on you to pay anything extra, so it is up to you to decide whether to tip and, if so, how much.

If you do decide to pay the bill inclusive of service in full, then you can pay **under protest** (put this in writing – on the back of the cheque, say) and write to the restaurant as soon as you can afterwards (p. 193). Make sure you keep a copy of the letter. By paying under protest you are keeping open the option of claiming the money back later, if necessary by taking the matter to the small claims court (pp. 245–8).

Q *We went to a local restaurant which had been recommended by friends. It was only when we sat down that we were able to check the prices and realised that everything was very expensive. Shouldn't information about prices be clearly displayed?*

A It is best to check prices before you sit down, and if you turn up without a booking you are within your rights to leave if you haven't ordered. However, if you have booked in advance but on arrival decide it is too expensive and leave, even if you haven't yet ordered, the restaurant may sue for loss of profit if it cannot re-fill the table (p. 189). If you are not sure you can afford it ask about the prices of the food and any extra charges, such as cover or service charges, before you book.

There are guidelines as to what information a restaurant or bar should give you before you make any commitment. If this information is not clearly displayed you should report the establishment to the Trading Standards Department at the local council offices:

- a restaurant must display prices on a menu at, or near, the entrance, so that you can see them before you sit down
- in a pub, the menu can be on or near the bar counter or at the table, depending on where you order the food
- all prices on the menus outside and inside a restaurant must **include VAT**
- the menu displayed at or near a restaurant entrance must also show any **service, cover** or **minimum charges** (p. 191).

Q *In a restaurant recently I was served chicken that wasn't properly cooked. The waitress took it away, but when it came back it was still almost raw and certainly inedible.*

A The Supply of Goods and Services Act 1982 (common law in Scotland) obliges restaurants to prepare food (and provide service) with reasonable skill and care: if they don't you are right to stop eating and tell the waiter. If you are unable to get things put right, you can deduct a reasonable sum from the bill – in this case, the cost of your chicken, for example – and refuse to pay some or all of the service charge if the service was not up to scratch (pp. 187–8). But you must pay for the food you did eat and the wine you drank, and the other parts of the meal which were all right. Alternatively you can pay the full bill **under protest** and effectively reserve your right to make a claim later (p. 188).

Q *We had booked a table for four but had to cancel because one of the party fell ill. The restaurant wants to charge us for the likely cost of our meal. Can it do this?*

A When you book a table, you are making a contract with the restaurant: it has to provide a table, and you have to turn up at or near the time booked. If you are very late – or don't turn up at all – the restaurant can claim reasonable compensation for its loss of business if it is unable to fill the table again. The restaurant must prove that it made reasonable efforts to fill the table to reduce its loss. If it does fill the table – because it is a very popular and busy restaurant, say – then it can't charge you.

Q *The restaurant asked for my credit card number when I booked over the phone. If I don't turn up, can it charge anything to my credit card account?*

A An increasing number of restaurants now ask for your credit card number when you book. They may then use it to deduct a sum to compensate them for loss should you fail to keep your booking. By giving the number over the phone, you may be authorising payment for the meal, or for compensation should you not arrive. And you may then find it harder to dispute the sum. If you do not want to leave your card number, try leaving your name and address as security instead: this shows good faith and the restaurant knows where to contact you to take the matter further.

Q *I had booked a table in advance for my mother's birthday, but when we arrived there was no table for us. It was such a disappointment. What are our rights?*

A When you book a table in advance, you make a contract with the restaurant and it is obliged to provide you with the table you have booked for the requisite number of people at the specified time. As there was no table for you, despite your booking, the restaurant was in breach of contract and you can claim a reasonable sum to cover any expenses you incur as a result, such as travel costs. You can also claim a reasonable sum as compensation for the disappointment and inconvenience suffered. The amount you claim depends on the importance to you of eating at that particular restaurant, whether it was a special occasion, and the trouble involved in making alternative last-minute arrangements.

Q *We went to a smart restaurant last week. The prices displayed outside said: 'Lunch – 3 courses – £12 all in.' Later we discovered that* *we would have to pay a* ***compulsory 15 per cent service charge*** *on top of the £12. Can the restaurant do this?*

A No. Any compulsory service charge that is automatically added to your bill must be displayed clearly on a menu at, or near, the entrance to the restaurant (pp. 188–9). If it was not on the menu and you were not informed at the time you made your order, then you can refuse to pay it as it does not form part of your contract with the restaurant. If it was displayed, you must pay it – unless the service was not of a reasonable standard for that type of restaurant (pp. 187–8).

By failing to mention the compulsory service charge, the restaurant risks prosecution for publishing misleading prices. You should tell the Trading Standards Department at the local council offices for the area where the restaurant is located.

Q *My lunchtime pot of tea set me back £5! It turned out that the restaurant had a* ***minimum charge*** *of £5 between 12 and 3 p.m. Could I have refused to pay the full £5?*

A Restaurants must display any **minimum** or **cover charges** as prominently as the prices of the food on the menu, at or near the entrance. If the minimum charge did not appear on the menu at all, and you were not told about it when you ordered your tea, you could have refused to pay it. Whether you can now claim it back depends on the conditions under which it was paid (see p. 188). If the minimum charge was not prominently displayed, contact the Trading Standards Department at the council offices local to the restaurant. The restaurant may be committing an offence for publishing misleading prices.

Q *We wanted a leisurely and relaxing meal, but this was not to be. The waiter brought each course before we had finished the last, and the coffee, dessert and bill all arrived at the same time. Was he within his rights to hurry us up like this?*

A You should be given a reasonable amount of time to finish your meal. This varies according to the type of restaurant and the price of the meal (you cannot expect to take as long in a burger bar as you would in an expensive restaurant). If you do feel you have been unreasonably hurried, and were not advised when you booked that the table would be needed for another sitting, complain about the bad service and deduct a sum from the service charge, or refuse to pay any service charge (pp. 187–8).

Q *We left our coats in the cloakroom at our local bistro. When we went to collect them both coats were gone. The owners say they are not responsible. Are they right?*

A When you leave your possessions in the care of a restaurant it is under a duty to take reasonable care of them. In law this situation is known as **bailment**. If your possessions were lost or damaged whilst in the restaurant's keeping it has to prove that it used reasonable care to prevent the loss or damage (p. 73). If it cannot prove this you are entitled to the value of the lost or damaged item.

If there was no clear notice in the restaurant excluding liability for loss or damage to customers' belongings, it is likely that you can hold the owners responsible. Even if they had such a notice, under the Unfair Contract Terms Act 1977 you may be able to challenge the notice as being unfair and unreasonable in all the circumstances. If a court finds such an exclusion or restriction clause unreasonable, it will be struck out (p. 72).

Q *The waiter was so clumsy that he spilled a bowlful of soup down my suit. Can I claim the cost of cleaning?*

A Yes. If you can prove that the waiter was **negligent** by failing to take reasonable care while serving you, the restaurant will be responsible for the cost of cleaning. And if the soup had been hot and scalded you, its liability would be much greater. Make sure you get evidence from witnesses and send the cleaning bill to the owner as soon as possible.

Q *We were most upset to discover pieces of bacon in a vegetarian salad which we ordered in a café. We did not eat it but the café insisted that as we had ordered the salad and it had been made for us we had to pay. We did pay as they threatened to call the police. It was all very nasty. Would I have been within my rights to leave without paying for the salad?*

A Yes, and as long as you paid for the food and drink you did eat, the police would have had no authority to get involved. It would only have been a matter for the police if you had gone to the café with no intention of paying for anything. You are entitled in these circumstances to complain and to refuse to pay for the dish. If you do pay, you should do so '**under protest**' so that you can still claim back the cost of the salad later (p. 188):

- descriptions of food and wine on the menu form part of your contract with the restaurant – 'home-made soup', for example, must be home-made, not canned or out of a packet
- under the Supply of Goods and Services Act 1982 (common law in Scotland) any food or drink you order should be as described. Your 'vegetarian' salad clearly wasn't
- if there is a genuine dispute, and the police are called, you should pay whatever you think is reasonable for anything else you did eat (the starter, drinks etc.) and deduct the cost of the disputed dish (p. 189). If you leave your name and address and show proof of identity the police cannot intervene as you are not committing any crime. It will then be up to the café to pursue you for the amount it says you owe
- a restaurant is misleading customers by not serving food (or drink) as described on the menu. The Trade Descriptions Act 1968 makes it a criminal offence to give a false description of food in menus or other promotional literature. So tell the local Trading Standards Department that the restaurant might be deliberately misleading customers.

Q *I had a meal recently to which had a 15 per cent service charge had been added. I was happy to pay this and used my credit card. I've now received my credit card statement which has a higher amount for the* *meal. I checked the voucher I signed and noticed that the total box had been left blank. It seems that the restaurant has filled in the total and added an extra charge after I signed it. Do I have to pay the extra?*

A No. This practice of leaving credit slips 'open' where service has already been charged is iniquitous because customers may fail to notice, as you did, or may feel morally obliged to add something extra. But under your contract with the restaurant you agreed to pay only the price shown on the bill and credit voucher you signed. Any extra would be unauthorised and the restaurant may not assume that you agree to pay more *after* you have signed:

- write immediately to the restaurant with a copy of the slip: the restaurant is legally obliged to reimburse you with the extra charged
- contact the credit card company straight away and send a copy of the credit slip you signed with the blank total. The company may agree to remove the extra charge from the statement and recover the amount from the restaurant on your behalf
- if need be you can take action against the restaurant under the small claims procedure in the county court (pp. 245–8) (sheriff court in Scotland).

Q *If I'm bothered by smokers at tables nearby, can I get the restaurant manager to stop them from smoking?*

A There is no legal obligation on restaurants to provide no-smoking areas. Normally it is at the manager's discretion whether or not to stop people smoking. However, if you specifically booked your table in the no-smoking area and other diners are smoking in that area the manager should ask them to stop or move them to a smokers' table. If not, you may be able to reduce the bill by a small amount for the effect the smoking had on your enjoyment of the meal. If there is no separate no-smoking area then you have no legal right to complain.

Q *A local wine bar refused to serve my sister, saying it would only take orders from a man. In the end I made the order to save embarrassment. But surely they weren't entitled to do this?*

A It is a criminal offence to discriminate against anyone in the supply of goods or services on the grounds of sex or race. This is clearly sex discrimination and as such is illegal. The wine bar can be prosecuted. Contact your local Trading Standards Department (at the council offices) and the Equal Opportunities Commission.†

Q *After eating at the local bistro, the whole family was ill for two days. The cause was obviously the food served at the bistro. Is there anything that we can do?*

A Yes. If your think the food you ate in the restaurant made you ill tell your doctor immediately. Although it can be difficult to pinpoint the cause of illness, since symptoms can take up to three days to appear, the fact that you were all ill after this particular meal makes it more obvious that the food was substandard.

You can claim compensation for your pain and suffering, and any loss of earnings and other expenses you incur as a result, including a refund of the cost of the meal. Tell your doctor and get a report on the cause of your illness.

The Food Safety Act 1990 makes it a criminal offence for a restaurant to serve food which is unfit for human consumption. You should also tell the local Environmental Health Department at the council offices for the area where the bistro is. The EHO can investigate the incident and the restaurant could be fined and forced to compensate you. The EHO can even close down the restaurant if it is found to be in a dirty condition.

CHAPTER 10

INSURANCE

WHILE you cannot prevent things happening by taking out insurance – possessions are stolen, accidents happen, whatever you do – proper and adequate insurance cover can soften the blow when problems arise.

It is important to decide what *you* want to insure and how much cover *you* need as opposed to what somebody wants to sell you. You may want to insure your home, its contents, your car, other specific possessions like a caravan or boat, your forthcoming holiday, yourself and your liabilities to others.

The insurance profession is highly regulated both by statute and by voluntary codes providing protection for the public. The right choice of insurance policy or scheme will depend on the circumstances of each individual case, so professional advice is essential. Whether you take advice from an insurance broker, an accountant, a solicitor or any other professional, it is preferable to choose an adviser who is personally recommended to you by a friend or colleague. It would be unwise to rely on someone who is not a member of one of the many professional associations in the insurance field.† If need be, take advice from more than one adviser.

All insurance policies have exclusions, so as well as checking that a policy offers the right level of cover, always insist that you see the full policy. You must tell the insurance company about *anything* that might affect its decision to insure you, even if the information is not specifically requested on the form (p. 202).

For claims on homes (buildings and contents), holidays, cars or private health insurance, this chapter explains the terms in frequent use and answers the most common queries on how to proceed, what hurdles you are likely to face, and whom to complain to in the event that you feel your claim is mishandled.

Q *I wish to make a claim on my insurance policy: what should I do?*

A First, obtain a **claim form** from your insurance company or your insurance broker without delay. Always check the terms of your policy for **time limits** within which claims must be reported or claim forms completed and make sure you comply with them. If you have doubts about whether to include information and/or certain items of claim, consult with your broker if you have one. In general, disclose everything that could possibly be relevant, and get the relevant **evidence** to back up any claim:

- you may need to show that a theft has been reported to the police, so get a police report or incident number from them
- if your luggage goes missing while you are travelling, fill in a 'property irregularity form' (pp. 166–7), and if you have to make emergency purchases, keep the receipts
- get medical evidence if your claim depends on this – a report from a doctor or specialist, for example. And if you are claiming for medical expenses, keep receipts for medication, etc.
- take photographs, and get statements from other witnesses to any event that may give rise to a claim.

Q *I've been arguing with my insurers for six months over my claim. Should I sue them?*

A An insurance contract is a contract like any other and you can take the company to court for breach of contract if it refuses your claim. If your claim is for over £1,000, the case would be heard in the county court or high court, which could be expensive, lengthy and risky. But there are some alternatives:

- if you are claiming £1,000 or less, use the **small claims procedure** (see pp. 245–8). You can pick up free leaflets from your local county court (sheriff court in Scotland). Even if your losses are for more than the small claims limit of £1,000 (£750 in Scotland), you are perfectly entitled to restrict the amount of your claim to that limit to take advantage of this informal and low-cost procedure
- if your insurers are part of the **Insurance Ombudsman Bureau** (IOB)† scheme your case can be looked at by an independent assessor who has the power to award up to £100,000 against the insurance company (£10,000 a year in permanent health insurance cases) (pp. 243–4)
- if your insurers are not members of the Ombudsman Scheme contact the **Personal Insurance Arbitration Service** (PIAS)† (see below). The arbitrator will look into the case and make a binding decision.

Q *Which is better in the event of a dispute over an insurance claim, the Insurance Ombudsman Bureau or the Personal Insurance Arbitration Service?*

A The IOB has two advantages over the PIAS. First, you do not need the consent of your insurers to go to the IOB but you do for the PIAS. Secondly, the IOB's decision is not binding on you, so you can still go to court afterwards if you are not satisfied (pp. 239–44). You have to bring your case before the IOB within six months of reaching a stalemate in your negotiations with the insurance company at Head Office level.

Q *By how much can the insurers increase the premium when I come to renew my policy?*

A As much as they like. Insurance contracts usually last for one year and every time you renew you make a new contract (although often on the same or similar standard terms each year). So at the date for renewal you can decide if you want to pay the premium, or accept any new terms the insurers may want to put into the agreement, or you can shop around for another company.

Q *Can I rely on the quote that I'm given by an insurer for cover?*

A If you accept the quote and pay your premium, a binding contract comes into existence so long as you have disclosed everything you should have (see p. 202). The insurer may not try to raise the premium after the event unless he has previously warned you that the quote is only provisional.

Q *The insurers say they want to send a* ***loss adjuster*** *round. How does this differ from a* ***loss assessor****?*

A **Loss adjusters** are independent professionals who are qualified to decide how much *insurers* should pay towards the cost of claims. For example, they may be called upon by your insurers to assess how much of the damage to a roof was done by a storm, and how much was due to poor condition in the first place.

Loss assessors specialise in negotiating the settlement of claims on behalf of *policyholders*. It is you, the insured, who pays the assessor (usually on a percentage basis). They are usually only necessary in complicated claims. The advantage of an assessor is that he will make sure the claim is properly prepared and dealt with quickly, and will be able to get values quickly for your damaged property, stolen jewellery etc.

Q *My insurance company is not paying my claim. They say I didn't take reasonable care to prevent the damage arising. What does* ***reasonable care*** *mean?*

A There is no fixed meaning, so it depends on the circumstances. In house buildings insurance, for example, it means that you've got to maintain the building to prevent avoidable accidents from happening – an insurance contract is not a maintenance contract, so wear and tear will usually be excluded. For contents insurance this means – among other things – that you must lock your doors when you go out. And if, for example, while on holiday you decide to lock your jewellery in the boot of the car and the jewellery is stolen, your claim might well succeed if you could show that you had considered the choices available and chosen what you thought best. You may, in this case, have decided that it would be unsafe to take your jewellery with you, and it might well be considered reasonable to have locked it in your boot; so as long as you can show that your decision was not 'reckless', it could be worth challenging the insurance company's refusal to pay (pp. 198–9).

Q *One of the clauses in my insurance policy seems very unfair. Can I challenge it?*

A Unfortunately not. Once the contract is agreed you are bound by all of the terms contained in it (see p. 18). In most contracts you make as a consumer, you can challenge certain terms which try to take away or limit your rights under the Unfair Contract Terms Act 1977 (see p. 72). Contracts of insurance are exempt from this Act, so you cannot have a clause in an insurance contract struck out as being unfair. But even if you are stuck with a 'get-out' term, it may be worth referring the matter to the Insurance Ombudsman Scheme† if the company is a member (pp. 199 and 243): often, the interpretation of a clause is crucial.

Q *I made a claim on my policy. The insurers have pointed to an exclusion clause, but I don't agree with their interpretation of it. The clause isn't entirely clear but I think I'm covered. Who's right?*

A It is up to insurers to make sure their policies are clear, and if they fail to do this they should bear the financial risk. A special legal principle, the **contra proferentem** rule, applies in cases like this. What this says is that where an exclusion clause in a standard form contract (which insurance policies always are) is ambiguous, that ambiguity must interpreted against the person who drew the contract up, and in the policyholder's favour. So the interpretation that favours you is the one that should prevail in this case. If the insurance company sticks to its own version, contact the Insurance Ombudsman Bureau† if the company is a member (pp. 199 and 243).

Q *My insurers say they won't meet my claim* and *they're going to declare my policy void because I didn't tell them about a minor conviction five years ago. Can they do this?*

A They probably can. A particular feature of insurance policies is that they are considered by the law to be contracts where the requirements of **utmost good faith** apply. So when you take out an insurance policy, you obviously have to answer truthfully all the questions you have been asked. Less obviously, you have got to tell the company about anything *not* asked which might possibly be relevant. If you do not the company can refuse to pay out. 'Relevant' means anything that could conceivably affect its decision to insure you, even if *you* do not regard it as relevant. And you are not only required to 'disclose' when you fill in the proposal form, but also when you confirm that you want to be covered and when you renew the policy. If you do not you could be guilty of making a **material non-disclosure** and your insurers always reserve the right to cancel the policy if this happens.

Q *What is the difference between third party cover, third party fire and theft, and fully comprehensive insurance?*

A **Third party cover** is the minimum cover for vehicle drivers required by the law. If you have no insurance you are committing a criminal offence by driving. Third party insurance covers you for any damage you cause to another person (the 'third party'), whether by injuring them or damaging their property. This includes not only other road users and pedestrians but also passengers in your own car. Any damage you or your car may suffer will not be covered.

Third party, fire and theft means that in addition to the basic third party cover you are also covered if your own car is stolen or destroyed by fire. Such a policy will not usually cover the contents of your car.

If you also want to cover accidental damage to your car or injury to yourself you will need **fully comprehensive** insurance. With this you also get cover for theft of car radios and cassette-players (often limited to a specific sum, see pp. 205–6), and cover for theft of personal possessions from your car; however, valuable items such as jewellery and cameras may be excluded from cover entirely, so always check your policy.

Q *Do I lose my* ***no-claims discount*** *if I have an accident but it is not my fault?*

A It all depends on how you seek to recover your losses:

- if you are comprehensively insured, you have the right to claim your own repair costs from your insurers. The advantage of doing so is that a claim against your own insurance policy will usually be paid more quickly. The main disadvantage of claiming on your own insurance is that to do so is likely to affect your no-claims discount (or 'bonus'), even though the accident was not your fault. This is because it is a **no-claims**, not a **no-blame**, discount. In some cases, claiming against your own policy may be the only practical option: for example, if the other driver is unknown or has no proper car insurance (pp. 206–7). If you know the identity of the other driver and you decide to claim for your repairs from your own insurers, you can try to recover your uninsured losses (such as your excess, loss of no-claims discount or transport costs while the car is off the road) from him or her
- if you are not comprehensively insured, or you simply decide to pursue the other driver for *all* your losses, including your repair bills, then your no-claims discount should not be

affected, as you are not making a claim. You are, however, under an obligation to notify your insurers of the accident

- traditionally, the large insurers have operated 'knock-for-knock' agreements between themselves. The effect of such an agreement is that in the event of an accident taking place between parties insured by the respective companies, the companies agree that each will meet its own policyholder's losses, regardless of fault. Although these schemes are now going out of vogue, if there is one in existence you may be put under pressure to agree settlement on these terms (see p. 207).

Q *What happens when insurers declare a car a* **write-off**, *and how can they be forced to increase their offer for the value?*

A If the garage estimate for the cost of repairs is more than about three-quarters of the value of the car, the insurance company may decide that the car is a **write-off**. This is because it is quite likely that when the garage starts repairs, it will find further damage, and a car that has been repaired after an accident will usually be worth less than it was before the accident. So you could end up with a car worth less than the amount spent to repair it.

If your insurance company decides to declare a car a write-off, it will pay the full value of the car and sell the wreck for scrap. The amount you are entitled to is the value of the car before the accident, i.e. the amount you would have to pay to buy an identical car in a private sale (second-hand car dealer prices will be higher than private sale prices). This may not be the amount you said it was worth when insuring it. Insurers simply use that as a guide.

When deciding the value of a written-off car, the insurer will start by looking in *Glass's Guide* to second-hand car prices. This is not available to the public but you can consult *Parker's*, a similar guide which is available in newsagents. To challenge the amount offered you will need proof that it is worth more. The following will all help to persuade the insurers:

- advertisements for similar models in newspapers
- a statement from a number of car dealers of its worth
- proof of modifications that would have added to its value.

The Institute of Automotive Engineer Assessors† will give you the name of a value assessor in your area. If you are a member of a motoring organisation such as the RAC or AA, either will help with your claim. But if the insurers will not budge you may have to take them to court or to the Insurance Ombudsman (pp. 243–8).

Q *Do I have to make a claim if I have a car accident?*

A No. If you want to preserve your no-claims discount and pay for the repairs yourself (or attempt to recover them from the other driver) you do not have to submit your claim to your insurers. Sometimes the cost of losing your no-claims discount is more than the cost of paying for repairs yourself. If so, you would be better off not claiming. However, you do have to inform your insurers that you have been in an accident. Send them a letter telling them what has happened, but make it crystal clear that it is for 'information only' and that you do not wish to make a claim. This should ensure that they do not make a knock-for-knock settlement without your knowledge (p. 207).

Q *Someone broke into my car whilst it was parked outside the house. As well as breaking a window they took my radio-cassette system. Is it worth claiming for this from my insurers?*

A It is not always advisable to make an insurance claim following this type of incident, even assuming you are comprehensively insured (p. 203). You should always report any incident involving your car to your insurers. But you are not obliged to make a claim for your resultant losses. Instead, look at your home contents insurance policy. You might find that this provides cover for your car radio/cassette-player. If you do claim on your motor policy, you may lose your no-claims discount, so you need to calculate whether it is worth doing so. It may be cheaper to replace the radio and the window yourself to protect your no-claims discount.

Q *Some of my losses aren't covered by my policy, such as car hire and the first £200 excess. Can I claim these back from anyone?*

A If the other driver involved in an accident with your vehicle was to blame, you can sue him for your **uninsured losses**. The most common of these are:

- your excess – any amount you have to pay for repairs
- cost of alternative transport while your car is off the road, so long as it is reasonable and justified (very few policies, if any, cover this)
- compensation for personal injury (most insurance policies pay out a small amount in the event of serious injury such as loss of limbs)
- loss of earnings
- loss in value of the car.

Start by writing to the other driver giving details of your uninsured losses and ask him to pass your claim on to his insurers. If he refuses to co-operate, you will have to take him to court. If the claim is for £1,000 or less (£750 in Scotland) you can use the small claims procedure (pp. 245–8). If you are successful and the courts make an award in your favour, but the other driver does not pay up, his insurance company *must* pay you.

Q *I was badly injured in a collision with another driver who was not insured. Is there any way I can get compensation without going to court?*

A If your injuries were due to the other driver's negligent driving, you are entitled to claim compensation through the courts. Even if he is not insured but you think he has the money to pay, this may be worth while. But if your claim is for more than the small claims limit of £1,000 (£750 in Scotland), taking a case to court can be very expensive, and there is a risk that the other driver may not be worth suing (p. 247). The **Motor Insurers' Bureau** (MIB)† was set up in 1946 to help people injured in road accidents who are having difficulty in obtaining the compensation to which they are entitled. All motor insurance companies are members of the MIB, which may meet a claim:

- for **personal injury** caused by an uninsured driver, whether or not the driver can be traced (this would cover, for example, a hit-and-run incident)
- for **damage to property** where the guilty driver is known but uninsured. You will have to pay first £185 of all property damage yourself, rather like an 'excess'.

Q *What does the insurance company mean when it says my claim will be dealt with on a* ***knock-for-knock*** *basis?*

A The so-called knock-for-knock agreements that exist between insurers mean that each company pays the expenses incurred by its own policyholder. If two people are involved in an accident and each holds a **comprehensive** policy with different insurers who are participants in a knock-for-knock scheme, each insurer pays for its own policyholder's damage, regardless of liability and blame. From the insurers' point of view, this avoids the cost that would be involved in arguing about liability (and in theory this allow premiums to be lower). But as far as a no-claims discount is concerned, the question of liability is relevant: if liability is clear and a recovery could have been made from the other insurance company had it not been for the knock-for-knock agreement, you can try to persuade your insurer to reinstate or preserve your no-claims discount. Evidence that you were not to blame will help (pp. 203–4).

But if liability is not clear, unless you show that the other party *is* to blame (by getting some payment, witness statements or other evidence of liability from the other driver) your insurers will reduce your no-claims discount after paying out under a knock-for-knock agreement. Where there is any doubt about who is liable, or where liability for the damage is clearly shared by both parties, your no-claims discount will be reduced in the ordinary way.

Q *The insurers' loss adjusters are reducing our claim to take account of the age of our stolen property. Can we argue about this?*

A Yes, but only if your policy stipulates that contents are covered on a '**new for old**' basis, which means you can go out and buy brand-new replacements. Many policies provide cover on an **indemnity** basis, i.e. to replace the lost item with an item of the same age and condition. Check your policy cover.

Q *Our neighbourhood is becoming a high-risk area for burglaries. Could the insurers decide to raise our premiums?*

A Insurers are always within their rights to raise the premium on renewal of a policy. Each year's renewal is a new contract and the offer of insurance can be made on any basis. The particular risks in your area are highly relevant to an offer of household insurance. But it is up to you to accept or reject as you see fit. If the amount seems too high, you will have to shop around for an alternative policy.

Q *The sofa forming part of my three-piece suite was completely ruined when my house was flooded. The two chairs were undamaged. We made a claim against our household insurance policy for a new three-piece suite, because the original style has been discontinued, but the insurers are only agreeing to replace the sofa. Are they within their rights?*

A As with any insurance case, much depends upon the written terms of your policy. But unless the policy specifically states that a three-piece suite should be seen as a single entity for insurance purposes, you are unlikely to be able to insist that the whole suite should be replaced. The insurance ombudsman† who deals with cases like yours takes the view that a policyholder should *not* be allowed to claim for a whole new suite when one item of it is damaged, or for the re-covering of the whole if one item is damaged and the material cannot be matched. This is worth bearing in mind if you decide to take your case to the ombudsman or to court.

Q *For what amount should I insure my house?*

A Most policies are geared to insuring you for the full cost of **rebuilding** the house rather than just its market value. You must ensure that it is insured to a sufficient value because if it is not any claim, even if it is not for complete rebuilding, will be *averaged*. This means the amount claimed under the policy will be reduced in proportion to the extent to which your house is under-insured.

The Association of British Insurers (ABI)† produces a pamphlet on insuring a house. Also, most insurers will supply a table based on the charts in this pamphlet, so ask your insurance company.

Q *Will index-linking guarantee that my house is always insured to a sufficient value?*

A Not necessarily. For example, if you have improved the house in any way, such as by extending it, this will increase the value in a way that is not reflected by simple index-linking. The best way to protect yourself is to check with the insurers on a regular basis that your house or flat is adequately insured for the full rebuilding cost.

Q *Without our knowledge, water was seeping into our cellar for a long period. Does this count as* ***flood damage****?*

A The risks covered by insurance policies are defined very precisely. In the case of flood, water seeping in like this does not come within the term. This will depend on what your policy says but it your property is unlikely to be covered: normally flooding is regarded as a relatively **sudden and substantial** influx of water. The damage may be excluded under the policy in any event because of your failure to maintain the property to a reasonable standard (pp. 200–1) as well as your failure to take necessary remedial steps to rectify the problem. The moral is that it pays to keep an eye on your property's general condition.

Q *We had* ***storm damage*** *but the insurers won't believe us. How can we persuade them?*

A You will have to prove that the property was damaged as a result of strong winds accompanied by rain. For this you should present evidence that there was a storm at the time that the damage occurred: the Meteorological Office† will be able to help you with this. In addition, it may help to have an independent expert opinion from a builder or a structural engineer confirming that the damage you have claimed for could only have been caused by a storm.

Q *My insurers say that my illness was a pre-existing condition and they won't pay for my treatment. Can I challenge them?*

A You can do this but you will need a report from a consultant or your GP supporting your claim. Unfortunately, this may not necessarily be enough to persuade your insurers if their expert says the opposite. There may be some connected illness in your past either which you disclosed but assumed was totally irrelevant to this particular claim, or a past condition or treatment which, if you failed to disclose it, could make your insurance policy invalid (p. 202).

Q *My doctor reckons my illness is covered by my private health insurance policy. Does this mean the insurers have to pay up?*

A Not necessarily. The insurers do not *have* to accept the recommendation of your doctor or consultant that the treatment is within the cover offered. They may get their own expert to examine you and base their decision on that. Your own doctor's opinion will help, but if the insurance company refuses your claim your only option will be to contact the Insurance Ombudsman† (although see p. 212), or the Personal Insurance Arbitration Service†, or to take the matter to court (pp. 199 and 245–8).

Q *Can I go to the ombudsman if I have a complaint about a private health insurer?*

A If the health insurer is a member of the Insurance Ombudsman scheme you can benefit from that service. However, most specialist private health insurers are not, although many subscribe to the Personal Insurance Arbitration Service (p. 199).

Q *I have been having treatment for the same illness for many years, and my private health insurance has been covering the cost. Now the insurers say my condition is a* ***chronic, long-term illness*** *and my policy does not cover me for this. Surely this can't be right?*

A Many policies do exclude treatment for conditions if they become chronic and in a sense the insurers are penalising you for turning out to be a bad risk. An insurance company can also insert exclusions for specific conditions when it renews the policy. If you have been receiving treatment and the insurance company decides to classify your condition as **long-term** or **incurable**:

- get evidence from your consultant that your illness is not incurable or long-term: for example, you could argue that each time you received treatment in the past the illness was 'cured' for a time, and that each flare-up is a separate and curable condition
- write, enclosing all your evidence, to the managing director of the insurance company

- note that most specialist health insurers are not part of the Insurance Ombudsman scheme. Instead, they belong to the Personal Insurance Arbitration Service (PIAS).† This is an inferior scheme for policyholders because they need the insurers' permission before a complaint can be heard; also, a PIAS decision is final, so the policyholder cannot go to court afterwards (p. 240)
- think about taking the claim to court instead of PIAS, especially if the amount of your claim is £1,000 or less (£750 in Scotland) (pp. 245–8) and can therefore be dealt with under the small claims procedure.

Q *What sort of cover should I look for in a holiday and travel insurance policy?*

A It is important that the level of cover offered by a policy is enough to meet your needs. The cover you should look for in a holiday policy includes the following:

- **for cancellation** This comes into operation as soon as the premium has been paid and should give you back everything you have paid out in advance. The minimum cover should be the full amount of your liability under the contract and should include cancellation in the event of (your) illness or death, or the illness or death of a close relative or business associate, or travelling companion; redundancy; jury service or being called as a witness in court; severe damage to your home by fire, flood, storm, burglary or other criminal acts against you which require you to stay at home
- **for curtailment** This covers you if you have to cut short your holiday for broadly the same reasons described under 'cancellation' above, or because of illness or accident while on holiday, and should also include the additional costs of earlier return travel
- **for medical expenses** This covers the possibility high medical bills for illness or an accident while abroad. The minimum you should look for is £250,000 in Europe and £1 million in the USA and the rest of the world

- **for belongings and money** This depends on how much you will be taking but in general a minimum of £1,500 is recommended to cover loss of, or damage to, your baggage and currency
- **for personal accident** A specified sum to be paid if as a result of an accident you should die, or lose a limb or an eye, or suffer permanent total disablement
- **for delays** In the event of your baggage being delayed you need minimum cover of £75 to buy emergency supplies. The delay usually has to be for 12 hours or more on the outward journey. Delayed departure should give you at least £20 after the first 12 hours' delay and the option to cancel and get a full refund of the holiday cost if you are delayed for more than 24 hours
- **for personal liability** This covers you if you have to pay compensation for accidentally injuring other people or damaging their property. Look for minimum cover of £1 million in Europe and the rest of the world, £2 million for the USA.

Q *When I was on a touring holiday I locked my camera in the glove compartment of my car while I went for a walk. The camera was stolen and the insurers are refusing to pay up. How can I get the money?*

A It is a general principle of insurance law, and it is often repeated in insurance policy conditions, that valuables are covered only if you took **reasonable care** of them – by keeping the jewellery, say, in a locked safe (pp. 200–1). There is no legal definition of what amounts to reasonable or due care, as it depends on all the circumstances, so you can certainly challenge the insurers' decision. Follow the procedures for making a claim (p. 198), and if the insurers still refuse to pay, consider the Insurance Ombudsman scheme, or the Personal Insurance Arbitration Scheme† (pp. 199 and 212).

Q *I booked a package holiday and filled in the booking form. When the confirmation invoice arrived I discovered that I'm being charged for holiday insurance. Do I have to pay this?*

A Usually you can choose whether or not to buy your tour operator's insurance, although the brochure and booking form do not always make it clear that you have a choice. But many booking forms use **negative option** selling. This means you will automatically be charged for insurance when you book unless you make it clear that you do not want it by deleting a word or phrase. So if you did not notice the 'option' and did not indicate that you did not want the tour operator's insurance, you will have to pay. Although this is unfair, it is perfectly legal. However, insurance obtained independently often provides better cover than that offered by tour operators, so shop around if you can.

CHAPTER 11

NEIGHBOURS

RELATIONS between neighbours are a rich source of dispute, and in these, unlike disputes over goods and services, it's often difficult to distance yourself from the cause of the problem – unless you move house. But be warned – what your neighbour does may annoy you, but may be perfectly reasonable and legal. So although there is some legal protection for you and your property, and it is possible to take formal legal action, it's always best to try a friendly approach first.

Before taking legal action try one of the many local mediation schemes available, which aim to resolve disputes through discussion (pp. 244–5). Mediation UK† will put you in touch with a scheme in your area. Alternatively, if the dispute is over boundaries, you may need to find a surveyor.

Q *Our neighbours often play music too loud. What rights do we have and can we force them to turn it down?*

A This depends on whether the noise is **unreasonable**. You are entitled to enjoy your property and can do whatever suits you, as long as you don't stop other people enjoying their property. The law calls an unreasonable disturbance of the enjoyment of property a **nuisance**. But just because *you* find the music a nuisance does not mean that the law is being broken. In flats and semi-detached houses some noise from neighbours in unavoidable. You have to put up with what is reasonable, and you yourself must behave reasonably. If you make a lot of noise in retaliation you could be just as guilty of nuisance. If you are unreasonably disturbed:

- don't assume your neighbours are aware that they're disturbing you, and try to sort it out on a friendly basis
- keep a detailed diary of each disturbance, noting the time, date and duration of the nuisance, and get other neighbours to write statements to back you up
- if the friendly approach doesn't work, send copies of your evidence to the Environmental Health Officers (EHO) at your local council. If they consider that your neighbour is causing a 'nuisance' they have the power to serve an **abatement** notice on the neighbour to prevent the nuisance continuing, or making the neighbour restrict it to certain days, or certain times. If this is not complied with, the neighbour can be fined up to £2,000
- it may sometimes be hard to persuade the EHO to take this action, but you can do it yourself. You will need to visit your local magistrates' court (sheriff court in Scotland) to ask for a 'nuisance order'. If you can persuade the court to grant one then the consequences are the same as above, so make sure you have evidence from other neighbours and your diary to support your case
- you can get an **injunction** in the county court (an 'interdict' in the sheriff court in Scotland) to prevent the noise continuing. The advantage of this over the magistrates' court process is that you can also claim compensation for the inconvenience you have suffered. But the process can be quite lengthy and expensive and any compensation is likely to be small.

Q *I work at night but can't sleep during the day because my next-door neighbours are noisy. Can I do anything?*

A Probably not. The law won't take into account your particular lifestyle if it differs from what is considered 'normal'. So, unfortunately, if the noise disturbs you only because you sleep during the day, and would not be considered a nuisance to someone who is awake at that time, you'll be unable to do much about it. The only answer may be to sleep in a quieter part of the house. But if the noise is severe enough to amount to a nuisance to anyone who is normally awake in the daytime, you will have a right at least to restrict the noise to more reasonable levels or to specific times of the day (p. 216). It is unlikely you will get the noise stopped altogether as a certain amount of noise is only to be expected during the day.

Q *We've repeatedly asked our neighbours to prune their tree. It hangs over the fence and the leaves block up our drain. As it is almost touching our house we're worried that it might damage the foundations. Can we prune it ourselves?*

A Trees certainly can cause damage to foundations. It is not so much that they cause direct physical damage, but rather that they take water from the soil, particularly clay, which then contracts and causes subsidence. The tree's owner is responsible for any damage caused, as long as it is proved that his or her tree was the cause. So if your foundations are damaged you may need expert evidence on the precise cause:

- you may well be covered for this damage by your house insurance policy. If you are, the simplest course is to make a claim under the policy, and let the insurers pursue the claim against your neighbour, or possibly against his insurance company
- chat with your neighbour – he may be persuaded to trim the whole tree, including the roots, so that it keeps its shape but stops being such a bother
- if a friendly word with the neighbour fails to do the trick, before you start cutting check with your local council whether the tree has a **preservation order** on it. If it does, and you prune it, you are committing an offence and could be fined. Also, if you live in a **conservation area** you must tell the council before you cut. It has six weeks to decide whether to put a preservation order on the tree
- if there's no such protection for the tree, you're entitled to cut off the roots and the branches at the point where they cross the boundary. You then have to offer them back to the

neighbour – just because they are on your land does not mean they belong to you. The same applies to tempting fruit that hangs over the fence. If the fruit has fallen into your garden the law assumes it has been abandoned by the neighbour, so it's yours. But don't be tempted to shake the branch!

Q *Do I have a 'right to light'?*

A If you find your garden plunged into darkness by the neighbour's new wall, or your garden becomes shaded by the trees next door, there may be little you can do. Not everyone has a **right to light**:

- if you have enjoyed a particular level of light for 20 uninterrupted years or more, you are entitled to keep a *reasonable* level of light for normal purposes – but you can't insist on getting the *same* amount of light as you have had in the past. The legal test is not 'how much light have I lost?' but 'how much light do I still have?'
- you can acquire a right to light to a particular window in your house, or a structure in your garden, like a greenhouse, but never to the garden itself, so if your garden has been cast into shade you can't complain
- you can complain only if an artificial structure, like another house or a wall, interferes with it – no complaint can be made when it is a natural obstacle like a tree that is in the way.

Q *The side wall of our house stands right on the boundary with our neighbour. We need to do some urgent repairs to the wall but we need to go into his garden to do the work. The neighbour has refused permission, and we don't want to trespass. What should we do?*

A Strictly speaking you cannot go on to the land without the neighbour's permission (p. 219). However, under the Access to Neighbouring Land Act 1992, where the neighbour has refused permission, you can apply to your local county court (sheriff court in Scotland) for an order giving access to do the work:

- you must identify the land, state why access is necessary, when it will start and its likely duration
- you will have to convince the court that the work you have in mind is necessary to maintain your property and that the only way to get it done is to go next door. This includes work to the house, drains, hedges, trees and ditches
- in return for access, you will have to make good any damage to the neighbour's land and perhaps pay a small sum of money for access or compensation
- you may have to take out insurance to cover injury to persons or damage to property during the proposed work.

Q *I have bonfires most weekends to get rid of garden rubbish. My neighbour objects to this. Am I not allowed to carry on with this perfectly reasonable activity?*

A In general there are no restrictions on when bonfires can be lit, but check with your local council for any by-laws. Whether it's a **nuisance** depends on whether the fires interfere with your neighbour's enjoyment of his property, and whether they're more frequent than an ordinary person would consider reasonable. Occasional bonfires, even the ritual burning of the Sunday papers, unwanted mail and circulars once a week, may not constitute nuisance. But listen to the objections and try to make an acceptable arrangement. Your neighbour is entitled to complain to the local Environmental Health Department or to the magistrates' court (sheriff court in Scotland) and you may receive an 'abatement' notice. If this happens you must comply with the notice or risk a £2,000 fine (pp. 215–16).

Q *Can I stop people coming on to my land?*

A Yes. Each time people come on to your land without your permission, they are **trespassing**. Some people have implied permission to be there for particular purposes – to call at the front door, to deliver the post and milk, or to collect the refuse. So, unless you specifically exclude everybody, by sign or fortifications, people can cross the boundary within certain limits. But even if those people start wandering over your garden or into your garage, say, or they stay after being asked to leave, they have gone too far.

You can build fences around your home. The general rule is that you do not need any planning permission to build your own fence up to 2 metres high where it joins your neighbour's land (1 metre where it joins a public road, path or pavement) – check with the planning department at your local council first, and also look at your deeds to ensure there are no 'restrictive covenants' preventing the building of fences. Here are some guidelines:

- if a friendly word doesn't stop unwanted visitors you're perfectly entitled to bar their way, by planting a hedge or putting up a fence, or by standing in the way!
- think carefully about what obstacles you put up. You can't set a trap (certainly not one that will harm trespassers or keep them against their will). Nor should you use barbed wire or broken glass around a domestic property because it may injure unsuspecting people, particularly children
- you must always be prepared for trespassers, especially young ones. Children cannot always read warning signs and may not realise how dangerous things like barbed wire are. If they injure themselves, even if they are not meant to be on your land, you could be responsible. The danger comes when you put something unnatural on your land
- when faced with repeated trespass, by a neighbour, say, you can apply to the county court for an injunction (an interdict from the sheriff court in Scotland). If the intruder has caused damage, you can claim compensation as well, but unless the damage is serious this is unlikely to be much. Keep a diary of each trespass and evidence of the damage caused
- trees can trespass (p. 217) and so can animals (p. 223): their owner, in each case, is responsible for them.

Q *My neighbour is building an extension. The noise of drills and cement mixers is intolerable. Can I stop the builders causing this nuisance?*

A Whether noise constitutes nuisance in law depends on the type of work, the methods used, and what steps have been taken to ensure that any annoyance to neighbours is kept to a reasonable level. An interference which is temporary may well escape being a nuisance on that ground. However, there always has to be a degree of give and take, and with construction work you will have to expect a certain amount of disturbance. But you don't have to put up with it 18 hours a day, seven days a week – it all depends on what is unreasonable (p. 215):

- check with the local authority planning department: it may well have imposed restrictions on the hours during which construction can take place, and the machinery to be used
- under the Control of Pollution Act 1974, a local authority has power to serve a notice on property owners restricting hours of working and the type of machinery used, to cut down the disturbance
- if all else fails, and the annoyance is excessive and happens at unreasonable times, you can seek an injunction in the civil courts – and you can ask for compensation (p. 216).

Q *What can I do about my neighbour's garden? It looks like a municipal dump.*

A There is no law which says people have to be tidy. So if the view from your window is spoilt by the state of your neighbour's garden, and a friendly word has no effect, there may be nothing you can do. But the local council has powers under the Town and Country Planning Act 1990 to clean up the areas it controls. It may consider a highly visible mess to be ruining the **amenity** and beauty of the neighbourhood – in which case you may even persuade the council to remove the rubbish (for which the neighbour will have to pay).

The law will certainly help if rats and mice are infesting the rubbish. Under the Prevention of Damage by Pests Act 1949, the council can serve a notice demanding its removal, and your neighbour could face a fine if he does not comply. Your local authority officials, such as the Environmental Health Officers, can enter a home if they suspect that there has been a breach of public health regulations, or of by-laws on sanitation. They also have the power to inspect houses for pests such as mice and rats, having given 24 hours' notice. If the householder does not admit them they can apply for a warrant authorising entry by force.

Q *I was walking across a field when the farmer pointed to a sign saying 'Trespassers will be prosecuted' and shouted that he would call the police if I didn't get off. I often walk that way. Can I be prosecuted?*

A No. Contrary to popular belief, trespassers cannot be prosecuted. It is not a criminal offence merely to walk on somebody else's land. If it is a public right of way you are entitled to be there, as long as you stick to the footpath. But if it is private land with no established right of way, the landowner can apply to a court for an injunction to prevent you walking that way again. If you ignore that you will be in contempt of court, and the penalty for contempt is gaol. You may also have to pay compensation for any damage you cause, although if you have been careful this is unlikely to be much (p. 220). Only if you are deliberately causing damage can the police intervene and prosecute for criminal damage.

Q *I have a* ***right of way*** *along a narrow passageway to my back garden. The lady down the street keeps parking her car there and blocking it. What can I do?*

A You have what is known in law as an **easement** ('servitude' in Scotland) – a right to use someone else's land for a specified purpose. This will be set out in the deeds of the property. And many other people may also have separate easements over the same land. Your neighbour probably has a specific right to park there. She may even own the land. But she cannot stop you exercising your right of way.

If the obstruction is serious and your neighbour refuses to move her car, you can apply to the county court for an injunction (or, in Scotland, to the sheriff court for an interdict) to prevent her parking there. Anyone who ignores a court order is in contempt of court and risks ending up in gaol.

Q *My neighbours have several dogs which are always making a noise and running in and out of my garden. One of them is particularly nasty and has already bitten me. Can I make my neighbours control their pets?*

A Noise problems can be dealt with effectively if they amount to **nuisance** (pp. 215–16). But you cannot easily prevent the dogs entering your garden, other than by putting up your own fence or wall (pp. 219–20); nor can you force your neighbours to fence in their animals. Dogs and cats are expected to roam, and, unlike most humans, they do not respect boundaries – a fence to a dog is something to jump over or tunnel under, and cats can climb just about anything.

If a dog injures you, or damages your property, you are entitled to compensation under the Animals Act 1971 if you can *prove* that your neighbour has:

- not taken **reasonable steps** to restrain the dog, or
- has **actively encouraged** the dog.

It would be difficult to prove that your neighbour has actively encouraged the dog to come into your garden or to bite you. And as there's no duty on your neighbour to fence the dog in, and dogs are expected to roam, there is no easy answer to what 'reasonable steps' to restrain the dog would be. But if any harm caused is due to the nasty or dangerous character of that particular dog, or breed of dog, and the neighbour knows it may cause harm not likely to be caused by an 'average' dog, the neighbour is legally responsible.

Under the Dangerous Dogs Act 1991, if you can show a dog is 'dangerous' and 'out of control', a magistrates' court can order that it be kept under proper control – for example, muzzled, kept on a leash, neutered or destroyed. The owner may also have to pay a fine of up to £2,000. One bite could be enough for a dog to be classed as dangerous. The court could also disqualify the owner from having a dog for a specified time.

To ignore this would mean another fine of up to £2,000. Contact the police or the RSPCA† for action.

Q *How do I know which of the fences around my garden are mine and which belong to my neighbour?*

A The first and obvious rule about fences is that the person who puts up the fence owns it. But this is not always clear. In many cases the matter can be settled by looking at the deeds relating to the property, which can be consulted at H.M. Land Registry if the land is registered, or at the lease. Often, you will see on the plan that there is a small 'T' marked against the various boundaries. The convention is that the fence belongs to the owner of the property on the side on which the 'T' is drawn. However, the T mark by itself has no meaning, and it is important to check its definition in the body of the deed.

If it is not clear from the deeds, then see if there is any record of who actually put up the fence or whether anyone in the neighbourhood can recall it. If there's no such evidence the law makes a presumption, although this is not a firm rule and evidence to the contrary would change it. The presumption is that a close-boarded fence with supporting posts every so often, or a timber lap fence or chain link fence built similarly, are assumed to belong to the owner on whose side the supports are. The reason for this is the presumption that anyone putting up a fence would erect it as near his boundary as he could, so that he fenced in the maximum amount of land. But if the fence line ran along the boundary, and the posts projected on the neighbour's side, the posts would be trespassing (pp. 219–20). The best the person putting up the fence can do is to run the fence along the boundary and have the projections on his side. The same applies to a garden wall which has supporting pillars every so often.

Q *I'm sure one of my boundary fences is in the wrong place, giving me more land than I should have. Has that extra land become mine?*

A It may have become yours through what the law calls **adverse possession** (sometimes 'squatters' rights'). If you are claiming land which is not legally yours, and the true owner has done nothing about it for 12 years or more, it becomes yours, as long as you have been using it without the real owner's permission. During that period, you have to act as if the land is yours: the most obvious proof that you are acting as if you were the owner is the fact that it is fenced in so that only you can be the owner and the 'true' owner is kept out. Your claim exists even if the fencing was put up (or moved!) by a previous owner of your land; the effect of the transfer is cumulative, so when you bought the land you got the benefit of the previous owner's annexation and the 12 years includes the whole period since the fence was put up – not just your own period of possession.

Once the 12 years have gone by, the land becomes yours, and the fact that the deeds may tell a different story (p. 224) does not alter that. If it is registered land you can get the deeds changed to include the extra land.

A word of caution when consulting a registered land certificate to decide where boundaries run: registrations are made with what are called 'general boundaries', which are approximate boundaries. So, although the Land Registry has very good plans, their accuracy is not guaranteed from this point of view except to about the nearest foot or two.

CHAPTER 12

OTHER PROBLEMS

THIS chapter deals with a variety of everyday problems which pose legal questions. Accidents, for example, will happen – but if they are somebody else's fault, what can you do? And can anything be done to stem the rising tide of junk mail? What should you do if you are sent goods you never ordered, or if you are worried about personal data being held on computer? That contract you just signed may not seem such a good idea in the cold light of day, but can you change your mind? And in what circumstances may your home be entered without permission? Your rights are explained in the pages that follow.

Q *The girl who delivers our papers fell off her bike and hurt herself on our drive. Are we responsible?*

A Every 'occupier' of property has a duty to ensure that it is reasonably safe for the people who are there by permission or who have a right to be there – so your duty does not just extend to your friends and relations, but also to people delivering post and milk, collecting rubbish etc. This is laid down in the Occupiers' Liability Act 1957 (in Scotland the Occupiers' Liability [Scotland] Act 1960). That does not mean that every time someone hurts himself you will be liable. Liability will depend on how the accident happened:

- if you have neglected repairs to your drive which you know or should have known were needed, then it is your fault

- if you had done all you could reasonably be expected to have done, then you are not to blame
- visitors are obliged to take reasonable care themselves. If they contribute to the injury by their own lack of care, the compensation you may have to pay will be reduced. For example, if there was an enormous pothole that was obvious to any visitor, or if you put up a warning sign, say, a court could decide that you were 70 per cent responsible for the injury, and the visitor was 30 per cent responsible
- you must expect children to be less careful than adults, particularly if you know children are likely to use the drive, or if you have 'allurements' on your premises, for example, a pond, pets, or anything that is likely to attract children. So, if a child is injured on your land because it was not reasonably safe, it will be difficult to argue that he or she contributed to the injury
- if you are responsible you risk having to pay compensation for the time the injured person has to take off work, and the pain and suffering caused (which could be substantial)
- check to see whether your household insurance provides cover for this kind of 'third party liability'.

Q *While shopping in a supermarket I slipped on some yoghurt somebody had spilled on the floor. I broke my wrist and tore my coat as I fell. The manageress told me that the supermarket is not responsible as the yoghurt was dropped by a customer. Is that correct?*

A Perhaps. It depends on whether you can prove that the supermarket was negligent. The Occupiers' Liability Act 1957 (in Scotland the Occupiers' Liability [Scotland] Act 1960) places on **occupiers** – people in control of premises – a legal duty to take reasonable care to see that visitors coming on to their land (and to a lesser extent trespassers – p. 220) are reasonably safe. But if the yoghurt had just been dropped by a customer and the supermarket staff were unaware of it, you would not be able to prove that the supermarket had been negligent; if, on the other hand, the staff had seen the breakage or been told of it by a customer and had failed to take immediate action, the shop could be held responsible.

Your compensation would cover the pain and suffering caused by your **personal injury**, plus the cost of repairing your coat. You may also get compensation for any loss of earnings that result.

Q *I knocked a teapot off a shelf as I was walking through a shop. The assistant pointed out a notice which read: 'All breakages must be paid for.' I hadn't seen the notice and I don't consider that the accident was my fault as the shelves were piled high and I stumbled on a loose floorboard. I didn't pay at the time but left my name and address. I've now received a letter demanding £60. Do I have to pay?*

A Notices like this are misleading as you only have to pay for breakages if the shop can prove that you were negligent or careless, and not otherwise, so it makes no difference whether you saw the sign.

Much will turn on the layout of the shop. If the display shelves were too close together, so that it would be difficult for the ordinary shopper to walk along the aisles without knocking off a piece of china, say, then you can argue that the accident occurred in spite of your being careful. Or it may be that the spout of the teapot was sticking out over the edge of the shelf. If, on the other hand, you were rushing through the shop with your clothes flapping, the responsibility would be yours. Often it is a bit of each – perhaps you were partly to blame, but a contributory factor was the loose floorboard, or the layout of the display shelving in the shop. If so, you would have to pay part of the price, taking into account the contributory negligence of the shop. You were absolutely right to leave your name and address and leave it up to the shop to contact you. Alternatively, had you felt under great pressure to pay up, you could have paid **under protest** and written this on the back of the cheque. You could then have tried to claim the money (or part of it) back later (p. 188).

Q *Last winter my car was showered with grit from the council's gritting lorry. The paintwork was badly damaged, but the council* *has refused to accept liability for its employees. Am I entitled to compensation?*

A If an employee, acting in the course of his or her employment, causes you to suffer damage or loss, you are entitled to claim compensation from that person's employer, in this case the local council. As long as you can prove that the damage was in fact caused by a gritting lorry driven by a council employee, you should write to the council with details of the damage caused. If it will not pay up you will have to consider either making a claim on your own car insurance, or taking the claim to court (pp. 203–5 and 245–8).

Q *I parked my car in the street next to some scaffolding. When I returned paint had been splattered over the roof and bonnet. I complained to the workmen, who told me that I shouldn't have parked so near the work site. Is this right?*

A If you are injured or your property damaged as a result of the carelessness of others, you can claim compensation:

- the workmen owed you and other passers-by a duty of care not to cause any damage when carrying out their work – for example, they should have taken precautions to shield pedestrians and road-users from paint and débris
- your claim will be against the company or business which employed the workmen, rather than the individual workmen, so you should address your written complaint to the managing director or partners as appropriate
- the trader could argue that you **contributed** to the damage by parking so close to the work, particularly if there were parking restrictions or other warning notices in the area of the scaffolding. If this is the case then any compensation you are entitled to will be reduced to reflect your own lack of care: a court would be able to divide up responsibility accordingly. If the repairs to your car cost £600, say, the court may decide that you were 50 per cent to blame, and you would only recover £300.

Q *I tripped and fell on the pavement and ruined a good pair of shoes. Luckily I was only shaken. Can I claim for the shoes?*

A If you can prove that the pavement needed repair and had not been properly maintained by the local authority, you will have a claim for negligence. There are no hard and fast rules as to what condition the pavement has to be in to give rise to liability, but as a rule of thumb, if paving slabs stick up by more than one inch from the general level of the pavement, this will indicate that it is in an unacceptable state of repair.

You can claim for any financial losses that result from the accident, such as the cost of repairs to your shoes, or their value if they are beyond repair. If the accident had been worse you would have been able to claim for any time off work, and for your personal injury, for which damages could have been high.

Q *I seem to get a load of advertising circulars and other junk mail, and I don't want them. Is there anything I can do about this?*

A You can write to the Mailing Preference Services† to request that your name and address be removed from the mailing lists of companies sending such material. You will be sent an application form to complete. This is a free service, set up and funded by the direct mail industry to give consumers the opportunity to have their names and addresses taken off (or added to) lists used by its members.

Q *I recently received a set of compact discs in the post. I didn't order them, but now I've been sent an invoice. What should I do?*

A If you receive goods that you haven't ordered and don't want, sent in the hope that you will buy them, you are certainly not obliged to pay for them. The Unsolicited Goods and Services Act 1971 (in Northern Ireland, the Unsolicited Goods and Services [Northern Ireland] Order 1976) makes this kind of sales technique illegal. Under the Act you should either:

- do nothing and keep the compact discs safe for six months, after which time the goods will be yours to keep. But if the sender wants the goods back during this period, he is entitled to them. You may not refuse to send them back if the sender pays for the postage, nor may you refuse to allow him to collect them
- write to the sender giving him notice that you didn't ask for the discs to be sent, that you don't want them, and that they are available for collection if he wants them. If the sender fails to collect them within 30 days they become your property.

If the sender demands payment or orders you to send the goods back without agreeing to pay the postage, ignore him. Report the matter to your local Trading Standards Department, which enforces the law in such cases. Demands for payment for unsolicited goods are a criminal offence for which the sender may be prosecuted and fined.

Q *I'm curious to know what information a company has on its computers about me. Can I find out?*

A Under the Data Protection Act 1984 you are entitled to see a copy of any **personal data** held on computer that is about you, provided you make a written request to the company. The company may make a charge of up to £10 for each register entry, but in some cases it will provide the information free of charge. Write to the company's head office. State that you are requesting information under section 21 of the Data Protection Act 1984. It may help if you state what relationship you have with the company (e.g. employee, customer, patient, student) and supply other relevant details. The company must respond within 40 days: if it does not, you should complain to the Data Protection Registrar†, who can enforce your right to know.

Q *If I suffer damage, such as credit blacklisting, because of errors in computer records, am I entitled to compensation?*

A Yes. You are entitled to seek compensation through the courts if damage (not just distress) results from any inaccuracy, loss, destruction (without authorisation from the data user) or disclosure held on computer. If you can prove damage, and there is no defence, the court may award compensation for the damage and any associated distress. If the court is satisfied that personal data held by a data user is inaccurate, it may order rectification or erasure of that data, or the inclusion of a supplementary statement clarifying the matter. Contact the Data Protection Registrar† if you have problems of this sort.

Q *Yesterday I received a visit from a double-glazing salesman who pressurised me into signing a contract to replace all my windows. I've just been told by a friend that the company has a bad reputation and is very expensive. Is there anything I can do about this?*

A Under the Consumer Protection (Cancellation of Contracts Concluded Away from Business Premises) Regulations 1987, if the visit was '**unsolicited**' then you will have a cooling-off period of seven days during which you have the right to cancel the contract you signed. An unsolicited visit is one that you have not expressly requested the salesman to make: this includes appointments made as a result of unrequested telephone calls, or after delivery of a card proposing the visit. If you initiated the double-glazing salesman's visit, then you will not be protected. To cancel the contract you should either write stating that you are cancelling the contract in accordance with your legal rights or send the cancellation notice to the salesman/person mentioned in the notice of cancellation rights. Keep any goods safe until they are collected by the trader (but see below).

Q *Can I cancel* any *contract signed at home?*

A No. The regulations don't apply to:

- contracts signed as a result of a home visit which you have requested
- most cash and credit contracts *under* £35

- agreements for the sale of food and drink, or other goods supplied by regular roundsmen such as a milkman
- agreements that relate to land (you *can* cancel contracts for repairs or improvements to property signed after an unsolicited visit: see p. 233)
- insurance agreements
- certain catalogue order agreements
- investment agreements and agreements for making deposits which are regulated by other legislation.

With any other agreement, if you sign following an 'unsolicited' visit at home (see p. 233) the salesman must give you a notice of cancellation rights at the time the agreement is signed. If he does not do this, the contract is null and void: you would be under no legal obligation to pay any money to the company and you may recover any money already paid.

Q *I cancelled the contract I signed at home but the trader says I must forfeit my deposit. Is this true?*

A No. Under the Consumer Protection (Cancellation of Contracts Concluded Away from Business Premises) Regulations 1987 (p. 233), you should not be penalised for exercising your right to cancel within the cooling-off period: your deposit should be returned in full.

Q *If I don't pay a bill, can the trader or company enter my home without permission and seize the goods in question – or anything else?*

A No. If you owe money, the trader must pursue the dispute with you through conciliation, arbitration or the courts. If he succeeds, he will be entitled to be paid the money you owe (and may also be entitled to the costs of pursuing you for the money). But there are some circumstances in which there *may* be a right of entry arising from an unpaid bill. The most common are unpaid bills from:

- British Gas or an electricity company (pp. 86 and 90)

- water supply companies (p. 93)
- telephone companies (p. 95), or
- where a court judgment has been obtained for the unpaid bill and bailiffs are sent to enforce that judgment (p. 255).

Q *Who, apart from gas, electricity, water and telephone company employees, and court bailiffs (as described above), can enter my home without my permission, and in what circumstances?*

A Generally, anyone who comes on to your land without your permission is a trespasser, which means that you can evict him and sue for compensation (pp. 219–20) in the event of any damage caused. Some officials can enter your home if they have got a warrant; others can enter anyway in certain circumstances, for example, if there is a gas leak (p. 86). Otherwise, the following personnel could have a right to enter your property:

- the local council (pp. 221–2)
- TV licence inspectors: as a last resort, they can get a warrant giving them the power to enter and search your home, if they reasonably suspect that you own a TV and have not got a licence, or have a black and white licence for a colour TV. The warrant lasts for a month and allows the TV licence inspectors to enter at a reasonable time. However, they are not allowed to use force to get in
- the police normally need a warrant to enter your property. However, in certain strictly defined circumstances, for example, if they are trying to stop someone from being seriously hurt, they can enter without a warrant. If they search your house while you are not there, they must leave a copy of the warrant behind, and if they force entry, they must leave your house secure. A warrant allows them to search your house for wanted people or stolen goods. If they want to take away items that they reasonably believe to be connected with a serious crime they must give you a receipt
- fire-fighters: they may, if necessary, force entry to your home to put out a fire or rescue anybody who is at risk from the flames. If they believe a fire has started, or need to get into your home in order to access a neighbour's, they may break in

- the Inland Revenue: for tax inspectors to be able to come into your home without permission, they will need to have obtained a warrant from a judge, who must be satisfied that there are reasonable grounds for suspecting serious tax fraud. If a warrant is issued the tax inspectors will be able to visit your home at any time, search it and remove any evidence that they reasonably believe to be connected with tax fraud. They are permitted to use force to break in if necessary, and to call in the police to help them. If they take documents or other evidence you are not entitled to an explanation about why they are being removed, but you are entitled to a receipt. If they take documents which you need to run your business, they should give you reasonable access to them.

CHAPTER 13

Taking your claim further

If the company or trader you are dealing with fails to answer your letters, or refuses to sort your problem out, don't be discouraged from pursuing your complaint further. Many traders are members of **trade associations** which have **codes of conduct** by which their members should abide (pp. 238–9), although there is no guarantee that members will follow the code in question; if they do not, the only effect this may have is that they are expelled from the association. Many associations offer a **conciliation** service to help resolve disagreements between consumers and members' companies, and others can offer **arbitration** schemes to sort out disputes (pp. 239–42).

There is now a wide range of **ombudsman** schemes in Britain. Using such a scheme to settle a dispute may be an alternative to going to court. They are completely free and aim to be less complex and time-consuming than legal proceedings, in many cases upholding the spirit and not just the letter of the law.

Going to court is nearly always an option, but should be considered only as a last resort. Court action can be lengthy and costly, and legal aid is available only to a few. The **small claims procedure**, which is an informal and simplified process, provides a comparatively quick and low-cost way of using the courts.

This chapter explains the various ways of sorting out a dispute and offers guidance on their pros and cons.

Q *Over a number of months I have been hassled by a doorstep salesman despite the fact that I have asked him on a number of occasions not to return. How can I stop him returning?*

A First, check whether the salesman's company is a member of a **trade association**, as the trade association will operate a **code of practice** to which the member should adhere. If it has breached the terms of the code, inform the trade association, which may be able to persuade the trader to comply and, in this case, adhere to proper selling methods. However, the trade association can only put pressure on members to comply: it cannot force them to do so. And if they do not follow the code they risk being thrown out of the association and losing the benefits that brings them. If the harassment is serious, contact the Trading Standards Department for the areas local to the trader, and also ask the police to intervene.

Q *I've got a dispute with a company over some work it did for me. It has suggested the matter be settled by* ***conciliation****. Does it prevent me going to court if a settlement can't be reached?*

A No. Conciliation is usually offered by the trade association to which the trader belongs, which will try to bring you and the trader together to reach a mutually acceptable compromise. Conciliation is free and informal and may result in the settlement of the dispute. It is often a prerequisite to arbitration in that many trade associations insist on the use of conciliation facilities before the dispute can be referred to their arbitration schemes. However, the outcome of conciliation is not legally binding and the trade association cannot force its members to reach a compromise. If conciliation does not resolve the dispute you can still go to court or refer the dispute to arbitration (pp. 253–4).

Q *My four-bedroomed house needs decoration. I have shopped around to get the best quotes. Of the best two, one firm is a member of a trade association and the other isn't. What would be the benefits in choosing the one that is?*

A Membership of a trade association will not necessarily guarantee you better work or fewer problems, but it may offer you some safeguards (p. 238): for example, conciliation facilities and low-cost arbitration schemes if something goes wrong; basic standards of workmanship may be set out in the code of practice; however, the recommendations in the code of practice have no legal force and no action can be taken in the court if the code is not followed by a member; and there may be a guarantee scheme which pays for work to be corrected or completed, if the original contractor goes out of business (p. 65).

Q *How do I know whether a trader is a member of a trade association?*

A The logo of the trade association should be prominently displayed at the trader's/firm's place of business and is usually displayed on the trader's headed notepaper. If so, check with the association that the membership is genuine. Otherwise:

- contact the trade association† which seems most likely to apply, or
- ask the trader if he is a member of a trade association, or
- contact the Office of Fair Trading.†

Q *I'm owed money by a firm but it doesn't belong to a trade association. Can I still have the matter settled by* ***arbitration****?*

A Yes. Any dispute can be sorted out by arbitration, whether through a scheme operated under a trade association code of practice (**code arbitration**) or arranged by you independently of any association.

In all cases, you can refer the matter to arbitration only if both sides agree. You can request it from the Chartered Institute of Arbitrators (Arbiters in Scotland)†, but because you won't be using one of the code arbitration schemes, the loser will be paying for the arbitrator's time, charged at an hourly rate, so it could be costly, depending on the complexity of the problem. With arbitration, you and the trader each put your side of the story to an independent person – an arbitrator (arbiter in Scotland), whose decision will be binding (see below). Although it is informal, a fee of some kind is payable. Most of the costs arising from arbitration schemes operated for trade associations are borne by the trader or trade association and consequently your costs should be relatively low. So it is best to deal with traders who are members of trade associations.

Q *The company claiming money from me wants the claim dealt with by an arbitration scheme run by the Institute of Arbitrators. Could I still go to court afterwards if I want to?*

A You have a choice as to whether you have the dispute settled by a court or an arbitration scheme:

- you can't be forced to go to arbitration. The Consumer Arbitration Agreements Act 1988 outlaws contract terms which state that disputes below £1,000 *must* be referred to arbitration: these are not legally binding
- arbitration schemes are offered as alternatives to court, not in addition, so you have to choose
- arbitration schemes generally use written evidence only, so you cannot present your case in person, and it's not always easy to put your problem clearly in writing. Court gives you the chance to put your side of the case (pp. 250–1, 253–4)
- once you have made your choice, the decision of the judge or arbitrator is binding, so you cannot have the case re-heard using the other option if you are unhappy with the decision.

Q *I'm owed a partial refund from the double-glazing company which did an inadequate job fitting new windows, but the company disputes this. We have signed the form agreeing to have the dispute referred to* ***arbitration*** *supplied by the company's trade association, but I'm concerned about the costs this will involve.*

A Many but not all arbitration schemes run for trade associations are operated on a low-cost basis so they should not cost you very much. Contact the individual association† for details. Generally:

- you will have to pay a registration fee on submitting your case. This varies depending on the trade association involved and the amount in dispute: for example, the fees for the Glass & Glazing Federation (GGF)† range from £23.50 (for claims up to £2,500) to £52.88 (for claims over £12,500). But if you win your case, the arbitrator is more than likely to refund your registration fee
- since most arbitration schemes generally decide cases on written evidence only, you won't incur travel expenses as there is no hearing to attend
- a number of schemes include site visits – for example, the GGF and BT – or expert examinations – for example, the Retail Motor Industry Federation† – which are free.

Q *What is the process of arbitration?*

A Generally, you and the trader will have to sign a joint application form, an **application for arbitration**, which you can get from the relevant trade association and/or the body that administers the scheme, for example, the Chartered Institute of Arbitrators.† The signed form together with relevant registration fee must be returned to the Institute. If the case is considered appropriate for arbitration, the Institute will send you (as the **claimant**) a **statement of claim** and an information sheet, detailing the process. After reading these carefully to ensure you comply with all the time limits and procedures:

- you must complete the statement of claim by setting out briefly but concisely the facts of your case. This, together with the appropriate **registration fee** and all supporting documentation, should be sent to the Chartered Institute of Arbitrators, or whichever organisation operates the scheme in question, as indicated on the form
- it is important to ensure that you send copies of all the documents which support your case, for example, receipts, invoices, contracts, brochures, expert reports and photographs, as the arbitrator's decision will, in most situations, be based on the information contained in the statement of claim,

and supporting documents. There will be no opportunity to clarify matters at an oral hearing
- the trader (called the **respondent**) will have to do the same by sending in a defence and supporting documents
- having received the documents, the arbitrator will read the papers and if necessary arrange an inspection or site visit. He will then make a decision and both parties will be notified in writing.

Q *I won my case at arbitration but the trader has failed to pay the amount he was ordered to pay me. Is there any way that I can force him to pay up?*

A Initially it is a good idea to inform the relevant trade association, which may be able to persuade the trader to comply with the arbitrator's decision. If this doesn't work, then you can go to court to enforce payment of the award as the arbitrator's decision is legally binding and enforceable at law. By agreeing to go to arbitration both you and the trader also agreed to accept the findings. So if either side fails to comply the agreement will have been broken (see pp. 254–5 for the various methods of enforcement).

Q *I've heard court action sometimes referred to as* ***'small claims arbitration'****. Is this the same as 'code arbitration' offered by trade associations?*

A No. The term 'arbitration' is used to refer to an informal means of arriving at decision on a dispute which is binding on both parties. But 'arbitration' operated by the courts is completely different from arbitration schemes organised by bodies like the Chartered Institute of Arbitrators.

When you start proceedings in the county court, claims of £1,000 or less are automatically referred to 'small claims arbitration', which is more commonly known as the **small claims procedure** (or, popularly, small claims court). It is operated by the courts as part of the legal proceedings and the case is heard by the district judge.

Arbitration schemes run for trade associations are operated by independent bodies such as the Chartered Institute of Arbitrators. The arbitrators appointed are independent of the trade association and are usually qualified professionals, for example, surveyors, architects, engineers or lawyers.

Q *My insurance company won't pay my claim. I've written to the head office but am now at an impasse. Could the* **ombudsman** *help me?*

A It is worth making your complaint to the relevant ombudsman to try to settle the dispute before considering going to court. There are a wide range of ombudsman† schemes in Britain. Some are statutory and cover everyone in that industry (e.g. Legal Services Ombudsman); others are voluntary and cover only those companies which have joined the scheme (e.g. the Insurance and Banking Ombudsmen) (p. 137). So if you have a complaint against a company that is not a member of a voluntary scheme you cannot take your case to the ombudsman. Generally the following apply to *all* schemes:

- they are completely free and aim to be less complex and time-consuming than legal proceedings, in many cases going beyond the letter of the law
- there are time limits for complaining, usually six months (as with the Insurance Ombudsman) or 12 months from reaching **deadlock** with the company (p. 244). Check with the relevant scheme
- some ombudsmen can **award** compensation, others can only **recommend** that the company pays up. Some have a maximum of £100,000, but most are unlimited
- these schemes are designed to be independent, accessible and, compared with going to court, quick.

Q *I've complained without success to the local branch of the company with which I'm in dispute. I want to write to the ombudsman, but if I do this, would his decision be binding, or could I still go to court?*

A Generally you have to exhaust all attempts at sorting out the dispute with the company first. So you must write to the head office of the company. If there is still no agreement, make sure the company is a member of the relevant ombudsman† scheme and send him all the details. An ombudsman's decision is binding on the organisation you have complained about, but it is not binding on you, so you can still go to court or to arbitration if you are unhappy with the decision.

Q *I wish to refer the dispute I have with my bank to the banking ombudsman but the bank has refused to issue the necessary 'deadlock' letter.*

A You should not be stopped by a company/organisation from referring your dispute to the ombudsman. If the company tries to stop you by refusing to provide a letter indicating that you have reached stalemate (a deadlock letter), complain to the ombudsman anyway about the way your complaint has been dealt with, as well as about the original matter over which the dispute arose.

Q *I've heard the term **ADR** mentioned. What does it stand for and how can it help me?*

A ADR stands for **Alternative Dispute Resolution** and means any method of resolving a dispute between two or more parties which does not involve complicated legal proceedings. Negotiation, conciliation, ombudsman schemes and arbitration both through the courts (small claims) and through arbitration schemes are all forms of ADR.

ADR can also mean **mediation,** in which a neutral mediator helps the parties in dispute to negotiate a settlement. The mediator does not make a decision on behalf of the parties and has no power to impose a view on them. The process differs from conciliation in that the mediator takes a more active role in the discussions and will suggest the terms of a possible settlement but neither side is obliged to accept any of the suggested terms. With conciliation, the conciliator aids or encourages the parties in dispute to reach their own agreement.

A number of organisations such as Mediation UK, the Centre for Dispute Resolution (CEDR) and IDR Europe Limited† offer ADR facilities. The fees they charge depend on the amount in dispute. CEDR offers a day's mediation for £350 plus VAT per party where the amount in dispute is under £20,000 and IDR Europe charges £175 plus VAT per party for one and a half hours of mediation where the amount in dispute is £25,000 or less.

Q *I am owed £600 by a trader, who has refused to give me the money even though I wrote asking for it. Can I sue him?*

A As long as you have a genuine dispute with a company or trader you can claim through the courts. However, even if the amount of your claim is below the small claims limit of £1,000 (£750 in Scotland) you should try to sort the matter out by using the alternative methods first, so contact any relevant trade association and ask if it will conciliate, or refer the matter to an ombudsman if appropriate (p. 243). If that proves unsuccessful, you will then have to decide between arbitration and court (pp. 240–2). If you do choose to start legal proceedings you need to send one last letter to the trader, stating that if he does not settle the matter within a reasonable time, usually seven to 14 days, you will issue a county court summons. Such a letter is known as a **letter before action**. If you do not hear from the trader within the time limit, you can issue proceedings.

Q *I want to issue proceedings in my local county court against a company based over a hundred miles away. Will it definitely be heard at a court local to me?*

A You can start the claim (**issue** proceedings) in your local county court. But if the company (or person) you are suing defends the case, then it will automatically be transferred to a county court nearer its place of business. Many cases settle out of court, but if you do have to travel a long way and you win your case you can recover reasonable travelling expenses and currently up to £29 (however long the case lasts, but it is likely to be only a matter of a few hours) for your loss of earnings.

Q *I had repairs carried out to my boat but the work was very shoddy and I have incurred further costs in having it put right. I want to sue the repairer but I'm worried about what it could cost me. Could I keep costs down by using the small claims court?*

A Claims of up to £1,000 (in England, Wales and Northern Ireland), or up to £750 in Scotland, are known as small claims. Such claims are automatically referred by the court to the small claims procedure – also known as arbitration (p. 242). The small claims procedure operates within the county court (sheriff court in Scotland) but it has simplified rules which makes it fairly speedy and straightforward for people using it.

The main advantage is cost. First, you won't have to seek the assistance of a solicitor so you won't incur solicitors' charges. Secondly, even if you lose, the only costs which can normally be awarded against you are:

- the defendants' and their witnesses' (if any) reasonable expenses incurred travelling to and from the hearing
- up to £29 each to cover the money the defendants and their witnesses would have earned that day
- up to £112.50 to cover the cost of any expert fees.

If you win you'll get back:

- the court fee
- your own and your witnessess' (if any) reasonable expenses incurred travelling to and from the hearing
- your own and our witnesses' (if any) loss of earnings of £29
- up to £112.50 if you paid an expert to provide evidence to support your case.

Q *What are the risks involved in starting legal proceedings for more than £1,000?*

A Claims over £1,000 are dealt with in the full county court (over £750 in the sheriff court in Scotland). These are subject to formal rules of evidence, and unless you have had experience of presenting cases in court and cross-examination you would be at a severe disadvantage. So legal representation, although not compulsory, is usually essential and as a result you will have to ask a solicitor to act for you. Furthermore, unlike in small claims cases, if you lose your case you face the prospect of having to pay not only your own solicitor's costs but those of the other side, which could run into several thousands of pounds. Therefore proceedings in the full county court can turn out to be very expensive.

In Scotland claims of between £750 and £1,500 are dealt with in the sheriff court by the summary cause procedure, which is intended to provide a quick, straightforward way of settling disputes that does not necessarily require a solicitor. However, using this procedure you risk having to pay legal costs if you lose, including those of the other side.

Q *I want to issue proceedings for £1,200. I want to avoid using a solicitor. Is there any way the case can still be heard in the small claims court, even though it is over the small claims limit?*

A It can still be heard in the small claims court if either you or the other side applies to the court and the court agrees. This way you can still benefit from the informal procedures (pp. 252–3). However, if you lose you will have to pay the other side's costs, as in the full county court (see above). Alternatively, you can limit your claim to £1,000 and make full use of the benefits of the small claims court. But you will have to accept that you will not recover the extra £200.

Q *I'm owed £1,800 by a double-glazing company. I want to sue them for the full amount but I know it won't be heard in the small claims court. How do I commence proceedings?*

A Issuing a summons in respect of a claim for over £1,000 is the same as in the small claims court but there are further steps which have to be taken before a hearing date is fixed. The court will inform you of what steps you should take as it tends to vary depending on the type of claim and its complexity. You should instruct a solicitor, and bear in mind that if you lose you may have to pay the other side's costs (pp. 246–7).

In Scotland claims for over £1,500 can be dealt with in the sheriff court but formal procedures apply and you start proceedings by issuing an initial writ. You will need the assistance of a solicitor to start such proceedings.

Q *How do I start a claim in the* ***small claims court****?*

A Free leaflets explaining what to do are available from county courts. You can also obtain a **default summons** from your local county court. There are two forms: Form N1, which you should use when claiming a fixed amount, as in this case, and Form N2, which you should use when you are not claiming a specific amount (for example, in holiday cases).

The court forms have recently been simplified so you shouldn't have too much trouble filling them in. If you do need any assistance, the court staff, your local Citizens Advice Bureau or Consumer Advice Centre will help you. Otherwise:

- complete the summons by inserting the full name and address of yourself (the plaintiff) and the other side (the defendant) and set out briefly the details of your claim. Finish by stating the remedy you require (see sample forms, pp. 257–60): these details are called the **particulars of claim**
- it is important that you sue the right person or company – a name on a letterhead, for example, may only be the trading name, not the name of the registered company
- check that the trader is still in business by contacting the Trading Standards Department for the area local to the trader, or, if it is a company, phone Companies House†
- once you have completed the summons, take it plus a copy to the court, or send it by first-class post. Also ensure you keep a copy for yourself. You will have to pay an issue fee

ranging from £10 to £65 for claims up to £1,000. If you pay by cheque or postal order, make it payable to 'HM Paymaster General'. You cannot pay by cheque if you are sending the documents by post as cheques are only accepted from individuals when presented personally and supported by a banker's card

- a few days later you should receive a note ('Notice of Issue of Default Summons') from the court telling you the number of the case. The court will send a copy of the summons to the defendant.

Q *I've received a court summons, form N1, from a company claiming £650 for work it did on my garden patio. This work was so bad that I don't want to pay anything. It's going to cost another £900 to put the work right. What should I do?*

A If you dispute the full amount claimed, you should send a **defence** to the court within 21 days from the date of the postmark by completing form N9B; if not, you risk having judgment entered against you (p. 250 below). This form and full instructions should be sent to you with the claim. The court will then send the defence to the person making the claim (the plaintiff). If a defence is not filed with the court within the time limit the plaintiff can apply for judgment to be given automatically ('in default'). As you will have to pay £250 more than the claim to put the inferior work right, you will have to fill in the form to make a **counter-claim** against the plaintiff. Always:

- read everything the court sends you very carefully: court forms and language are not as clear as they could be. If in doubt, ask for help. The court staff should be able to answer your queries
- put your evidence and arguments together carefully and avoid irrelevant elements
- keep receipts for all expenses you intend to claim and make sure you have all the evidence you need to support your arguments, such as estimates, bills and written reports.

Q *I issued proceedings approximately three weeks ago in my local county court for compensation for a spoilt holiday. Although I received a note from the court indicating the case number, I've heard nothing from the defendant. What should I do next?*

A When sending you notification of the case number, the court will also have sent you documents setting out what happens if you hear from the defendant and what you should do if you don't. These documents should be read carefully.

You should ring up the court and find out whether the defendant has sent a **defence** to the court. If he has, then the case will proceed in a set way (pp. 251–2). If he has not you can apply to have **judgment in default** entered. You do this by obtaining from the court and completing Form N30 or by filling in the form attached to the Notice of Issue which the court will have already sent to you (Form N205A). Send or take the completed form to the court, which will enter judgment for you. You will be sent a copy of the judgment, which will indicate a time within which you require payment from the defendant. A copy of the judgment should be sent to the defendant.

Q *Should I be represented by a solicitor at the hearing? If I'm not, and the other side is, will I be disadvantaged?*

A This depends on whether the case is a 'small claim' or not:

- if the case is being heard under the **small claims procedure**, you will not need the assistance of a solicitor in preparing or presenting the case. The small claims procedure is specifically designed for you to take your own case to court and operates by simplified rules. Therefore, even if the other side is represented by a solicitor you should not be disadvantaged
- if the case is being heard in the **full county court** (sheriff court in Scotland for claims over £1,500), strict rules of evidence and presentation apply and the case is heard in a formal atmosphere, so legal representation is very important. Unless you have had experience of this type of thing before, you may find it difficult to present your case and cross-examine

effectively. Clearly, if your opponent is professionally represented you would be at an unfair disadvantage.

Q *I've issued a summons. Will I have to attend a court hearing?*

A Issuing a summons does not necessarily mean that you have to go to court. You can always pull out if, for example, the defendant pays up, or makes an offer that is acceptable. The threat of proceedings in a letter before action and/or the issuing of a summons shows you mean business and often results in the settlement of the matter.

Q *I issued proceedings and I have now received a form from the defendant in which he admits he owes me money, together with a cheque for the full amount. What should I do?*

A You should write to the court and the defendant acknowledging receipt of the cheque in settlement of the case and confirm that the case is withdrawn.

Q *What are the main stages under the small claims procedure once I've received a defence from the defendant?*

A On sending you a copy of the defence, the court will tell you how the case is to proceed. The documents which the court sends to you should be read carefully and the procedures followed. The case may proceed in a number of ways.

The court will provide you with a list of steps (**automatic directions**) which have to be taken by both parties before a hearing date can be fixed. The directions, which usually have to be carried out within specified time limits, are normally contained in a standard form and include the following:

- the preparation of a list of the documents which you have relating to the case (for example, letters between you and the defendant), which you should then send to the defendant

within a specified time limit. The directions will also state that these documents will be available for inspection by the other side. The defendant will have to prepare a similar list
- the exchange of experts' reports
- the exchange of photographs and sketch plans, if any
- sending a certificate of readiness to the court within six months and requesting a date be fixed for the hearing.

Alternatively, the court will fix a date for the hearing and request both parties to provide each other with copies of all the documents they intend to rely on to support their case, as in the first three stages above.

In exceptional cases the court may decide that automatic directions are not appropriate and will fix a date for a preliminary hearing which both parties will have to attend. It will at this hearing be decided how the case should proceed and specific directions will be agreed.

Q *I'm due to attend a small claims hearing in few days' time to defend a case. What can I expect?*

A If you are familiar with the details of your case, the hearing should be informal and quick, so there is no need to be nervous. Taking the following steps should make matters easy for you whether you are bringing or defending a case:

- the day before the hearing you should read your documents so you are clear about the facts of your case
- make notes in point form of the main facts you have to raise in order to prove/defend your case, and flag the documents which cover those points, so you can find them easily during the hearing
- make sure you take with you to the hearing all the documents relating to the case
- ring your witnesses the day before to remind them of the time and place of the hearing
- arrive at the court in plenty of time
- at the hearing keep matters simple and stick to the points you mentioned in your summons/defence.

The clerk of the court will call both parties into the room where the hearing is to take place. It will take place in **private** in an **informal** atmosphere before a **district judge** (**sheriff** in Scotland). District judges differ in their approaches: some ask questions and intervene a great deal, while others simply listen. In any event the plaintiff will be asked to give his side of the story and call his witnesses, if any. The defendant will then be given the opportunity to ask the plaintiff any questions. The defendant will then give his side of the story and call any witnesses. The plaintiff will then have the opportunity to ask the defendant questions. Once each side has presented evidence, the district judge will give his decision. This will be confirmed in writing a few days later by the court.

Q *If I don't agree with the district judge's decision, can I appeal?*

A There is no appeal as such but you can apply to have the decision set aside on the basis that there has been an error of law or there has been misconduct by the district judge. But if you merely disagree with the outcome, there is nothing you can do.

Q *I have failed to reach an agreement with a company that owes me £950. It is a member of a trade association which offers arbitration. I don't know whether to go to arbitration or sue in the small claims court. What are the advantages/disadvantages of arbitration?*

A The advantages of having your claim dealt with by arbitration are:

- generally there is no hearing to attend so you need not take time off work or incur travel expenses
- if you're worried about presenting your case in person, arbitration is better as it is based on documents only
- financial ceilings are usually higher than the small claims limit of £1,000.

The disadvantages are:

- you won't be able to argue your case in person
- it's not always easy to put your problem in writing and include all relevant facts
- the trader must be a member of the relevant trade association to enable you to use the scheme.

Q *What are the pros and cons of taking court action in the small claims court?*

A The advantages of pursuing a claim through the small claims procedure are:

- costs (see p. 246)
- you present your own case in an informal hearing. It may be easier for you to get across the extent of your case by giving a verbal account of your troubles
- it is relatively easy to make a claim
- issuing a summons shows you mean business and often leads to a sensible offer.

The disadvantages of court action are that:

- you may need to take time off work to attend the hearing
- you may incur travel expenses
- you will have to present your own case at the hearing (some people find this difficult and daunting)
- there is a financial limit under the small claims procedure of £1,000 (£750 in Scotland).

Q *I obtained judgment in the court for payment of a debt and although I sent a copy of the judgment to the defendant and have requested payment on numerous occasions, he has failed to pay up. How can I force him to pay?*

A You will probably have to take further court action to get your money. The various procedures open to you are set out and explained in a free booklet from your local county court. The court will do nothing at all on its own initiative so it is up to you to take enforcement action and to choose the best method. The key to successful enforcement is to find out what assets there are and to select a method of enforcement to get at them. The methods of enforcement are as follows:

- **attachment of earnings** Payment is extracted from the wages or salary of an employed (as opposed to a self-employed) judgment debtor. The employers are obliged to make specified deductions from pay on a week-by-week or month-by-month basis and pay it to the court
- **warrant of execution** This orders bailiffs to remove and sell sufficient goods belonging to the judgment debtor to pay the debt. Items on hire purchase or belonging to someone else may not be seized. The judgment debtor's clothes, bedding and trade tools up to a certain value may not be seized
- **garnishee proceedings** This process directs moneys that are due to the judgment debtor to be paid to you instead. For example, it can be used to access money held in the judgment debtor's bank or building society account or a trade debt
- **charging order** This can be placed on property, domestic or business, owned by the judgment debtor, by himself or jointly with someone else. The object of such an order is to have the property sold to pay the judgment debt.

If you do not know anything about the financial position of the judgment debtor or his business it may be in your best interests to find out as much as you can on this before opting for one of the above methods of enforcement. You can do this by applying to the court for an **oral examination of the judgment debtor's means**. This procedure allows you, or the court, to ask the debtor a series of questions to find out how much money/assets he has and how much he can afford to pay. Once you have such information it will then be easier for you to decide whether it is worth enforcing the judgment and, if it is, to choose the best method.

Q *I was just about to sue a company when I heard that it had gone out of business. Is it worth taking the company to court?*

A Unfortunately, once a company has gone into liquidation it is very difficult to recover any money unless the company is solvent and merely ceasing to trade. Usually the only people who have a chance of recovering any money from such a company are preferential creditors such as the Inland Revenue or those who have secured loans to the company. These groups will be the first to be paid out should there be any money and only if there is some money left over will unsecured creditors be paid.

In the circumstances, your only course of action is to notify the liquidators of the nature and extent of your claim as soon as possible so that they are fully aware of all outstanding debts (p. 25). If you paid on credit you may have a claim against the lender or credit card company (p. 132). And if you took out an insurance-backed guarantee you should not lose out. (p. 65).

County Court Summons (NI)

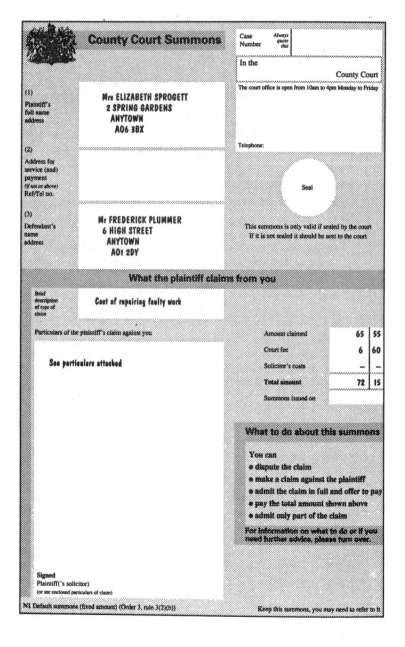

County Court Summons

Case Number *Always quote this*

In the

County Court

The court office is open from 10am to 4pm Monday to Friday

Telephone:

(1) Plaintiff's full name address

Mrs ELIZABETH SPROGETT
2 SPRING GARDENS
ANYTOWN
A06 3BX

(2) Address for service (and) payment *(if not as above)* Ref/Tel no.

(3) Defendant's name address

Mr FREDERICK PLUMMER
6 HIGH STREET
ANYTOWN
A01 2DY

Seal

This summons is only valid if sealed by the court
If it is not sealed it should be sent to the court

What the plaintiff claims from you

Brief description of type of claim: Cost of repairing faulty work

Particulars of the plaintiff's claim against you

See particulars attached

Amount claimed	65	55
Court fee	6	60
Solicitor's costs	–	–
Total amount	72	15
Summons issued on		

What to do about this summons

You can
- **dispute the claim**
- **make a claim against the plaintiff**
- **admit the claim in full and offer to pay**
- **pay the total amount shown above**
- **admit only part of the claim**

For information on what to do or if you need further advice, please turn over.

Signed
Plaintiff('s solicitor)
(or see enclosed particulars of claim)

N1 Default summons (fixed amount) (Order 3, rule 3(2)(b))

Keep this summons, you may need to refer to it

Court Particulars – claiming the cost of repairing faulty work

Case No. ______

IN THE **[Name]** COUNTY COURT

BETWEEN:

[PLAINTIFF'S NAME] Plaintiff

AND

[DEFENDANT'S NAME] Defendant

PARTICULARS OF CLAIM

1. At all material times the Defendant carried on business as a **[describe business]** at **[address]**.
2. By a contract in writing made between the Plaintiff and the Defendant, contained in or evidenced by the Defendant's estimate dated **[date and reference number]**, the Defendant agreed to **[describe nature of work]** for the sum of **[£.....]**.
3. It was an implied term of the contract that the Defendant would carry out the work with all due care, skill and diligence and in a good and workmanlike manner and with materials which were of a reasonable quality.
4. In breach of the implied term set out in paragraph 3 above, the Defendant failed to carry out the work with all due care, skill and diligence and in a good and workmanlike manner and with materials which were of a reasonable quality.

Particulars of Breach

[Precise details of faulty work]

5. By reason of the matters set out above the Plaintiff has suffered loss and damage.

Particulars of Loss

Cost of remedial work **[£.....]**

AND THE PLAINTIFF CLAIMS:

Damages limited to **[£.....]**

Signed ______________________ Dated ______________

To: The Defendant

The District Judge

Court Particulars – claiming the cost of repairing faulty goods

Case No. ______

IN THE **[Name]** COUNTY COURT

BETWEEN:

[PLAINTIFF'S NAME] Plaintiff

AND

[DEFENDANT'S NAME] Defendant

PARTICULARS OF CLAIM

1. At all material times the Defendant carried on business as a **[describe business]** at **[address]**.
2. By a contract in writing made between the Plaintiff and the Defendant, contained in or evidenced by the Defendant's estimate dated **[date and reference number]**, the Defendant agreed to supply the Plaintiff with a **[describe goods]** for the sum of **[£.....]**.
3. It was an implied term of the contract that the goods should be of merchantable quality.
4. In breach of the implied term set out in paragraph 3 above, the goods were not of merchantable quality.

Particulars of Breach

[Precise details of faults in goods]

5. By reason of the matters set out above the Plaintiff has suffered loss and damage.

Particulars of Loss

Cost of repairs to goods **[£.....]**

AND THE PLAINTIFF CLAIMS:

Damages limited to **[£.....]**

Signed ______________________ Dated ________________

To: The Defendant

The District Judge

Notice of issue of Default Summons (N205A)

Notice of Issue of Default Summons - fixed amount

In the	
ANYTOWN County Court	
The court office at COURT BUILDINGS 6, WEST STREET, ANYTOWN is open between 10am & 4 pm Monday to Friday Tel 00 765 – 1234	
Case Number (Always quote this)	91/16254
Plaintiff (including ref.)	MRS E SPROGETT
Defendants	MR FREDERICK PLUMMER
Issue date	22/7/91
Date of postal service	31/7/91
Issue fee	£ 6.60

For further information please turn over

To the plaintiff ('s solicitor)

MRS E SPROGETT
2 SPRING GARDENS
ANYTOWN
A06 3BX

Your summons was issued today The defendant has 14 days from the date of service to reply to the summons If the date of postal service is not shown on this form you will be sent a separate notice of service (Form N222)

The defendant may either

- Pay you your total claim
- **Dispute the whole claim.** The court will send you a copy of the defence and tell you what to do next
- **Admit that all the money is owed.** The defendant will send you form of admission N9A You may then ask the court to send the defendant an order to pay you the money owed by completing the request for judgment below and returning it to the court
- **Admit that only part of your claim is owed.** The court will send you a copy of the reply and tell you what to do next
- **Not reply at all.** You should wait 14 days from the date of service You may then ask the court to send the defendant an order to pay you the money owed by completing the request for judgment below and returning it to the court

---

Request for Judgment

In the	
ANYTOWN County Court	
Case Number (Always quote this)	91/16254
Plaintiff	Mrs E SPROGETT
Defendant	Mr FREDERICK PLUMMER
Plaintiff's Ref.	

- *Tick and complete either A or B Make sure that all the case details are given and that the judgment details at C are completed Remember to sign and date the form Your signature certifies that the information you have given is correct*
- *If the defendant has given an address on the form of admission to which correspondence should be sent which is different from the address shown on the summons you will need to tell the court*

A ☐ The defendant has not replied to my summons

Complete all the judgment details at C Decide how and when you want the defendant to pay You can ask for the judgment to be paid by instalments or in one payment

B ☐ The defendant admits that all the money is owed

Tick only one box below and return the completed slip to the court.

☐ **I accept the defendant's proposal for payment**

Complete all the judgment details at C Say how the defendant intends to pay The court will send the defendant an order to pay You will also be sent a copy

☐ **The defendant has not made any proposal for payment**

Complete all the judgment details at C. Say how you want the defendant to pay You can ask for the judgment to be paid by instalments or in one payment The court will send the defendant an order to pay You will also be sent a copy

☐ **I do NOT accept the defendant's proposal for payment**

Complete all the judgment details at C and say how you want the defendant to pay Give your reasons for objecting to the defendant's offer of payment in the section overleaf Return this slip to the court **together with the defendant's admission** N9A (or a copy). The court will fix a rate of payment and send the defendant an order to pay You will also be sent a copy

C Judgment details

I would like the judgment to be paid

☐ (forthwith [illegible])
☐ (by instalments of £ 20.00 per month)
☐ (in full by)

	£	p
Amount of claim as stated in summons (including interest at date of issue)	65	55
Interest since date of summons (if any) Period ...... Rate ......%	–	–
Court fees shown on summons	6	60
Solicitor's costs (if any) on issuing summons	–	–
Sub Total	72	15
Solicitor's costs (if any) on entering judgment	–	–
Sub Total	72	15
Deduct amount (if any) paid since issue	–	–
Amount payable by defendant	72	15

I certify that the information given is correct

Signed E Sprogett **Dated** 13/8/91

N205A Notice of issue (default summons) and request for judgment (Order 3, rule 2(d)(i), Order 9 rules 3 and 6) Dd 8252220 200M 5/91 Ed(209481)

Glossary

Bailment A common law *q.v.* rule which applies when you leave goods with another person or organisation to be kept safely, taken care of and returned to you on demand. If goods are lost or damaged while the other person or organisation has them, that party is obliged to compensate you – unless it can prove that the loss or damage was caused through no fault on its part.

Breach of contract A refusal or failure by a party to a contract to fulfil an obligation imposed on him under that contract.

Caveat emptor 'Let the buyer beware.' This legal principle applies to the sale of property, and means that the onus is on the buyer to ascertain the quality and condition of a property before proceeding with its purchase. In this instance, purchasers do not have the right to seek redress subsequently.

Civil law Law which is concerned with rights and duties that pertain to individual citizens. If you suffer loss because someone else transgresses these laws then you have a right to redress and are entitled to take that person to court.

Common law This kind of law is based on the decisions of the courts in actual cases and amounts to the use of precedent.

Contract Any agreement that can be enforced by law. It gives the parties who have made the contract certain rights and obligations. Contracts can be made in writing, by word of mouth or even without a single word being spoken or written. Every day people make contracts without putting them in writing – buying food in supermarkets or travelling by bus, for example. These have the same standing as written contracts and, like all contracts, are governed by the law of contract.

Cooling-off period The interval in which you are legally entitled to cancel a deal or contract without being financially penalised.

Criminal law Law which is concerned with offences against the public, such as the Trade Descriptions Act 1968. Criminal law affecting consumers is enforced by public authorities like Trading Standards Departments. You cannot get compensation directly by reporting a criminal offence such as a false trade description, but it will give you added leverage with your complaint.

Defendant The person against whom a civil court case is brought, *cf* plaintiff.

Estimate A rough, provisional guide to the price that a tradesman will charge once the work is complete.

Fitness for purpose If you inform a retailer that you want goods for a specific purpose, then as well as being fit for their more general purpose, the goods should also be reasonably fit for the specific purpose. If they are not, you have a claim against the retailer.

Guarantee A manufacturer's promise to resolve manufacturing problems in its products free of charge. Some offer your money back, others offer a free repair or replacement. Always check the wording of a guarantee to see what is included. Guarantees are in addition to your rights under the Sale of Goods Act and are not in any way an alternative to these rights.

Injunction A formal court order requiring a person or organisation to do, or not to do, a particular act. If an injunction is not obeyed, the party concerned may be fined or sent to prison. The injunction lasts as long as the court so decrees.

Judgment The formal decision of a court.

Letter before action A final letter giving the defendant, whether an individual or an organisation, one last opportunity to settle a claim before a summons is issued.

Negligence The breach of a legal duty to take reasonable care, resulting in damage to the plaintiff.

Nuisance The unlawful interference with someone else's enjoyment of his home.

Paying under protest If a purchaser makes it clear, preferably in writing, when paying for goods or services that he or she is 'paying under protest', the purchaser retains the right to bring a claim later if something is wrong, or subsequently goes wrong, with the item or service purchased.

Plaintiff The person bringing a civil case in court, *cf* defendant.

Quotation A firm indication, given before any work is started, of the price that a tradesman will charge once his work is complete.

Reasonable Description used in legislation to give some definition to the period of time within which certain parties have rights to redress. In consumer matters it is used in legislation to describe the time during which goods can be rejected and a full refund demanded. As 'a reasonable time' is not a precise interval, but depends on the circumstances of each case, it is advisable for consumers to act to seek redress as soon as they can.

Rejecting goods Indicating to a retailer that the purchaser does not want the goods in question and in accordance with legally defined rights is seeking a refund.

Reserving rights Preserving the consumer's right, in letters or in verbal complaint, to bring a subsequent claim, if the problem is not resolved at this stage.

Satisfactory quality A legal requirement that goods should work properly, be free from minor defects, safe, durable and, if new, look new and be in good condition.

Statute law Legislation which consists of Acts of Parliament (for example, the Sale of Goods Act 1979) and Regulations and Orders made under the general authority of Acts of Parliament.

Summons A formal document issued by a court informing a defendant that a court case has been started and instructing him to do something: generally to defend the case, or to pay an amount of money to the plaintiff.

Time is of the essence An expression used in contracts to make time a crucial element of that contract. It entitles the consumer to cancel it and insist on a full refund of the price paid if goods are not delivered by the due date or if a service is not performed on time.

Without prejudice A term added to documents, usually letters, which attempts to protect the writer from having the letter construed as an admission of liability or willingness to settle. Generally, nothing said in 'without prejudice' correspondence will be allowed in evidence should the matter come to court. It should not be used on any documentation which may be needed to prove a case, should the lack of appropriate response to a complaint mean that the issue is taken to court.

Addresses

Building

Building Guarantee Scheme Ltd
143 Malone Road, Belfast BT9 6SU
Tel. 01232 661717

Federation of Master Builders
14–15 Great James Street, London WC1N 3DP
Tel. 0171–242 7583

Guarantee Protection Trust Ltd
27 London Road, High Wycombe, Bucks HP11 1BW
Tel. 01494 447049

Independent Warranty Association
21 Albion Place, Northampton NN1 1UD
Tel. 01604 604511

Joint Contracts Tribunal
RIBA Publications Ltd, 66 Portland Place, London W1M 4AD
Tel. 0171–580 5588

National Federation of Roofing Contractors
24 Weymouth Street, London W1N 4XL
Tel. 0171–436 0387

National House Building Council (NHBC)
Buildmark House, Chiltern Avenue, Amersham, Bucks
HP6 5AP
Tel. 01494 434477

Carpets

British Carpet Technical Centre (BCTC)
Wira House, West Park Ring Road, Leeds LS16 6QL
Tel. 01532 591999

Cars

Institute of Automotive Engineer Assessors
Mansell House, 22 Bore Street, Lichfield, Staffs WS13 6LP
Tel. 01543 251346

Retail Motor Industry Federation
201 Great Portland Street, London W1N 6AB
Tel. 0171–580 9122

Scottish Motor Trade Association
3 Palmerston Place, Edinburgh EH12 5AF
Tel. 0131–225 3643

Commercial services

British Association of Removers
3 Churchill Court, 58 Station Road, North Harrow, Middlesex HA2 7SA
Tel. 0181–861 3331

Glass & Glazing Federation
44–48 Borough High Street, London SE1 1XB
Tel. 0171–403 7177

Hairdressing Council
12 David House, 45 High Street, South Norwood, London SE25 6HJ
Tel. 0181–771 6205

Institute of Plumbing
64 Station Lane, Hornchurch, Essex RM12 6NB
Tel. 01708 472791

Institute of Trichologists
228 Stockwell Road, Brixton, London SW9 9SU
Tel. 0171–733 2056

National Association of Plumbing, Heating and Mechanical Services Contractors (NAPHMSC)
14 & 15 Ensign House, Ensign Business Centre, Westwood Way, Coventry, West Midlands CV4 8JA
Tel. 01203 470626

National Inspection Council for Electrical Installation Contracting (NICEIC)
Vintage House, 37 Albert Embankment, London SE1 7UJ
Tel. 0171–735 1322

Society of Master Shoe Repairers Ltd
St Crispin's House, 21 Station Road, Desborough, Northants NN14 2SA
Tel. 01536 760374

Textile Services Association Ltd
7 Churchill Court, 58 Station Road, North Harrow, Middlesex HA2 7SA
Tel. 0181–863 7755/9177

Domestic services

Electricity
Office of Electricity Regulation (OFFER)
Hagley House, 83–85 Hagley Road, Edgbaston, Birmingham B16 8QG
Tel. 0121–456 2100

Gas
CORGI (Council for Registered Gas Installers)
4 Elmwood, Chineham Business Park, Crockford Lane, Basingstoke, Hants RG24 8WG
Tel. 01256 708133

British Gas Region head offices
Eastern
Star House, Mutton Lane, Potters Bar, Herts EN6 2PD
Tel. 01707 651151

East Midlands
PO Box 145, De Montfort Street, Leicester LE1 9DB
Tel. 01162 551111

British Gas Leeds
New York Road, Leeds LS2 7PE
Tel. 01132 436291

Northern
PO Box 1GB, Norgas House, Killingworth, Newcastle Upon Tyne NE99 1GB
Tel. 0191–216 3000

North Thames
North Thames House, London Road, Staines, Middlesex TW18 4AE
Tel. 01784 461666

North Western
Welman House, Golf Road, Altrincham, Cheshire WA15 8AE
Tel. 0161–928 6311

Scotland
Granton House, 4 Marine Drive, Edinburgh EH5 1YB
Tel. 0131–559 5000

South Eastern
Segas House, Katharine Street, Croydon CR9 1JU
Tel. 0181–688 4466

Southern
80 St Mary's Road, Southampton SO9 7GL
Tel. 01703 824100

South Western
Riverside, Temple Street, Keynsham, Bristol BS18 1EQ
Tel. 01179 861717

Wales
Helmont House, Churchill Way, Cardiff CF1 4NB
Tel. 01222 239290

West Midlands
5 Wharf Lane, Solihull, West Midlands B91 2JP
Tel. 0121–705 6888

Gas Consumers Council
Abford House, 15 Wilton Road, London SW1V 1LT
Tel. 0171–931 0977

Office of Gas Supply (OFGAS)
Stockley House, 130 Wilton Road, London SW1V 1LQ
Tel. 0171–828 0898

Telephones
Office of Telecommunications (OFTEL)
Export House, 50 Ludgate Hill, London EC4M 7JJ
Tel. 0171–634 8700

Water
Office of Water Services (OFWAT)
Centre City Tower, 7 Hill Street, Birmingham B5 4UA
Tel. 0121–625 1300

Electrical goods

Radio, Electrical and Television Retailers' Association Ltd (RETRA)
Retra House, St John's Terrace, 1 Ampthill Street, Bedford MK42 9EY
Tel. 01234 269110

Finance and credit

Association for Payment Clearing Services
Mercury House, Triton Court, 14 Finsbury Square, London EC2A 1BR
Tel. 0171–711 6234

The Banking Ombudsman
70 Gray's Inn Road, London WC1X 8NB
Tel. 0171–404 9944

Insolvency Service
Official Receiver's Office, Commercial Union House, 22 Martineau Square, Birmingham B2 4UZ
Tel. 0121–233 4808

The Building Societies Ombudsman
Grosvenor Gardens House, 35–37 Grosvenor Gardens, London SW1X 7AW
Tel. 0171–931 0044

Companies House
Crown Way, Cardiff CF4 3UZ
Tel. 01222 380801

Department of Trade and Industry
Companies Investigation Department, Ashdown House, 123 Victoria Street, London SW1E 6RB
Tel. 0171–215 5000

Hire Purchase Information plc (HPI)
PO Box 61, Dolphin House, New Street, Salisbury, Wilts SP1 2TB
Tel. 01722 422422 (8 a.m.–8 p.m. Monday–Saturday)

Investment Management Regulatory Organisation Ltd (IMRO)
Broadwalk House, 6 Appold Street, London EC2A 2AA
Tel. 0171–628 6022

Finance & Leasing Association
18 Upper Grosvenor Street, London W1X 9PB
Tel. 0171–491 2783

Personal Investment Authority (now deals with business of FIMBRA)
Hertsmere House, Hertsmere Road, Marsh Wall, London E14 4AB
Tel. 0171–538 8860 (use this number for the PIA Ombudsman, too)

Personal Investment Authority (now deals with business of LAUTRO)
Centre Point, 103 New Oxford Street, London WC1A 1QH
Tel. 0171–379 0444

Occupational Pensions Advisory Service (OPAS)
11 Belgrave Road, London SW1V 1RB
Tel. 0171–233 8080

Pensions Ombudsman
11 Belgrave Road, London SW1V 1RB
Tel. 0171–834 9144

General

Advertising Standards Authority (ASA)
2–16 Torrington Place, London WC1E 7HW
Tel. 0171–580 5555

British Standards Institution
BSI Enquiries, Linford Wood, Milton Keynes, Bucks MK14 6LE
Tel. 01908 226888

The Commission for Racial Equality
Elliot House, 10–12 Allington Street, London SW1E 5EH
Tel. 0171–828 7022

Commission of Local Administration in Scotland
23 Walker Street, Edinburgh EH3 7HX
Tel. 0131–225 5300

The Data Protection Registrar
Wycliffe House, Water Lane, Wilmslow, Cheshire SK9 5AF
Tel. 01625 535777

Department of Economic Development for Northern Ireland
Trading Standards Section, 176 Newtonbreda Road, Belfast BT8 4QF
Tel. 01232 253900

The Equal Opportunities Commission
Overseas House, Quay Street, Manchester M3 3HN
Tel. 0161–833 9244

General Consumer Council for Northern Ireland
Elizabeth House, 116 Hollywood Road, Belfast BT4 1NY
Tel. 01232 672488

Office of Fair Trading
Field House, 15–25 Bream's Buildings, London EC4A 1PR
Tel. 0171–242 2858

Royal Society for the Prevention of Cruelty to Animals (RSPCA)
Causeway, Horsham, West Sussex RH12 1HG
Tel. 01403 264181

The Timeshare Council
23 Buckingham Gate, London SW1E 6LB
Tel. 0171–821 8845

Health services

Accident Line
The Law Society, Freepost, London WC2A 1BR
Tel. 0500–192939

Action for the Victims of Medical Accidents (AVMA)
Bank Chambers, 1 London Road, Forest Hill, London SE23 3TP
Tel. 0181–291 2793

Association of Community Health Councils for England and Wales
30 Drayton Park, London N5 1PB
Tel. 0171–609 8405

Association of Personal Injury Lawyers (APIL)
10a Byard Lane, Nottingham NG1 2GJ
Tel. 01159 580585

College of Health (Waiting List Helpline)
Helpline tel. 0181–983 1133

General Dental Council
37 Wimpole Street, London W1M 8DQ
Tel. 0171–486 2171

General Medical Council
44 Hallam Street, London W1N 6AE
Tel. 0171–580 7642

General Optical Council
41 Harley Street, London W1N 2DJ
Tel. 0171–580 3898

Health Service Ombudsman
Church House, Great Smith Street, London SW1P 3BW
Tel. 0171–276 2035

Health Service Commissioner for Scotland
1 Atholl Place, Edinburgh EH3 8HP
Tel. 0131–225 7465

Health Service Commissioner for Wales
Fourth Floor, Pearl Assurance House, Greyfriars Road, Cardiff CF1 3AG
Tel. 01222 394621

NHS Chief Executive
Quarry House, Quarry Hill, Leeds LS2 7UE
Tel. 01132 545000

Northern Ireland Commissioner for Complaints
Freepost, Belfast BT1 6BR
Tel. 01232 233821

Patients Association
8 Guilford Street, London WC1N 1DT
Tel. 0171–242 3460

Patient's Charter
Freepost, London SE99 7XU

Complementary medicine

The British Chiropractic Association
29 Whitley Street, Reading RG2 0EG
Tel. 01734 757557

The British Complementary Medicine Association
St Charles Hospital, Exmoor Street, London W10 6DZ
Tel. 0181–964 1205

The Council for Acupuncture
179 Gloucester Place, London NW1 6DX
Tel. 0171–724 5756

The General Council and Register of Osteopaths
56 London Street, Reading, Berks RG1 4SQ
Tel. 01734 576585

Institute for Complementary Medicine
PO Box 194, London SE16 1QZ
Tel. 0171–237 5165

National Institute of Medical Herbalists
56 Longbrook Street, Exeter EX4 6AH
Tel. 01392 426022

The Society of Homeopaths
2 Artizan Road, Northampton NN1 4HU
Tel. 01604 21400

Holidays and travel

Air Travel Organiser's Licence (ATOL)
Room T506, CAA House, 45–59 Kingsway, London WC2B 6TE
Tel. 0171–832 5620/6600

Association of British Travel Agents (ABTA)
55–57 Newman Street, London W1P 4AH
Tel. 0171–637 2444; info line 0891 202520 (49p per min)

Association of Independent Tour Operators (AITO)
133a St Margarets Road, Twickenham, Middlesex TW1 1RG
Tel. 0181–744 9280

Insurance

Association of British Insurers (ABI)
51 Gresham Street, London EC2V 7HQ
Tel. 0171–600 3333

British Insurance and Investment Brokers Association
BIIBA House, 14 Bevis Marks, London EC3A 7NT
Tel. 0171–623 9043

Institute of Public Loss Assessors
14 Red Lion Street, Chesham, Bucks HP5 1HB
Tel. 01494 782342

Insurance Ombudsman Bureau
135 Park Street, London SE1 9EA
Tel. 0171–928 7600

Meteorological Office
Johnson House, London Road, Bracknell, Berks RG12 2SY
Tel. 01344 854565

Motor Insurers Bureau (MIB)
152 Silbury Boulevard, Central Milton Keynes MK9 1NB
Tel. 01908 830001

Personal Insurance Arbitration Service (PIAS)
see Chartered Institute of Arbitrators

Legal services

Council for Licensed Conveyancers
16 Glebe Road, Chelmsford, Essex CM1 1QG
Tel. 01245 349599

General Council of the Bar
3 Bedford Row, London WC1R 4DB
Tel. 0171–242 0082

Law Society of England and Wales
Law Society House, 113 Chancery Lane, London WC2A 1PL
Tel. 0171–242 1222

Law Society of Northern Ireland
Law Society House, 98 Victoria Street, Belfast BT1 3JZ
Tel. 01232 231614

Law Society of Scotland
26 Drumsheugh Gardens, Edinburgh EH3 7YR
Tel. 0131–226 7411

Legal Services Ombudsman
22 Oxford Court, Oxford Street, Manchester M2 3WQ
Tel. 0161–236 9532

Scottish Legal Services Ombudsman
2 Greenside Lane, Edinburgh EH1 3AH
Tel. 0131–556 5574

Solicitors' Complaints Bureau
Victoria Court, 8 Dormer Place, Leamington Spa CV32 5AE
Tel. 01926 820082

Solicitors' Indemnity Fund
100 St John Street, London EC1M 4EH
Tel. 0171–566 6000

Mail order

The Direct Marketing Association UK Ltd
Haymarket House, 1 Oxendon Street, London SW1Y 4EE
Tel. 0171–321 2525

Mailing Preference Services
Freepost 22, London W1E 7EZ
Tel. 0171–738 1625

Mail Order Protection Scheme (MOPS)
16 Tooks Court, London EC4A 1LB
Tel. 0171–405 6806

Mail Order Traders' Association
100 Old Hall Street, Liverpool L3 9TD
Tel. 0151–227 4181

Newspaper Publishers' Association Ltd
34 Southwark Bridge Road, London SE1 9EU
Tel. 0171–928 6928

Newspaper Society
Bloomsbury House, 74–77 Great Russell Street, London WC1B 3DA
Tel. 0171–636 7014

Periodical Publishers Association Ltd
Imperial House, 15–19 Kingsway, London WC2B 6UN
Tel. 0171–379 6268

Scottish Daily Newspaper Society
Merchants House Buildings, 30 George Square, Glasgow G2 1EG
Tel. 0141–248 2375

Scottish Newspaper Publishers' Association
48 Palmerston Place, Edinburgh EH12 5DE
Tel. 0131–220 4353

Mediation and arbitration

Centre for Dispute Resolution (CEDR)
100 Fetter Lane, London EC4A 1DD
Tel. 0171–430 1852

Chartered Institute of Arbitrators
International Arbitration Centre, 24 Angel Gate, City Road, London EC1V 2RS
Tel. 0171–837 4483

Alternative Dispute Resolution Group
Equity and Law Building, 36–38 Baldwin Street, Bristol BS1 1NR
Tel. 01179 252090

Mediation UK
82a Gloucester Road, Bishopston, Bristol BS7 8BN
Tel. 01179 241234

Property

Incorporated Society of Valuers and Auctioneers
3 Cadogan Gate, London SW1X 0AS
Tel. 0171–235 2282

National Association of Estate Agents
Arbon House, 21 Jury Street, Warwick CV34 4EH
Tel. 01926 496800

Office of the Ombudsman for Corporate Estate Agents
Beckett House, 4 Bridge Street, Salisbury SP1 2LX
Tel. 01722 333306

Royal Institution of Chartered Surveyors
12 Great George Street, London SW1P 3AD
Tel. 0171–222 7000

Small claims offices (Northern Ireland)

Armagh
Court Office, Courthouse, The Mall, Armagh BT61 9DJ
Tel. 01861 522816

Ballymena
Court Office, Courthouse, Albert Place, Ballymena BT43 5BS
Tel. 01266 49416

Belfast
The Royal Courts of Justice, Chichester Street, Belfast BT1 3JF
Tel. 01232 235111

Craigavon
Court Office, Courthouse, Central Way, Craigavon, Co. Armagh BT64 1AP
Tel. 01762 341324

Downpatrick
Court Office, Courthouse, 21 English Street, Downpatrick BT30 6AD
Tel. 01396 614621

Enniskillen
Petty Sessions Office, Courthouse, East Bridge Street, Enniskillen BT74 7BW
Tel. 01365 322356

Londonderry
Crown and County Court Office, Courthouse, Bishop Street, Londonderry BT48 6PY
Tel. 01504 363448

Newtownards
Court Office, Courthouse, 3 Regent Street, Newtownards BT23 4LP
Tel. 01247 814343

Omagh
Court Office, Courthouse, High Street, Omagh BT78 1DU
Tel. 01662 242056

Enforcement of Judgments Office
7th Floor, Bedford House, Bedford Street, Belfast BT2 7DS
Tel. 01232 245081

INDEX